W9-BUQ-764

Praise for *Agile Project Management*

This book is the missing link for large enterprises seeking to apply an agile approach to portfolio management.

—Mike Cohn, Author of Agile Estimating and Planning

Jochen Krebs has written a book that demystifies what happens in large organizations where various interdependencies can mystify and confuse teams making the journey to agile methods. It belongs on the bookshelves of forward-thinking executives and project managers at all levels.

—Peter Rivera, SVP, Executive Creative and Program Director, AOL Programming

This book addresses a sorely neglected area in the overall discussion of Agile methods. The solutions to many of the issues organizations face when adopting Agile methods like Scrum and XP lie in effective portfolio management, and Jochen has done well to bring this topic to the fore.

—Sanjiv Augustine, President Lithespeed, Author of Agile Project Management, Co-Founder of Agile Project Leadership Network

This is an absolute must read. Jochen simplifies a very complex concept and delivers a book that is easily read and provides a very pragmatic approach to Agile Portfolio Management.

—Robert Eagan, Director of Global Project Management Methodology for a major New York Financial Organization

Jochen Krebs' new book, Agile Portfolio Management, breaks new ground in the Agile canon by providing specific techniques for organizing work in Agile organizations at the program and portfolio level. As larger IT organizations adopt Agile broadly, many find that their legacy project selection, budgeting, and portfolio management processes are impediments to realizing the full competitive benefits their Agile development organizations can support. Joe's book will provide organizations with some specific options for organizations to consider to increase the cadence and quality of portfolio planning and management practices to match the speed of modern Agile development shops.

—Evan Campbell, VP of Professional Services, Rally Software Development

In this unique and standard-setting book, Jochen Krebs gives the IT community a much-needed, practical, and comprehensive roadmap for creating and managing the agile portfolio.

—Doug DeCarlo, Principal, The Doug DeCarlo Group, and author of eXtreme Project Management: Using Leadership, Principles & Tools to Deliver Value in the face of Volatility

Finally, a practical Agile Project Management book for IT leadership and business stakeholders alike. Jochen's comprehensive review of Agile principles covers the financial, process, and people perspectives of three crucial vectors in portfolio management: Project, Asset, and Resource. A valuable reference book I will keep at my desk, great for Agile champions in any organization, and a must read for CIOs, PMO leaders, and product owners alike.

—Tiran Dagan, Director/Engagement Leader, Strategic Initiatives & Analysis, GE/NBC Universal

In a global, hypercompetitive marketplace, we are now forced more than ever to find ways to continuously identify, prioritize and execute software projects that routinely result in rapid deployment of compelling products and services that also routinely deliver improved enterprise innovation and profits. While Agile Software Development practices have emerged to meet this growing imperative, organizational decisioning and governance methods have remained rooted in old-school management practices that cling to big design upfront funding and execution models. Agile Portfolio Management successfully outlines a broad, practical, and well-conceived framework for aligning organizational thinking and practices that are purpose built for achieving maximum organizational agility and value creation in a change-driven world. Jochen's book is one I will ask all my CXO clients to read as they strive to better understand how best to effectively govern and exploit emerging Agile engineering practices so crucial to both survival and systematic innovation.

—Brad Murphy, CEO North America, Valtech

Agile Portfolio Managment

Jochen Krebs

PUBLISHED BY
Microsoft Press
A Division of Microsoft Corporation
One Microsoft Way
Redmond, Washington 98052-6399

Copyright © 2009 by Jochen Krebs

All rights reserved. No part of the contents of this book may be reproduced or transmitted in any form or by any means without the written permission of the publisher.

Library of Congress Control Number: 2008927279

Printed and bound in the United States of America.

1 2 3 4 5 6 7 8 9 QWT 3 2 1 0 9 8

Distributed in Canada by H.B. Fenn and Company Ltd.

A CIP catalogue record for this book is available from the British Library.

Microsoft Press books are available through booksellers and distributors worldwide. For further information about international editions, contact your local Microsoft Corporation office or contact Microsoft Press International directly at fax (425) 936-7329. Visit our Web site at www.microsoft.com/mspress. Send comments to mspinput@microsoft.com.

Microsoft, Microsoft Press, Excel, and Windows are either registered trademarks or trademarks of the Microsoft group of companies. Other product and company names mentioned herein may be the trademarks of their respective owners.

The example companies, organizations, products, domain names, e-mail addresses, logos, people, places, and events depicted herein are fictitious. No association with any real company, organization, product, domain name, e-mail address, logo, person, place, or event is intended or should be inferred.

This book expresses the author's views and opinions. The information contained in this book is provided without any express, statutory, or implied warranties. Neither the authors, Microsoft Corporation, nor its resellers, or distributors will be held liable for any damages caused or alleged to be caused either directly or indirectly by this book.

Acquisitions Editor: Ben Ryan
Developmental Editor: Devon Musgrave
Project Editor: Lynn Finnel
Editorial Production: Waypoint Press
Illustration by: John Hersey

Body Part No. X14-95062

To Melanie, with love and gratitude

Contents at a Glance

Table of Contents

What do you think of this book? We want to hear from you!

Microsoft is interested in hearing your feedback so we can continually improve our books and learning resources for you. To participate in a brief online survey, please visit:

www.microsoft.com/learning/booksurvey

What do you think of this book? We want to hear from you!

Microsoft is interested in hearing your feedback so we can continually improve our books and learning resources for you. To participate in a brief online survey, please visit:

www.microsoft.com/learning/booksurvey

Acknowledgments

I would like to thank the following individuals for their invaluable feedback and in-depth review during various stages of this project: Denise Cook, Marie Kalliney, and Roman Pichler. Roger LeBlanc edited this book to completion throughout many review cycles and didn't stop when I thought it was done. Steve Sagman and Lynn Finnel edited and coordinated this project and had an endless repertoire of good ideas to improve the product. The book would not be what it is without your comments and passion for this topic. Thank you all!

Completing a project like this is not possible with just pure know-how. My family and friends, especially, gave me the morale and support I needed: my Mum, Ute and Dad, Frieder; my sister,Iris ,and Rainer Löw, Markus Löw, Torben Löw, Reinhold and Sieglinde Oppenländer, Noreen and Charles Bramman, Rita O'Grady, Christopher Bramman, Gregory Bramman, Lauren, and Richard French. Another very special thank you goes to Gerhard Mauz, Markus Knierim, and Marcus Zimmermann—friends who keep me focused on what is important in life.

Introduction

If you have studied economics, you have seen the difference between tactical and strategic planning. During the 1980s, the tactical window of actions was three to five years of planning, whereas strategic planning was beyond five years, up to ten. After the information age took off during the 1990s, the rate of change with all its side effects significantly reduced this planning window, and software development cycles decreased. By now, I don't think that you will find any organization that plans in the cycles of the 1980s anymore, especially not in the information technology sector. As a matter of fact, I have heard managers tell me the joke, "Tactical is what you do today; strategy is when you plan for tomorrow." As with many jokes, some truth lies in it.

The new rate of change also affects the way we will develop systems in the future—in particular, the larger ones. The longer the project schedules, the higher the chance the scope of the project will be part of a strategy. And we know from many past experiences that a system that results from a two-year project might not do what it was intended to do. One of the reasons for this is that the planning accuracy in traditional projects is very coarse.

To address this problem, many organizations adopt or experiment with agile development—an approach based on iterative-incremental development that breaks the project's scope into smaller, manageable pieces. From managements' perspective, this approach is ideal because even the longest strategic project will have a tactical component: the iteration ahead. And it is exactly this component that will allow executives, project managers, and the project team to steer the project toward an imprecise vision. The transition to agile is not always easy, but it is the same with every change. Change bears risks and opportunities, and agile development offers many of them. This book will explore the opportunities agile presents for the development organization and its leadership, and it will address the potential risks.

One of the motivations for writing this book was to share observations I have made throughout my career, either inside or outside the project team. Many of these observations trace back to the same root cause: the lack of trust I witnessed in all aspects of an organization.

During long-term traditionally managed projects, many project status reports—especially in early phases of the project—are highly optimistic. First, it is extremely difficult for business analysts or software engineers to know that they are behind schedule. Before or during analysis, it is impossible to know how much analysis there is in total. If they don't know the total, how can they know whether they are on track? Later in the project, if the project is delayed because of new findings, the people who performed the analysis are long gone, having moved on to new projects.

Second, we were long taught that project managers are "in charge." They manage the team, give assignments, and bear responsibility for the overall success of the project. All this pressure and all these expectations are directed toward one person, who is also in charge of project communication. Given this scenario, how can we expect project communication to be neutral? Isn't it already an underlying form of mistrust for senior executives to ask for additional detailed weekly status reports? I saw these symptoms of dysfunction and mistrust over and over again in my career.

Agile portfolio management does not eliminate written communication, but it ensures that communication is based on existing agile metrics that are produced while the project is in flight. Agile portfolio management establishes a clearly defined interface between the project team and the executives, and this interface is based on agile principles. These principles are based on trust and will have a positive impact in any transition toward organizational agility.

I called the book *Agile Portfolio Management* because it is exactly the portfolio of active projects in an organization that represents the future of the enterprise—tactically and strategically, whatever your definition of those terms is. The term "agile" should highlight not only that the projects inside the portfolio are agile projects but also that the portfolio is built upon agile principles and managed dynamically. This book shows that the modern agile enterprise is transparent and that it has clearly defined communication channels; therefore, this book targets project managers and executives the same way.

This book is divided into the following three parts:

Part I: Agile for Managers

This introductory part is written for managers who want to know why agile software development has become so popular within the past several years. It explains the most important agile practices commonly applied in agile software development and agile project management.

Part II: Defining, Planning, and Measuring Portfolios

The second part is the largest section of the book. It explains practices relevant to agile portfolio management. Practices included in this section are compiling metrics, establishing a project selection process, evaluating resources, and calculating the return on investment. These chapters capture the practices of modern portfolio management.

Part III: Organization and Environment

The last part of the book provides some hands-on advice about how to orchestrate the most popular agile development processes with agile portfolio management. I highlight how Scrum-managed projects fit into the portfolio management process. In addition, this section investigates the new role of the project management office (PMO) in an agile organization.

Who Is This Book For?

This book is primarily targeting project managers, portfolio managers, business analysts, members of the PMO, and executive managers who are interested in adopting agile practices and portfolio management. I hope it will give exactly this audience an easily digestible introduction to this topic, with enough material to sponsor agility across the entire enterprise.

Although this book is not intended primarily for technical audiences, it might help them to appreciate the motivations of individuals at various levels within an organization and to better understand how factors external to the project factor into their work within the enterprise.

Beyond being a benefit to the professionals in the audience, I hope that this book will also help students currently pursuing business and science degrees to understand the importance and impact of agile development in our industry. They are the project managers of tomorrow.

Find Additional Content Online

As new or updated material becomes available that complements this book, it will be posted online on the Microsoft Press Online Developer Tools Web site. The type of material you might find includes updates to book content, articles, errata, sample chapters, and more. This Web site will be available soon at *http://www.microsoft.com/learning/books/online/developer*, and it will be updated periodically.

Support for This Book

Every effort has been made to ensure the accuracy of this book and the companion content. As corrections or changes are collected, they will be added to a Microsoft Knowledge Base article.

Microsoft Press provides support for books and companion content at the following Web site:

http://www.microsoft.com/learning/support/books/

Questions and Comments

If you have comments, questions, or ideas regarding the book or the companion content, or questions that are not answered by visiting the sites above, please send them to Microsoft Press via e-mail to

mspinput@microsoft.com

Or via postal mail to

Microsoft Press
Attn*: Agile Portfolio Management* Editor
One Microsoft Way
Redmond, WA 98052-6399

Please note that Microsoft software product support is not offered through the above addresses.

Part I
Agile for Managers

The first part of this book is intended for managers who would like to learn more about the benefits and motivations for agile software development. It is an introduction to what agile is and why agile development works especially well in dynamic marketplaces. The three chapters in this first part will set the stage for agile portfolio management which we will explore in the second part of this book in more depth.

Therefore the following three chapters will give an introduction to agility from a managers' perspective:

- Chapter 1, "Motivations," uses real-world examples, trends, and facts from the business world to illustrate why agile development has received so much attention recently.

- Chapter 2, "Agile Software Development," introduces the core agile values, key practices, and key techniques applied in agile projects.

- Chapter 3, "Project Management," showcases the role and responsibilities of agile project managers and the relationship to their stakeholders, as well as the challenges of traditional project management practices.

Chapter 1
Motivations

In the beginning of this new millennium, there is an obvious trend toward a global marketplace, especially in the information technology (IT) sector. Even local IT entrepreneurs, who long thought they would be excluded from this trend, face more and more international pressure to compete for value and price. But stakeholders not only expect higher quality for less money, they expect the development organization to achieve faster delivery and in shorter cycles. Managing requirements in this fast-paced environment, delivering products in a timely manner to the market, and being price-cautious are the motivations for agile development. Let's explore some of the challenges of traditionally managed IT projects in an unstable, unknowable, and unpredictable world. This chapter unveils common challenges of enterprises using a traditional development approach (also known as *waterfall*) from an enterprise's perspective and from management's perspective.

Every challenge imposed through traditionally managed projects introduces significant risks to the development organization. Some of these risks are so overpowering that modern organizations can no longer tolerate their existence or the strategies used to mitigate these risks.

Managing Expectations

I decided to use the word *expectation* instead of *requirements*, for one good reason. Requirements are a set of business rules and organizational policies combined with needs stakeholders have expressed. Expectations include requirements, but they might be less tangible, and they might not be expressed at all. However, expectations are, at the end of the project, the measure for success, not necessarily the requirements. For example, a business analyst might not go the extra mile and document with the utmost attention to detail the requirements for a system. As a result, the system might still not be "liked" by its audience. Was the project successful? The answer might be yes. Does the system do what the users wanted? Most likely not. Late changes, the unstable scope of the system, and ambiguity about requirements constantly cause the project to detour from the original plan, and these things are typical symptoms of a project that will fail to meet expectations. The reason projects don't achieve success despite the developers paying careful attention to detail is that it is impossible to capture all the expectations of a complete group of stakeholders. This ideal world simply does not exist.

Late Changes

Traditionally managed projects are characterized by phases separated by milestones, which usually require a sign-off in between. This sign-off signals that the project team has passed the milestone and can proceed to work in a new phase. Similar to legally binding contracts, once the sign-off is agreed to, it will be hard to get back to the project's previous state. Although these signed legal contracts make sense in many circumstances to get agreement on certain conditions, the model is challenged when applied in the context of software development. Let's see why.

Figure 1-1 outlines a traditional software development approach, where common engineering activities such as requirements, analysis and design, coding, testing, and deployment are divided into individual phases.

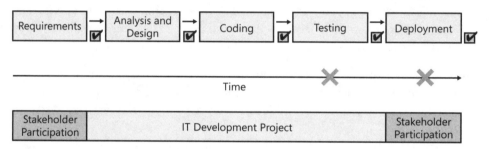

FIGURE 1-1 Late requirement changes

The transition from one phase to the other is enforced through a sign-off, approval, and hand-over to the next team of specialists. As soon as the next phase is entered, the previous phase is complete. Here is exactly where the problem begins.

In the traditional process, each project flows once through the process, which concludes with the deployment of the system. Imagine a two-year project, going through the phases illustrated in Figure 1-1. By the time we enter the coding phase, our requirements could already be 10 months old. Then, let's say after 16 months, the system finally enters the testing phase. But it is exactly here, during the testing phase, that missing requirements are uncovered, if they have not already been discovered earlier. The worst-case scenario is that the missed requirements are not uncovered during testing either, and the system is deployed. After deployment, the stakeholder will judge the implementation of their earlier requirements. The discovery happens here because this is the phase in which the initial stakeholders are back in the game. However, changes are hard to incorporate at this point, for two reasons. Economically, the project has already spent the majority of the allocated resources, and also the architecture and design have not been built with these requirements in mind.

Traditionally managed projects come in many different flavors, but they have this one problem in common; late changes are extremely difficult to digest. The degree of difficulty depends, of course, on the severity of the introduced change. I have even seen projects fail entirely because of one changed requirement. That's why, for humorous reasons, I often add a new phase after the deployment phase that I call the *finger-pointing phase*.

Please remember that the traditional model was developed in the 1960s, when mainframe computers dominated the IT landscape. The technologies used at that time did not embrace change. Programming during that period of time was procedural, top-down. If a change was required, the entire program or system needed to be recompiled and reassembled. Every compilation, on the other hand, required a new complete test to be on the safe side. The model worked for its particular technology, and people heroically tried to get things right the very first time.

Although development organizations have adopted new, component-oriented technologies, the underlying development process is still often the same traditional approach. It is exactly this process that reflects the culture of the entire development organization. Changing a well-established culture requires much more energy than adapting to a new programming language.

In contrast, modern software development commonly uses object-oriented technologies. These object-oriented systems are assembled from smaller pieces and elements that are highly cohesive and loosely coupled. That allows the development team to develop, test, and integrate in smaller steps and units. Because of newly available technologies, we are now in a position to focus on modern development processes and their management. As a result, agile development and agile project management invite change early and frequently, and these approaches build software in small, gradual steps.

Requirements Paralysis

In contrast to late requirements changes that can be implemented (although with great difficulty), some requirements are so dynamic or contradictory that they will never be resolved. In a situation where the rate of change in the requirements occurs faster than a large specification can be agreed upon, the project team will never find the exit out of the requirements phase. The frustration that occurs with this circle of events is that the project team will never produce any tangible progress other than documentation.

Valuable time and resources are wasted while stakeholders and business analysts try to work through the ambiguities to get the scope stable enough for the sign-off. This phenomenon is especially common in dynamic industries, where the rate of change is very high, or in innovative projects, where the fluctuation of requirements is very volatile. The media and advertisement industries, as well as the financial industry, are examples of these dynamic business sectors. In situations like these, a requirement today might no longer be important tomorrow.

This type of environment in particular is very frustrating to work in because all parties involved clearly know that no progress has been achieved. The longer the team is in such a state, the better the facilitation skills must be to get them on the right track. Fundamentally, requirements paralysis traces back to the same root cause: trying to get requirements "finalized."

Ambiguity

Ask three team members about their favorite pizza and they might talk about totally different pies. One might favor a thin crust versus thick, the other a calzone versus a slice, and the third team member might select a red-sauce pizza over white pizza. Making a pie for all three without clarifying expectations might be like playing the lottery. When we talk about ordinary items such as pizza, it seems that such things do not require any explanation. Gause and Weinberg illustrate this example with a simple statement, "Mary had a little lamb," where the word "had" could have been misinterpreted in a variety of ways. She could have given birth to a lamb, possessed a lamb, or actually eaten a lamb, among other possible interpretations.

The same is true for managing expectations. The problem with mental pictures is that everybody has their own version of the subject at hand. In the same way that people have different mental pictures when you say, "The weather will be nice tomorrow!" they might have different pictures about "The system generates a receipt." Some people think about a piece of paper; others assume receipts to be electronically recorded. As a result, the finished system might do what the documentation specified but not what the users had in mind. If your users are actually customers (for example, online shoppers), removing ambiguity must be a top priority. Ambiguity is expensive. Barry Boehm, for example, estimated that if ambiguity fixed during the requirements phase has a cost ratio of 1, the cost of ambiguity uncovered during testing increases to 15 to 40 times that amount, and the cost is 40 to 1000 times higher when ambiguity is found after the deployment phase, when the application or system is in operation. Keep in mind that these statistics are related to traditionally managed projects.

Agile development will keep the users involved, and it asks the stakeholders frequently to validate the achievements with their mental pictures. As a result, agile development tackles ambiguity and its expensive price tag.

Too Many Requirements

Many IT project teams take the requirements specification very seriously. So did I in the beginning of my career. After I did a small exercise with the business users, however, I learned that requirements are often simply personal wish lists. These wish lists are often individual requirements based on personal work routines. I have interviewed stakeholders who insisted on certain requirements. When we ran the requirements by the other stakeholders, we found out that the stakeholders who stated the requirements actually used an outdated company policy. Can you imagine if we had regarded the requirement as absolutely necessary and implemented it? We discovered the issue in this case, but I am sure we unknowingly implemented it somewhere else. Lesson learned: negotiate with the requirements, take polls, have the stakeholders work with you, and keep them involved.

Stakeholders want a lot, but what do they really need? When you prioritize the so-called requirement specification, you will learn that many requirements drop down in the list or out of scope entirely. This is particularly true if you have price tags for these features estimated already. Remember, requirements are expressed as the common needs of the stakeholders. Some requirements, however, might have emerged from one stakeholder only. They have to be negotiated, accepted, and validated by other stakeholders as well. Developing features will cost time and money. Not only that, some features are not worth developing—they will take valuable time away from the more important features.

Many traditional projects go through the initial step of prioritizing and filtering requirements. Unfortunately, this step is performed only once. Once requirements are considered to be outside the scope of the project, it will require a lot of energy to get them back into the scope at a later point.

Throughout this book, you will see how powerful open-scope requirements management is with agile project management. And you'll see that real needs will find their way into the final system.

Too Few Requirements

So far all our issues about requirements management had one positive aspect: we had requirements to start with. We either had too many, had to cope with ambiguity, had to incorporate late changes, or had to deal with requirements paralysis. The scenario we discuss next is probably the worst situation a traditional project can be in: too few requirements. Ironically, having too few requirements is something that agile development is very good at dealing with.

The lack of requirements has a dramatic impact on traditional projects, though. First, the initial project scope does not reflect what the stakeholder really wanted. Second, the estimated scope causes internal change-control churn because stakeholders will express their needs eventually. We see change-control churn as a high number of changes based on low-quality requirements. That also includes changes to the previously approved changes. Last but not least, the scope is limited to the requirements expressed in the first part of the project. Therefore, many newly uncovered requirements are collected for so-called enhancement projects following the actual project. Very often, these enhancement projects are so essential for an organization that without them the benefits are not achieved. In other words, the enhancement projects contain the "real" requirements, unleashing the real potential. I can only imagine how much business potential is hidden in those projects in the *standby* list.

With too few requirements, it will be challenging to get to an early or initial estimate or plan an iteration. The fact is, however, that the requirements will eventually emerge. The worst case for traditional projects occurs when the requirements emerge at the end of the project. This situation often occurs when a project team continues working on a new release even though the first or major release was just delivered. Most likely, the team works and fixes the things that were not thought of initially.

As a result, the project team works off of a high-level list of visionary features, which opens the door for other requirements issues—specifically, ambiguity and late changes. Too few requirements are a typical scenario for traditional projects in a dynamic marketplace. In dynamic industries, a stakeholder's time is usually so limited that workshops are brief, but also business analysts cannot invest the time needed for exploring and detailing requirements—not even the requirements that are most important to begin with.

Agile projects do not aim to establish a perfect set of requirements either, but you will see how the model dynamically incorporates newly uncovered important requirements early in the development life cycle. As a result, the plan of an agile project will adapt to incorporate newly identified but very important requirements early in the project.

Change Control Board

To address the issues resulting from requirements management in traditional managed projects, organizations establish so-called change control boards (CCBs). As the name indicates, these are the people who control the change that occurs to the scope throughout the project. That could be a change to existing requirements, or it could be new requirements that appear early or late in the project. The board, which commonly consists of a few strategic project team members (for example, project manager, architect, lead business analyst), decides about each change request on a case-by-case basis. The CCB discusses the change request, puts forth a plan of action, and votes on it.

Investing in a change control board is expensive. Not only does the change control board need to organize and hold meetings, it also needs to set aside significant time to prepare for (clarify the change request, perform risk assessment, gain a common understanding of the current scope, and perform administrative tasks) and wrap up the meetings. The latter task requires re-communicating the decisions and clarifying the changes to the scope. Most likely, the initial decision will result in more detailed meetings and breakout sessions within the project team.

For an organization to admit that a change control board is necessary is its first step toward adopting a more modern engineering process. It demonstrates that the organization is starting to embrace change. However, deciding that the change control board will meet weekly or biweekly is rarely dynamic enough for either the developers or the business. We will discuss in subsequent chapters how agile projects integrate the change control mechanism directly into the development process as day-to-day activities.

Time to Market

Initiating a project is an investment in the future. Projects take time and consume resources, and in most cases the sponsor of the project expects that the project will pay back more than it will cost. In other words, projects should be treated and seen as regular investments. IT systems, for example, should make information travel faster, and they are very good at automating slow and manual business procedures. That is one reason why IT projects have huge investment potential for any organization. After the opportunity is identified and the investment quantified, the project is initiated. In an ideal world, the project is executed, the system delivered, and the benefits of the solution are received. In reality, it is not so easy because every project carries risks. Some of them are very basic and obvious, and they all are fundamental to the discussions in the remainder of this book. Therefore, let's explore a few of them.

Technology can become a bigger bottleneck to a solution than originally anticipated. The expected performance of an application could run 50 percent slower than estimated in the business case. Deploying the solution in the marketplace could eliminate the profit margin, or even worse, it could be counterproductive. For example, think about performance issues related to a new stock-trading system. Fewer transactions every second means less profit, and customers might turn to alternative brokers with a better infrastructure to conduct their business. The bigger question around this scenario is, "Would the project have been sponsored if it were known that the system would be 50 percent slower?" Probably not.

Most companies have competition, and they are not acting independently in their marketplace. Initiating a project introduces a new cost center. Only the delivered project will add value to the company and bring it into a unique or better position that could possibly be lucrative. However, the duration for which the company can harvest the benefits is limited, because competition is likely to catch up over time. (See Figure 1-2.)

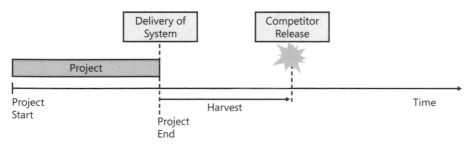

FIGURE 1-2 Time to market and time-limited benefits

Let's say a company announces a medication to cure a specific virus. The company's stock price might go through the roof because the company just increased its value in the market. Bankers at Wall Street buy into the future, and it is the potential of a company that drives the value of a stock. Now it is the responsibility of that company to prove itself and deliver the promised product to the market. With every day the project is late, there is a chance for another organization to be first. The race has begun.

Software development is not much different, even though internal projects of a large organization might not have the same obvious competition as in the example just given and are generally not announced beforehand to the public. What IT projects struggle with, however, is that the business is usually ahead of IT. This is natural, but it is a challenge because, internally, we can see that the business group is in competition with IT.

Let's illustrate this scenario. An organization provides certain services and products to clients by using sales representatives working directly with the clients. A business analysis uncovered, however, that 80 percent of the orders from the customers are periodic and identical. An IT project designed to automate and expedite the processing of orders was initiated. Automating this existing business process is a typical scenario for software projects. After the decision is made and the funds are allocated, the clock starts ticking for the developers. The problem with these kinds of projects is that IT projects are constantly following the business vision and rarely leading it.

While time is elapsing for the IT project, the business is evolving. The delivered system, upon completion, might not serve the business need anymore. For example, the competitor had a similar idea and already released a similar system shortly after the project started. The project team cannot ignore the fact that the project might be right on track internally but behind the market schedule.

Innovation

In 2006, the online movie rental company Netflix announced on NPR a one-million-dollar award to anyone who could improve their movie recommendation system by at least 10 percent. A year later, in November 2007, no one had earned the cash award.

Going public with this award is in many ways a new and unique way of innovating business for a company. Let's see what makes it so creative by comparing it with traditionally executed projects.

First, the company admits that the public could do a better job of recommending movies to Netflix customers. Netflix also admits that it cannot solve this issue itself, which is a tremendous psychological factor. Think about how protective some companies are when intellectual property is involved. This example involves much more than just gathering feedback and ideas from a customer base. The contest is asking for a clever solution to solve one particular problem.

Then, instead of outsourcing this solution to a subcontractor, Netflix takes an approach similar to open-source development. Everyone is invited and can contribute, with one big difference: the winner will be generously rewarded. Instead of limiting themselves to a few partners, Netflix uses the power of a global network of engineers, who are now tackling the issue.

Third, the company has quantified this feature internally—that a 10-percent improvement in the recommendations will increase revenue and customer satisfaction enough so that it will easily pay for the large award.

Last but not least, the example also demonstrates to competitors how Netflix is keen on improving one element of its system and which area of customer service it is focusing on. With this announcement, the innovation has turned public.

In return, and I believe this is as creative as the entire contest itself, the award creates a lot of hype and conversation about Netflix. Perhaps it even generates new business from people attracted by the openness and creativity of the company's vision.

Innovation requires creativity and constantly rethinking existing business processes. The use of new technologies applied in modern business processes is probably still in its infancy. While IT was automating manual, tedious exchanges of information in enterprises in the last century, it also brought up a new generation of professionals who have high expectations about IT systems. The Netflix example shows that the discussion is shifting from technology-motivated development to a business-motivated solution.

Most organizations live on the attention they get from the outside world. That attention includes end consumers and also partnerships and distribution channels with other operations. Marketing and public relations are typically used to bundle a company's efforts to direct attention to a certain product or service. Both of these strategies are dependent on news. That could include an entire marketing strategy for a launch of a new product or new release that provides more benefits to its customers. Hypothetically, Netflix could launch a campaign for its new system called, "We already know your next good movie!" that includes television advertisements, flyers, and online advertisement. Although the IT project is only a small piece of the entire strategy, it is such an integral part of it that all other parts of the project are dependent on the success of the IT project first. IT is the engine of the campaign.

The same is true for many projects executed inside an organization. The news that tends to attract attention is news related to innovation. Based on innovation, third parties either invest in the company's vision or purchase the products or services. Without innovation and interesting news about its offerings, the organization will lose its competitive edge and eventually be just an average player in the marketplace.

Planning innovation is very hard; planning for innovation is easier. The organization has to create an environment that embraces and encourages innovation. In terms of project and portfolio management, we will need to "plan" a platform for everybody to introduce change and innovative ideas. As Alan Kay once said, "The best way to predict the future is to invent it." This platform must include a process for initiating and executing projects that invite change and therefore innovation. Traditional descriptive process models with a rigid and enforced flow of events are less likely to embrace change than empirical adaptive approaches. Agile is adaptive and embraces innovation.

In addition to generating brilliant ideas for new products and services, technology itself is often the motivator for the business. For example, think about the use of GPS devices as a tracking mechanism for a parcel courier or scanners that read electrical meters. My local energy company recently started reading its meters by driving by the house. Although I am sure many people before were dreaming about a way to read meters without the necessity of entering the buildings, the invention of laser, bar-code, and infrared technology opened the doors for a broader use of technologies in a business environment.

Funding

Monetary streams inside organizations are also organized in a way that they target tradition-ally managed projects. When future IT budgets are planned and negotiated at the end of a fiscal year, the portfolio of future projects is evaluated and estimated. The result is a very static and inflexible financial model to accommodate new additional projects. This budgeting procedure is very difficult to change in the middle of the fiscal year because the initial bucket of budget dollars has already been determined. Then this bucket is dedicated to select projects. Needless to say, new and innovative projects are postponed because of budget constraints.

Instead of increasing or decreasing the previous year's budget by a percentage, management usually demands hard data for forecasts and estimates. Meeting this demand turns into a situation similar to traditional requirements. The organization does not know exactly what, when, and how much it will need for a new project. Projects are vaguely defined, and situa-tions will change. General Dwight Eisenhower once said, "Plans are worthless, but planning is everything." This saying is also true when applied to the financial planning for projects.

Instead of laying out a master plan of projects for the upcoming year, organizations are better off allocating resources (financial and human) to the upcoming fiscal year as rough parameters. This advice is especially true with regard to resource allocations for innovative and creative projects, as IT projects usually are.

With traditional funding procedures in place, a troubled project (Project A) continues to consume more and more resources because it is delayed. Following projects dependent on the resources from its predecessor need to wait. See Figure 1-3. The reason for this is that the project is on the radar of the organization and serious money has already been invested. Organizationally, it will be very hard to unplug the project and free the resources for more promising projects.

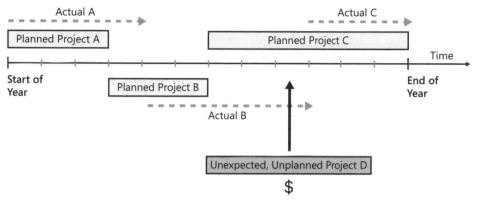

FIGURE 1-3 Budget changes

The impact is that the increased budget takes away resources from other projects that are lined up later. All subsequent projects (Projects B and C in Figure 1-3) might even drop out of the portfolio completely because of the lack of resources. But what if that project is one that can provide even more benefits to the organization than any other project? What if a new project appears (Project D in Figure 1-3) that promises great potential but cannot compete for resources because of an outdated budget plan? Wouldn't it be wise to increase the budget and get Project D started as well or instead?

Agile projects allow for a much more dynamic project selection and funding process, which we will investigate in the subsequent chapters.

Summary

The goal of this first chapter is to establish a common understanding of the challenges associated with traditionally managed projects in a dynamic business world. To illustrate the challenges, I covered four common areas in which organizations are challenged with their IT projects: managing expectations, speeding up the time-to-market delivery, encouraging innovation, and providing funding. For each area, I pointed out the challenges associated with traditional project management. These challenges will set the stage for the two subsequent chapters, in which we look at agile development and its project management techniques. The next two chapters will give managers detailed answers and solutions to the issues outlined within this chapter.

Chapter 2
Agile Software Development

In this chapter, I will define what agile software development stands for and look at the key practices of agile development from a manager's perspective. I'll tie these practices to the motivations introduced in the previous chapter.

Definitions

Let's take a look at the agile lingo before we dive into the practices of agile software development.

What Is Agile?

An agile methodology is a framework for software engineering that embraces change. For example, software development is often complex, and requirements are, especially in the beginning of a project, unknown or ambiguous. Therefore, an agile framework must have built-in mechanisms to allow the project to tackle and reduce these uncertainties. These mechanisms are listed as the key practices covered in this chapter. If only one of these key practices is left out, an agile project is incomplete.

But agile also means that the framework itself is flexible and adapts to any situation. That means that the same framework applied to two projects will have two different interpretations. The agile approach is best described as *empirical* because the process itself must be adapted to its environment, which is not necessarily the organization but could be the individual project. Agile is not a "one size fits all" solution.

Agile Processes

The following agile processes have been successfully adopted in the past in a wide range of industries. Publications, training courses, and a substantial user community exist for each of the processes listed. During this introductory part of the book, written for managers, I'll provide a quick definition of each of the popular agile processes and information about their origin. Later, in Part 3 of this book, we'll take an in-depth look at Scrum as an example of a popular agile project management process.

Extreme Programming

Extreme Programming (XP) was developed by Kent Beck, Ward Cunningham, and Ron Jeffries during the 1990s as a set of dynamic programming practices. Today, XP is the most often adopted agile methodology in the high-technology industry. The most noticeable practices of XP are pair programming and test-driven development, which we will discuss in more detail later in this chapter. Although XP provides planning practices for project management, it is often seen as an agile engineering process.

Scrum

Ken Schwaber and Jeff Sutherland, who developed Scrum in the 1990s, define it as a framework for agile project management rather than an agile process. Scrum has its origins in lean manufacturing (which is described later in this section), iterative-incremental development, and the Smalltalk engineering tools. Scrum provides a simple set of rules. Aside from these simple rules, Scrum is extremely flexible and adaptive to emerging situations. *Scrum* is a term used in rugby and not an acronym. In a nutshell, Scrum is quite different from existing project management practices. First, the role of a traditional project manager is shared among three different roles: the product owner, the scrum master, and the team. Second, two different backlogs are used to manage scope: the product backlog, which captures the scope of the product, and the sprint backlog, which contains the detail work for the current iteration. A sprint, which is the Scrum synonym for an iteration, is four weeks long. The entire Scrum team meets daily for 15 minutes so that each member can give other team members a quick update. Scrum is very popular in the agile industry. For that reason, I have dedicated Chapter 11 to providing a more detailed overview of the framework—in particular, when it is applied in the context of agile portfolio management.

Dynamic Systems Development Method

Also developed in the mid-1990s, the Dynamic Systems Development Method (DSDM) has its roots in Rapid Application Development (RAD), an iterative-incremental process model that uses prototypes at each stage of development. Compared with agile development, which strives for working software at the end of each iteration, the prototypes might be incomplete and not functioning. The prototypes do provide, however, a great way of including all stakeholders early in the requirements work, because the prototypes might be enough to get feedback—for example, from end users. Prototypes can be created for all aspects of the system, including its architecture. In reality, they are often used with graphical user interfaces. DSDM consists of the following nine principles:

- Active user involvement
- Addressing business needs
- Baselining of high-level scope

- Communication and collaboration among all stakeholders

- Frequent delivery

- Team decision making

- Integrated testing

- Iterative-incremental development

- Reversible changes throughout development

Lean Development

Lean development, originated by Bob Charette, applies the principles of lean manufacturing to software development. The result is a kit of 22 *tools*. The names of these tools still reflect their manufacturing origin—for example, "eliminate waste." Mary and Tom Poppendieck are leading advocates of lean development in the agile software development industry, having spoken and written extensively about it.

Unified Process

Listing the Unified Process (UP) here as an agile development process is not entirely correct. Compared with the other processes, the Unified Process is a descriptive process rather than an empirical one. That means the UP describes in text, like a hyperlinked version of a book, what particular roles are required to do, when they do it, and how they do it. As with any book, changes to it are more challenging to redistribute. Although the Unified Process is based on architecture-centric, iterative-incremental development principles, the project phases, disciplines, and relationships between roles and responsibilities provide less flexibility. On the other hand, it is exactly the somewhat fixed description of the process that appeals to large organizations that need to comply with a variety of standards and need to outline, for example, a companywide policy for a software development process. Nonetheless, the UP provides a tremendous step forward from the traditional waterfall process (large, separated, and sequenced software engineering phases) and is often an intermediate step between traditional processes and agile processes. There are two noteworthy flavors of the Unified Process:

- **IBM Rational Unified Process (RUP)**   The RUP is a result of merging three methodologies (Booch, Objectory, and OMT) during the early and mid-1990s into one unified approach. After Rational was acquired by IBM in 2003, an eclipse-based[1] process authoring tool called the IBM Rational Method Composer (RMC) was developed. The eclipse framework provides a consistent platform for all toolmakers to develop and deploy software products. By using such a framework, developers can organize different

---

[1]   www.eclipse.org

tools under one umbrella and view them through *perspectives*. Therefore, RUP can easily be modified using the RMC.

- **OpenUP**   OpenUP is an open-source process released in October 2006. A year earlier, IBM Rational donated a significant amount of its "RUP for Small Projects" to the eclipse community (which you can learn more about at http://www.eclipse.org/epf) with the goal of developing a simple iterative-incremental process framework for small projects. Like the commercial version of RUP, OpenUP comes with an eclipse-based free process authoring tool called the Eclipse Process Framework (EPF).

Crystal Clear

The father of the crystal clear process is Alistair Cockburn. Crystal clear, like the other agile processes, is rooted in iterative-incremental development. Alistair's work is also heavily focused on humans, invention, and the idea of developing software as a corporate game. Interesting in this process is the emphasis of product and methodology fine-tuning at the beginning and in the middle of the iteration. This approach enables every project to evolve not only the system deliverables but also the chosen process itself. The ceremony of project documentation is also delegated to the project level.

Crystal clear also requires the team members to be in close proximity, the identification of real users, and that the team use basic code-versioning tooling. A major differentiator from other processes is the consideration of project communication. The larger the team, the more communication has to be factored in. Whereas a team of 5 or 10 members might easily fit into a team room with very effective communication channels, this setup might not be applicable for a team of 50 or more members. Based on the size of the team, different flavors of the crystal clear family can be adopted.

Agile Manifesto

The agile manifesto (which you can read at *http://www.agilemanifesto.org*) is the result of a meeting at the Snowbird ski resort in Utah in 2001. Prior to that date, the individual agile processes were referred to as *lightweight*. I think it was a good idea renaming it to *agile* because *lightweight* could have given the impression that it is easy to do and that heavy things were left out. Lightweight could also lead someone to believe that it was incomplete. Once you implement agile development practices, you will see that doing so can actually be difficult and that agile practices are not incomplete. The word *agile*, however, presents a challenge for the community. Nobody likes to admit that they are not agile, so some developers who call themselves agile are, in reality, not agile in our definition of the practices.

Despite any small misgivings about the name, all 17 participants at the ski resort defined the process and signed the manifesto, which was to become the measure of agility in the years to come. I remember the release of the manifesto, which immediately gave the industry a tangible definition of agile and ground rules for adding new ideas in the future. Still today, the manifesto provides clear direction and is used to discuss and compare agile methodologies, including those in this book. More important in my opinion, the manifesto provides one common roof for all agilists, whatever their favorite agile methodology might be. Here are the core values of the manifesto:

- Individuals and interaction take precedence over processes and tools.

- Working software takes precedence over comprehensive documentation.

- Customer collaboration takes precedence over contract negotiation.

- Responding to change takes precedence over following a plan.

Please note that the left side of each statement is valued more than the right side. What is important and often misunderstood is that the manifesto does not recommend neglecting the values of the right side—for example, project documentation. It simply means that the values on the left are valued more highly. Every agile project team has to find the right balance as a team, but also they must find balance within the organization. Figure 2-1 illustrates a value system for a sample project or organization when it interprets the agile manifesto. In Figure 2-1, the arrows indicate how strictly or loosely the values on the left are balanced compared with the values on the right. But even if the arrow is placed toward the right end, it does not imply that the values on the left are overruled. It means that the organization needs to consider other elements as well.

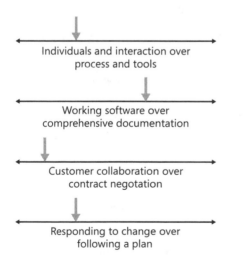

Individuals and interaction over
process and tools

Working software over
comprehensive documentation

Customer collaboration over
contract negotation

Responding to change over
following a plan

FIGURE 2-1 Example of a value system for an agile project

By the end of 2007, more than 4,700 professionals across the information technology (IT) industry had agreed to and signed the manifesto. Among the 17 authors of the manifesto were representatives from the Scrum, Extreme Programming, DSDM, and crystal clear methodologies.

Agile Alliance

The goals of the Agile Alliance (which you can read more about at *www.agilealliance.org*) are to promote agile development in the software industry. With approximately 4,000 members in December 2007, the Agile Alliance is the largest nonprofit community of agile profession-als in the industry. The alliance promotes agile methodologies that comply with the agile manifesto, offers funds to members who promote agile development, offers a library of agile publications, and announces local events in the industry. The flagship of the Agile Alliance is the yearly *Agile* conference. This five-day conference offers several programs, depending on your interest, and a variety of speakers. The interest in this conference seems boundless. Attendance increased from 675 participants in 2005 to 1,100 in 2006 and to more than 1,600 in 2007. Every year, the conference is sold out, and it seems the topics create a degree of interest limited only by the size of the venue. I agree, large does not necessarily mean bet-ter quality, but I believe the attendance records demonstrate that agile development has become a mainstream approach.

Agile Project Leadership Network

Just as the Agile Alliance represents the agile manifesto, so does the Agile Project Leadership Network (APLN) represent the *project management declaration of interdependence* (PMDOI). The core values of the PMDOI are as follows:

- We increase return on investment by making continuous flow of value our focus.
- We deliver reliable results by engaging customers in frequent interactions and shared ownership.
- We expect uncertainty and manage for it through iterations, anticipation, and adaptation.
- We unleash creativity and innovation by recognizing that individuals are the ultimate source of value and creating an environment where they can make a difference.
- We boost performance through group accountability for results and shared responsibility for team effectiveness.
- We improve effectiveness and reliability through situation-specific strategies, processes, and practices.

The APLN is a nonprofit organization consisting of a community of project leaders organized into local chapters. During the remainder of this book, I'll connect the principles of the agile manifesto with the principles of the PMDOI. Furthermore, I'll apply these principles in the context of portfolio management in Part 2.

Key Practices of Agile Development

"I am breaking my two-year projects into two major phases: requirements and coding. Does that make my project agile?" The answer to this question is clearly no. Beyond that simple answer, we need to deliver an explanation of what will give a project an agile spin. The various agile processes have some successful patterns in common, which are isolated as key practices. These key practices are so essential to any agile project that they will affect the energy, spirit, and eventually the success of the agile project. These practices are, in no particular order:

- Iterative-incremental development.

- Test-driven development.

- Continuous integration.

- Face-to-face communication.

Let's explore each of the key practices in more detail in the following subsections.

Iterative-Incremental Development

This practice is, from a management perspective, the most noticeable change toward an agile approach. Instead of executing every software development cycle (requirements, design, programming, and so on) only once in the entire project (which is the traditional or waterfall way of doing it), iterative development enforces repetition and semi-parallelism of the development activities. That means the activities are extremely narrow and close to one another. They seem to blend, and the order of activities can change. That might sound strange, but you will see later in this chapter why this is a very good idea.

As a rule of thumb, the shorter the iterations, the better. That's why agile processes require a time frame for each iteration that is typically between 2 and 6 weeks.

The second aspect of this practice is the actual increment. Whereas the *iteration* provides the rhythm for the project, the *increment* demonstrates the actual progress of the project, as illustrated in Figure 2-2. Viewed in that way, it looks as if the project progresses by stepping up a staircase.

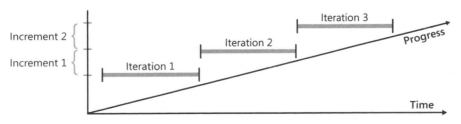

FIGURE 2-2 Incremental development and progress

In agile development, progress is measured in working software. For example, a project that focuses on a throwaway prototype during the first iteration and defining requirements in the next iteration has not demonstrated progress, based on the definition of agile. Similar to a pizza, a project must be cut in slices. The difference is, however, that we won't know in the beginning how many slices we will need and what kind of pizza it will be. We will figure it out as the project continues, slice by slice.

To state it another way, a project will have a few very high-level requirements, and the project team will take one of these requirements (for example, the highest-priority item first) and drill down into more detail. Then the team approaches the more detailed requirements, writes unit tests (as described in the "Test-Driven Development" section), designs and programs the code, and executes test cases periodically. At the end of the iteration, one high-level requirement, a slice of the project, is completed. Now, this is where iterative-incremental development really shines. One requirement is converted into working software and can be demonstrated to the customer just two weeks after the project was kicked off. Think about where your waterfall project would be two weeks into the project. Even better, by taking this approach, we opened an early feedback loop to the customer, who can now make changes and help navigate the project in the right direction (as illustrated in Figure 2-3) according to their expectations.

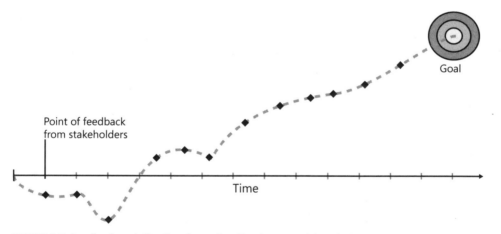

FIGURE 2-3 Feedback and direction for an iterative-incremental project

In my experience, I've seen many projects implement an iterative-incremental approach, but the majority of the customers have not taken advantage of this feedback loop. We have told so many users (wrongly) in the past that software requirements have to be complete and clearly defined up front that we will have to bring customers back to the natural way of building applications—that is, back to an agile way. The feedback loop has huge potential for many projects and shows that transitioning to agile development is a process that includes the customer as well.

Within each iteration, stakeholders will shape the direction of the increment for the scope of the iteration. In between iterations, more significant (and less disruptive) adjustments to the scope of the project are possible and often welcome. Stakeholders who are not involved in the progress of the project on a day-to-day basis are required to take part between iterations. That way, the development team also gets important feedback from peripheral stakeholders and can meet their expectations as well. According to authors Gause and Weinberg (mentioned in Chapter 1, "Motivations"), this is also called the "Yes, but..." syndrome. Whatever follows the *"but..."* are changes in the direction of refining the project. The shorter the cycles between the input and the feedback from stakeholders the better. That is one of the motivations to keep the iterations very short.

We will make heavy use of this feedback loop when agile projects are part of the portfolio.

Besides being able to better manage expectations, the customers and the project team also benefit from iterative-incremental development in many different ways. Nothing is more rewarding than hearing, iteration by iteration, that the team did a good job. Even if they did not, negative feedback allows the team to rectify things in the next iteration or even within the current one. In contrast, in the traditional approach, the verdict comes in so late that the project team cannot take corrective actions. Iterative-incremental development also overcomes requirements paralysis and the issue of ending up with too few requirements. It might sound surprising, but agile, in some respects, introduces more discipline into the process than other project methodologies—such as the discipline to deliver working software in two-week increments. What customer does not like that?

Other advantages of iterative-incremental development include the following:

- The highest risks can be reduced or eliminated in early iterations.
- Confidence in planning and estimation increases iteration by iteration.
- Based on past iterations, trends for a completion date can be determined.
- Completed means completed, not 90 percent done.
- Morale is increased through constant feedback.

Iterative-incremental development is a tremendous change to the traditional development processes currently in place in most organizations. However, this degree of change is worth undertaking, as it immediately provides invaluable benefits.

Test-Driven Development

I know this might make a lot of executives nervous, but many organizations have a lot of untested software code in production. To be fair, though, not even the software engineers are aware of that. One of the reasons is that developers write their code, debug it, make corrections to it, and so forth. What emerges is a network of classes, objects, and methods with a variety of conditions and loops. Nested within these clauses are statements that might never be executed because the conditions that guard (and protect) these statements from execution will never be fulfilled. But who says the condition will go unfulfilled forever?

Agile development promotes a practice of test-driven development (TDD). The idea behind this practice is that the developer writes the unit test prior to the actual code. If you don't know what to test, how do you know what to code? The result is a unit test that tests the actual object but does not interfere with the object itself. The test object contains messages for all the various guards and conditions and makes sure the object acts as planned.

In agile projects, these unit tests are commonly automated, including the code coverage. That way, the project team can monitor the number of classes and the number of unit tests. If the unit tests are falling behind the number of classes, somebody on the team is not practicing test-driven development and unverified code might have entered the code base.

Test-driven development will have a significant positive impact on the quality of a project. The test cases evolve alongside the iterations; therefore, the code base that exists after each iteration is tested. Remember the waterfall approach, where the writing and execution of test cases are commonly performed at the end of the project? And that is exactly when budgets get tight and resources begin transitioning out to other projects.

The idea behind TDD is to capture the unit test code in its own component, separated from the component that implements the functionality. The activity of writing the test code and the functionality are almost parallel, with the test code slightly ahead of the game. Often the unit test as well as the functionality is developed by the same developer (pair). Then both components are compiled and the unit test executes behavior on the component. The results either pass or fail and are recorded. Through the separation of the test and the functionality, a build and, eventually, the release can be easily assembled by simply leaving the test object behind. That also means that the component does not need to be recompiled, which assures that the component with the last time-stamp is the component that passed the test.

With the test cases stored parallel to the actual code using an agile approach, it takes only a small step to automate the execution of these unit tests. This is exactly what agile developers do by using tools to execute the tests when certain triggers occur.

But even if teams are more casual about the timing of writing unit tests, tremendous organizational value can still be achieved. Once the behavior of the team has changed to make writing unit tests a common practice, the team can make a relatively easy transition to the final step—writing them prior to the actual code.

Without any unit tests, regression testing would be extremely challenging and tedious, if not impossible. The automation of the unit tests, and therefore regression testing, must be the basis for test-driven development, which will bring us to the next topic—continuous integration.

Continuous Integration

The integration of components and the testing that goes along with it is nothing new for software engineers. Where agile development substantially differs is in its continuous approach. One of the major issues with the traditional approach is that the testing of the integration is deferred to late phases in the project, and the architecture is expected to just fall into place. In reality, projects can blow up right at the worst possible moment, when little project budget and time are left. Patching problems with workarounds and mediocre approaches might help get the system out the door, but new issues are just waiting to pop up again. There has to be a better way.

One approach with iterative-incremental development is to integrate items at the end of each iteration, but that means that you have this peak and stress at the end of each iteration. So why not, instead, implement ongoing integration? That is exactly what agile teams do. Figure 2-4 shows steps in a continuous integration approach. All of these steps are commonly automated.

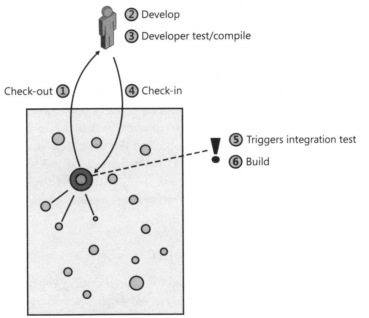

FIGURE 2-4 Continuous integration

Even the trigger for performing the integration can be linked to regular software engineering activities—for example, checking code in through a configuration management system (subversion or CVS [Concurrent Versioning System]). With a continuous integration infrastructure in place, the team, management, and executives in the organization know what the most recent successful version of the system is. When a developer on a waterfall project reports

100 percent done for a certain requirement, that means something totally different than when an agile developer reports something as being 100 percent done. In agile projects, *100 percent* means developed, tested, and integrated.

Continuous integration is relatively easy to achieve from a technical perspective. Many open-source tools have been developed to support the agile development team with its continuous integration efforts. Once the environment is in place, source and version control, execution of tests, creation of software builds, and the continuous deployment of builds are delegated to reliable tools.

Face-to-Face Communication

When I began working with IT projects, there was no such thing as electronic communication. Yes, there was e-mail, which was used to distribute information to the masses, but project team members were usually located in close proximity to one another, if not in the same room. Although we did not have the alternatives we have today, there is something about verbal and nonverbal communication that electronic communication cannot replace. Think about foreign accents or body language, for example. Agile development factors in this loss in communication and forces team members to collaborate directly with one another, person to person, without electronic firewalls. Especially when business analysts and software developers work together, face-to-face communication is essential. Anonymously sharing requirements documents just opens the door to misinterpretation and misunderstandings—not to mention that written information travels so much slower than verbal communication. Just to be clear, I'm not saying that no requirements are documented—they are co-developed, clarified, or negotiated between team members. Last but not least, we are all humans, and a project is a social network. We need these networks to increase morale and fun. I have never come across a project team that worked in an exclusively distributed way and actually had fun.

Things You Observe in an Agile Project

If we compare our agile toolkit with a menu in a restaurant, the foregoing key practices are entrees. In addition, many agile projects make heavy use of complementary tools (side dishes) that either support or enhance the impact of the key practices. Although they seem optional, they should not be ignored.

Pair Programming

Two people work together at the same time on the same code using one keyboard. Pair programming has often had a stigma attached to it in traditional organizations. "Why would I pay two people to do the job of one?" Well, in reality two people often do the job of three!

In the past, I've taught developers in training courses for Java or Smalltalk. During the course, I offered every student the opportunity to pair up with another student during the exercises. Some thought it was a good idea; others argued that they did not pay good money to not have access to the keyboard all the time. Of course, I did not force anybody either way; I just offered the option. I admit, originally the idea was a bit selfish, because I could not assist 10 engineers with individual feedback all the time. It turns out that some of the pairs helped each other with the most basic questions and needed less attention from me. Because they did work out so many things together, they used the instructor time for the tougher questions. At the end of the week, the pairs completed much more course work than the individuals. As a matter of fact, the individuals often held the pairs up in their learning goals. And as a positive side effect, the pairs usually had more fun and shared more laughs.

One of the secrets of pair programming is psychological. Adults, especially, learn most effectively by doing rather than listening or reading. The knowledge is internalized by the learner the first time someone explains or demonstrates it to that person. That is exactly what happens in pair programming. One person does a thing the other person might not know about. Through the question and answer process, the expert explains and the listener receives the knowledge. Now, equipped with the knowledge, the former listener practices it, and so forth. As a positive side effect, two people then know the same code. Think about the benefits of that in terms of sick days, vacation time, and other employee fluctuation.

Building pairs to increase productivity is not new. As a matter of fact, the army uses pairs of soldiers especially during battle at the front. Two soldiers together are more likely to stand up to an attack than individuals. Police departments also often operate with pairs of officers assigned to a case. That reduces slack but it also provides support in the event of a critical situation.

Daily Stand-Up Meetings

Short daily meetings are commonly practiced in Scrum projects, which we will focus on in a later chapter. The art of these projects is that no other meetings are scheduled besides these daily stand-up meetings, which should not last longer than 15 minutes. If you have ever tried to keep a meeting with 5 to 8 people in the 15-minute range, you know how difficult it can be. In Scrum, for example, every team member provides answers to three questions only:

- What have you done since the last meeting?
- What are you planning on doing until the next meeting?
- What issues and impediments are you facing that prevent you from accomplishing these things?

What an agile project manager is interested in are the deliverables and tangible results. That is, in my experience, the point where the daily stand-up meeting most frequently fails. Because we are used to weekly or monthly status reports, we like to elaborate on accomplishments to justify our existence in the project. But seriously, how much tangible output can someone produce in eight hours of work? But these small accomplishments demonstrate daily progress to other team members. Also, quite an important difference from other, traditional, status meetings is the fact that the team members report to each other, not to the project manager.

Stories About Requirements

Stories on index cards are a very common practice in extreme programming. They can be estimated and planned for, and picked up by pairs of developers. Using the following template

<as a > *I want* <the feature> *so that I can* <business value>

the team can produce requirement cards and post these cards in the team room. Once reviewed and prioritized, the cards are subject to iteration planning, and team members sign up to test and develop the items on the cards. Stories just seem to have the right style and are the right size for agile teams to work with requirements.

Writing these stories is not as easy as it might first look. Many project teams struggle with coming up with the right size for the story. Some stories are too granular and user interface focused (for example, "As a customer, I want an OK button so that I can save the changes made to my account information"); other stories are too broad (for example, "As a customer, I want to order a product online so that I can save time going to the store myself").

Team Rooms

The majority of agile projects are based in a single team room, which makes face-to-face communication very easy. In the past, project teams posted their index cards on the wall or on whiteboards and signed up for pair programming by simply looking around the room. Even today, with more tools and technology available to facilitate agile projects, the team room still plays an integral part. Instead of physical index cards posted on the wall, stories are captured on electronic "cards" and projected against the wall or against whiteboards turned into smart-boards with more features to store results more quickly and more conveniently. The idea behind all this innovation, however, is the same. The entire project team always shares and works with the same information and collaboratively works toward the same goal. Therefore, electronic communication across continents is less efficient than communication among team members in the same room. In addition to overcoming difficulties in conducting the daily meetings, geographically distributed projects are challenged by meeting the goals of continuous integration, stakeholder feedback, iteration planning, and pair programming.

Frequent Releases

A *build* is a collection of tested and integrated software components that can be released either internally for verification or externally in a production environment. A build process—which includes the compilation, testing, and integration of all software—can either pass or fail. When a build passes, it represents the last good build. That build is something a test engineer, business analyst, or other stakeholder can work from and use as a test against the original story. A *release*, on the other hand, is a good build that has enough functionality to be released—internally or externally. For example, consider a project that is estimated to last for 12 months. During the first phase, a group of stories is aligned to create a release after 8 months of the project. The second phase of the project (months 9–12) include the other logical group of requirements. The first release can be used inside the organization or unleashed externally. The concept of builds and releases has tremendous influence on agile portfolio management, which I'll discuss in the second part of this book.

Self-Organized Teams

When you observe an agile project, you'll notice, for example, that a pair of developers agree during the daily meeting to tackle a story card—taking ownership and responsibility for a story card for at least a few hours or until the story is implemented. They refer to themselves as *self-managed* or *self-organized*. Surprisingly, at the end of each stand-up meeting, you'll notice that almost magically the work got divided and distributed without any top-down commands. During the next stand-up meeting, team members will report their progress to one another, which means they are also controlling one another. The traditional command-control paradigm we are so used to working in has shifted to a team-organized approach. Does that mean a manager is not needed anymore in an agile project? Because the team is already self-managed, all it needs is a *leader*. The person in that role will drop duties and responsibilities that the team has already taken over, but he or she will pick up new challenges, especially those related to project leadership. Here are just a few examples:

- Facilitating the iteration retrospectives
- Prioritizing the stories for the project and iteration with the business
- Estimating requirements
- Communicating the progress of the project
- Removing organizational and technical obstacles for the team

You might argue that these are responsibilities project managers already had in the past. Yes, but please remember, the leader's sole responsibility is to inject the vision into the project and keep the team focused without a command-and-control style. It sounds like an easy job for future project managers in agile projects, but reality shows that the opposite is the case. Good leaders can steer a project without the team feeling that it is being led. Team members can just do their jobs while the leader creates an environment where everyone feels that everybody is working toward the same goals.

Summary

This chapter covered the most fundamental principles of agile development. These are iterative-incremental development, test-driven design, continuous integration, and face-to-face communication. Additionally, we discussed the techniques that enable agile development—for example, requirements captured in stories, the use of team rooms, and the use of pair programming. After reading this chapter, you should have a sense of the culture in an agile development team and have a vision of how these practices tackle the most common challenges in today's businesses.

Now that we've viewed the world through the glasses of an agile developer, we'll look at agility from a different angle in the following chapter—from the perspective of the agile project manager.

If you are interested in drilling down into more detail in one of these key practices, you will find cross-references for additional recommended reading in the bibliography section at the end of this book.

Chapter 3
Project Management

During the first two chapters, agile software development was introduced from a manager's perspective and we discussed why organizations are getting more and more interested in agile development. Following agile principles requires a rethinking of the traditional project management style as well. In this chapter, I'll showcase why certain project management practices need to be removed or adjusted while new agile management practices need to be acquired. These new skills are necessary for a true agile organizational transformation. Therefore, this chapter focuses on two major topics: the challenges with traditional project management in an agile environment, followed by a new agile-based definition of the role of project manager. Only the correct interpretation of agile development and agile project management will enable agile portfolio management. This chapter will be our bridge to the next part of the book.

Traditional Project Management

Project management is a well-established discipline across all industries. I once met a senior project manager who managed large enterprise information technology (IT) projects. Within his organization, he was extremely successful and had a great reputation. As it turned out, he had actually very little knowledge of information technology. His background was in manufacturing.

First I thought that, because of the size of the projects, his position was so elevated that knowledge in IT might not be necessary. But then he told me that he had experiences with all sizes of IT projects. The keys of his success were that he trusts the team and focuses on leadership and stakeholder management. He also gave me a clear understanding of why project management is a discipline on its own, which is not necessarily dependent on knowledge inside a particular industry. Too many insights can even block the real view of the project, he explained.

I thought about my meeting with him for a long time. I was skeptical and tried to imagine myself in a situation where I was, for example, managing a project in the construction industry. I then realized that even though agile project management was far from being an established concept, he had created his own recipe for project management. Years later, it did not surprise me that agile project management was founded on very similar principles: trust, shared ownership, and stakeholder collaboration. Ironically, the Project Management Institute (PMI), which takes a lot of heat from the agile community, promotes project management as a cross-industry discipline. The issue is that several concepts from the PMBOK are difficult to endorse when applied in an agile context. The PMBOK is short for the *Project Management Body of Knowledge*, which is the framework released by the PMI. According to this process, a project steps through clearly defined and separated phases. This proves to be extremely challenging for IT projects, where requirements and expectations frequently change.

The following are four typical deliverables that are commonly created in traditional projects and promoted through the PMBOK:

- Work-breakdown structures
- Gantt charts
- Critical path analyses
- Project reports

Let's take a look at them in more detail and see what challenges they might present if applied in an agile context.

Work-Breakdown Structures

In traditional development processes, breakdown structures are hierarchical decompositions, often used in the context of work. With a work-breakdown structure (WBS), work is broken down into activities and tasks, and then these work items are broken down into more detail. (See Figure 3-1.) Sometimes cost-breakdown structures and product-work-breakdown structures are created in parallel to the WBS, always using the same approach, which is to drill down into more detail from the top down.

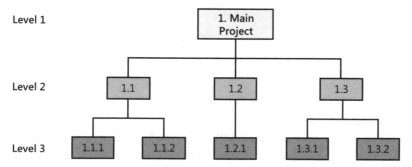

FIGURE 3-1 Work-breakdown structure (WBS)

The lowest level in the WBS hierarchy is also called a *work-package*, which is the level at which estimation is performed and assignments are done. The levels higher in the hierarchy are always combinations of the lower elements. So the bigger the project scope, the more branches there are in the WBS. The challenge with work-breakdown structures traces back to the problem of producing at an early stage a so-called master plan of work. Any work that is not listed in the WBS won't be estimated. As a result, any work performed that is not in the WBS will produce cost overruns. We could argue that the WBS could be constantly updated to reflect the changes caused by scope changes, but that is hardly done in practice. The structure is difficult to adjust.

Another issue with estimating work up front is that the development team has not had the chance to work together and verify the estimates. If one estimate is significantly off, there is a chance that the other estimates are also out of line. Corrections of estimates while the project is under way are difficult to incorporate.

From a psychological perspective, the WBS is owned and managed by the project manager. Work is assigned to team members, and completion is controlled. This top-down, command-and-control management style does not work with agile teams, and it violates the principle of using a team-managed and team-organized approach.

I've met project managers who have told me that they will need the WBS for their own benefit, even though they won't tell the agile team about it. These managers were so accustomed to this work product that they continued using it. It is hard to be against something that gives the project manager confidence, but if the team is not using it, why bother? Are the costs of creating and maintaining a WBS for a project manager justified? Shouldn't the agile project manager work on something else and make better use of her time? Shouldn't she work on something more important and relevant for the project team—for example, removing organizational impediments or facilitating a planning session?

Instead of seeing the project from the perspective of "work to be performed," the agile team takes a different view. They look at the features and functionality of the system and document them as stories on index cards. Because the tasks in every iteration are the same, the focus of work is the story card. The activities for the iterations run parallel to one another; there is no requirements iteration or testing iteration in agile development. The activities are merged together and are continuously performed in parallel. The cards are estimated and prioritized, and the ones found relevant for the business are assigned to iterations. Remember, the feedback loop established through iterative-incremental development easily allows for this.

Gantt Charts

A Gantt chart illustrates the orchestration of the tasks according to timing and dependencies. In traditional projects, this format is frequently used to depict the project schedule. (See Figure 3-2.)

FIGURE 3-2 A Gantt chart

Very much like the WBS, the Gantt chart lays out the project schedule up front. The problem is the lack of predictability and accuracy of the schedule, especially for tasks late in the project. The planning window with the highest accuracy is the short time frame ahead of the day of planning. That is why iterations are so intuitive for many managers. Imagine a project manager in the beginning of a new long-term project. Ask him what the scope of work will be in iteration 20? It seems almost ridiculous to expect the manager to know, right? It is human nature that we think about the first iteration, the second iteration, and maybe a rough sketch of iteration 3. Iteration 3 will be refined once we start with iteration 2, and so forth.

Agile teams, however, know the project goals and have a rough estimate of how to get there. They know where the features and requirements stand at any given moment and the amount of progress expected to be achieved in an iteration.

Try the following experiment the next time you meet with a traditional project team. Ask for the project schedule, which is most likely shown as a Gantt chart. Then compare the actual day (the present day) with the plan. Ask a team member, "Based on this plan, you are currently working on task XY, correct?"

Based on my experience, the answer is most commonly an excuse for why the team is not working on that task, such as the schedule being outdated. The team's good spirit and best instincts are directed most of the time to working dynamically with the project manager instead of following a plan. Developers follow their instinct and trust their common sense. Without those, the project schedule would collapse anyway, because there are so many tasks unaccounted for in the original schedule that just seem to pop up. I have also never seen a project team start work in the morning by looking at the latest edition of the schedule. "Based on the schedule, I should be working on XY." Call it unprofessional or undisciplined; it just hasn't happened in my world.

In all fairness, maintaining the schedule is a full-time job on its own because projects are naturally very dynamic. Occasionally, especially when executives like to get an overview of the progress of the project, it is a team effort to get the Gantt chart up to date. I call this *pastcasting* (instead of *forecasting*) because the schedule's past is put back in order. For various reasons, the plan's history might be put back in order, but it provides no value to the project itself.

In agile projects, which embrace change and a dynamic way of building systems, planning with Gantt charts encounters limitations and is too expensive to maintain. Most important, such planning does not reflect what is really going on in the agile team. An agile team can tell you, however, what its plan for the next iteration is and, possibly, the plan for the following iteration also.

Critical Path Analyses

Performing a critical path analysis is a technique used to identify the shortest way through the project schedule. Any delay of any task on the critical path will delay the completion date. Figure 3-3 demonstrates that activity E cannot start before C and D are completed.

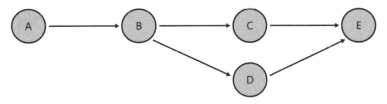

FIGURE 3-3 Task dependencies

Knowing and monitoring the critical path allows project managers to control the progress of the project. One form of illustrating the project schedule and its critical path is the activity-on-node diagram. Each node carries the following information:

- Earliest start
- Latest start
- Earliest finish
- Latest finish
- Duration
- Number
- Name of the activity

By subtracting the earliest start from the latest start, the *float* is determined. If, for example, the earliest start is day 12 in a schedule and the latest start is day 18, we have a float of 6 days. That means this task could be delayed up to 6 days without having to sacrifice the overall schedule. Therefore, this task is not on the critical path. Every task without any float is, however, on the critical path.

Although this technique seems extremely powerful for controlling projects and puts emphasis on the critical tasks in the project, it has its shortcomings when applied in an agile project. A typical sequence for traditional project management is to have the up-front planning followed by the execution. The controlling mechanism of the critical path analysis does not include the adaptive development that takes place in an agile project. As a matter of fact, in agile projects tasks are performed in parallel—for example, writing small units of tests followed by the appropriate messages and methods in objects. A clear separation of tasks is not possible. The detailed level of the tasks would be measured in minutes rather than in hours and days, which are typically the unit of measure captured on an activity-on-node diagram.

In addition, agile projects are not considered to be late as long as the iteration is completed on time. Instead, agile teams measure how much progress has been accomplished within the last iteration. This approach creates a totally different perspective about a project's schedule.

On agile projects, the critical path is nested inside the iteration, and every iteration is on the critical path. Daily stand-up meetings expose the most critical impediments. Suppose a team planned 50 story points and completed 55. They made more progress than planned. If they again plan 50 points for the following iteration and then complete 58, the team seems to be able to deliver more than planned. Having a rough estimate for the entire project, the average progress can be used to draw conclusions on the final delivery. Having each iteration serve as feedback about progress based on tangible output seems to be more effective than projecting the completion of tasks on paper.

Project Reports

Project reports present the state of the project to stakeholders. They provide information about how the project is doing compared with its original plan. In a perfect world, a project manager can ask her team members about the progress of a task. We know by now that IT projects are often far from a perfect world. So there are basically two problems with this approach. First, the plan is often outdated and cannot be compared with reality, and second, the tasks are too broad to measure as "done" or "not done."

For example, a broad schedule might include a task of "Write User Guide," which is estimated to take 100 person-days. It is extremely difficult for a technical writer to give a status report on this task not knowing what is left to complete. A typical answer is 50 percent, 80 percent, or 90 percent done. Also, the last 10 percent might take three times as long as the first 90 percent. So how predictable is this form of status reporting?

Executives who believe in status reports might be disappointed when they realize that a project that was reporting positive figures all of a sudden has to report the breaking news, *"We are running late..."* Whoever believes that the project status reports are exclusively created by the project manager is misinformed. Usually, status reports are a team effort that takes a lot of energy out of the entire team. But worse, while the team is providing status updates and explaining the work it has performed, team members are not making progress on the project itself.

Again, agile project teams use the increment and the iterative rhythm to report their status. For example, using two-week iterations, a project team can demonstrate its accomplishments in producing executable software. The features and requirements are either done or not done, and every claim or measurement is tangible. Using the earlier example, a team can report that a feature was not only converted to running software during an iteration, but it was also documented in the user-guide documentation. Executable software, a build, automated test cases, and a piece of documentation have been completed. All aspects of a manageable piece of functionality have been completed.

In addition, executives and stakeholders can always sneak into the daily stand-up meetings and observe the mood, progress, and issues of the project firsthand.

Summary About Challenges

By examining four typical work products found in traditional project management, you saw the challenges that arise when they are applied in the context of agile projects. The way that scope (via WBS), schedule (via Gantt charts), and progress (via progress reports) are managed and controlled (through critical-path analyses) must be adjusted to techniques that are easier to apply in the context of agile project management. The fundamental idea of project management is, however, still the same. We are still planning work, but agile projects plan around requirements, provide schedules through iterations, analyze the progress (iteratively and daily), and report on the progress to stakeholders through demonstrations and tangible progress.

Keep in mind that the challenges presented here concerning the traditional work products are based on their use in agile IT projects. In other, more predictable and reliable, industries, or in very short projects, their use and application might be appropriate. This is, however, outside my judgment.

Agile Project Management

By now, we know we want to make use of agile development practices in our IT organization, but we also know that the traditional project management techniques just do not map 1:1 to our style anymore. So let's take a look at the role of an agile project manager and that person's responsibilities and techniques for carrying out those responsibilities. Before we do that, let's look at the principles of the project management declaration of interdependence (PMDOI) to reiterate fundamental differences in agile project management.

Project Management Declaration of Interdependence

In addition to adhering to the agile manifesto, agile project managers agree to the project management declaration of interdependence. The following six core values of the PMDOI will give you a good idea of the role of an agile project manager. The PMDOI is consistent with the agile manifesto, but the core values provide a much clearer definition of agile project management. Let's see how the core values relate to the fundamental motivations for agility (which were presented in Chapter 1, "Motivations"). Please note that each core value starts with "We." Agile project managers are a community of professionals who signed the declaration. Also notice that the core values are heavily influenced by the key principle of iterative-incremental development.

- **We increase return on investment by making continuous flow of value our focus.**   Instead of delivering the value of a project in one single piece, agile projects deliver in increments. Therefore, agile projects not only tackle the issues imposed by traditional project management, they also provide a cost-benefit standard as well. This is possible because the value of the project is continuously evaluated. Instead of hoo-raying because "We got it done!" agile project teams hooray because "The right thing is done." The "right" thing is determined by the stakeholders, who define the value of the project to the organization. The agile project manager leads the team to this goal, iteration by iteration.

  Increasing the return on investment requires feature-thinking by all participants. Features add benefits to an organization. The positive impact of some features might be stronger than others. Therefore, the sooner the benefits can be put to use, the higher the return on investment. We will see in subsequent chapters how we can schedule high-priority features to be developed early in the project to increase the return on investment.

- **We deliver reliable results by engaging customers in frequent interactions and shared ownership.**   The end of an iteration is a technical and functional checkpoint for all participants of the project. Equipped with the latest successful build, the project team can demonstrate what functionality has been completed. Delivering in small intervals showcases the reliability of the project team and makes executives confident in the ability of the team. Teams and stakeholders together compare the delivered functionality with the desired outcome. After five iterations, it will be challenging for your customer to argue that the system does not meet his expectations because he agreed to significant portions of the requirements during the previous four iterations. The customer plays an integral part in these interactions and owns the direction of the project.

- **We expect uncertainty and manage for it through iterations, anticipation, and adaptation.**   Remember the "Yes, but..." syndrome from the previous chapter? Your team delivered, but it did not deliver the right thing. Iterative development is the pattern used to close the feedback loop. In agile projects, the customer decides how significant the progress of an iteration was; the customer does this through feedback, redirection, and change requests. Change is common, especially in early iterations. It is the responsibility of the project managers to steer the project toward the vision.

- **We unleash creativity and innovation by recognizing that individuals are the ultimate source of value and creating an environment where they can make a difference.** Every project team member provides value. However, sometimes team members just don't search hard enough to find their best possible role. Generally speaking, software engineers have a good work ethic and like to add value to a project. I can't recall meeting anybody at any time in my career who did not want to deliver something great. As a project manager, you should embrace interesting ideas and suggestions and create a stage for anybody to submit them. Google, for example, encourages their employees to work 20 percent of the time on projects that interest them. Great innovative solutions, such as Gmail and Google News, were the result of this policy. Make this source of ideas your strength.

- **We boost performance through group accountability for results and shared responsibility for team effectiveness.** My favorite question to pose to project teams is, "Who estimates work?" When the answer is not "We do," some work needs to be done to improve project management. Agile project managers need to be facilitators and moderators who lead the team to success. They should not be the estimators. The team estimates the work, which is prioritized by the business. It is also a team member's (or a pair's) responsibility to sign up for work. Think about this. Someone estimates work and then voluntarily signs up for it, and this initiative is combined with good work ethics. These are major ingredients for a successful delivery. Additionally, every team member reports to the rest of the team, not to the project manager.

- **We improve effectiveness and reliability through situationally specific strategies, processes, and practices.** There is a huge difference between being efficient and being effective. We can streamline a development process and make it highly efficient, but it might not be effective. Effectiveness contains results that have an impact on goals—for example, the implementation of a feature can have a cost-effective result. Knowing that effectiveness is the higher standard, the project goals can change over time, and so can the development process itself. Adapting to new situations is essential to your team's success, but the agile project manager must lead in this regard. Watching the effectiveness and reliability of the process and project are an integral part of the project manager role. As a simple example, a project team thought it would be a good idea to start the day with the daily stand-up meeting. They scheduled it for 9:00 a.m. Although penalties were assessed for late arrivals, team members had a tough time being on time. The organization had this early-arrival culture tattooed onto it, so the team had adopted it even though it was not effective for them. In the first retrospective, the team decided to have the daily stand-up meeting later in the day. They adjusted, became more effective in their meetings, and moved on.

Roles and Responsibilities

Now that you know the challenges of traditional project management and the key principles of the PMDOI, it is time to focus directly on agile project managers—who they are and what their duties are. The following roles and responsibilities define what agile project managers are.

Roles

There are primarily two roles in agile project management: the project manager and lead business analyst. Scrum has developed the de facto standard for many agile project managers. I decided to provide a definition for both terminologies.

Project Manager

The term *project management* is deeply rooted in our professional world. Even though in the agile world the project manager would be better described as a project leader, I'll go along with this widely used term. The distinction between *manager* and *leader*, however, is still important for defining the role of an agile project manager. Instead of managing projects, the project leader steers the project team and constantly shapes the vision. The definition of the Agile Project Leadership Network (APLN) reflects this fact. An agile project manager creates a team-managed platform, which encourages the values of the PMDOI. In addition, the project manager applies the key practices for agile development.

Becoming a project manager is often falsely seen as receiving a promotion. Yes, someone with special skills, which we will discuss in more detail soon, was appointed to play this role, but the role is as specialized as any other role taken on by team members. In traditional projects, the team often sees the project manager as an outsider who controls the team's progress and gives out work assignments. Good project managers who follow the agile project management approach are part of the team and are within the team's social boundary. Instead of having a command-control role, the agile project manager collaborates with the team as part of a unit.

The difference between *manager* and *leader* might appear to be subtle, but it has a significant impact on team morale. As a result, the agile project manager's role is probably best described as facilitator or moderator.

In Scrum, the scrum master assures that the rules of scrum are correctly interpreted. In this case, the scrum master executes the daily scrum meeting, conducts the retrospectives, and plans the iteration with other roles by using the project backlog. Chapter 11 takes a closer look at Scrum and how scrum principles are implemented for portfolio management. It also includes an explanation of the terms used in Scrum.

Scrum Master

In Scrum, the role of a project manager is gone. Instead of managing and leading the development effort of the project, the scrum master implements the rules of Scrum in a project and makes sure the team's path is clear so that the team can stay productive. This emphasis on *leading* becomes clear in what is known in Scrum as *sprint backlog planning*, where the project team is empowered to plan and schedule its own work. The sprint backlog contains a list of tasks to be tackled throughout the upcoming sprint, which represents in Scrum a fixed-length iteration of 30 days. The backlog contains a to-do list of activities and deliverables the team needs to tackle. Once the team has entered the sprint, the scrum master facilitates the daily scrum meeting and removes impediments for the team, such as environmental, administrative, or team-related hurdles. Especially in large organizations in which a large project spans organizational hierarchies, the scrum master must be an influential mediator and determined to facilitate the project across departmental boundaries. In such projects, the scrum master must also stand up for the team so that its requests are met; a compromised resolution is often the least desirable outcome.

The role of a scrum master translates probably best to that of a change agent or servant leader who works for the team so that it becomes more productive and effective over time. In Scrum, the responsibilities of traditional project management are divided among three different roles: the product owner, the scrum master, and of course the team.

Business Analyst

Remember the principle of shared ownership and engaging customers at frequent intervals? In internal and large-scale projects, business analysts often serve as the voice of the customer. Agile projects are so dependent on them that they are an integral part of any agile process. In an ideal world, the business analyst works full-time on the project, also inside the team boundary.

Based on my experience, defining this role in an organization is the most challenging of all. Because of the structure of the organization, the business analyst is often part of a different reporting chain. In situations like that, the business analyst is part of or reports to product management, marketing, accounting, and so on, whereas the project team reports to the chief information officer (CIO) or chief technology officer (CTO). This separation creates a gap between these two parties that has to be bridged during the project. The challenge for the project manager is to make the business analysts feel comfortable around all the technical specialists. Sharing the same project room and having direct communication channels is a major element in the agile success story.

Still today, I see so-called agile projects where requirements are handed over from the business analysts to the software development team for implementation. Organizations interested in offshore development even have to deal with language, time, and cultural barriers. In situations like this, the interpretation of agile is often just a little too loose.

Think about the difference in time and money consumed when a developer has a quick question to clarify a requirement. Asking the person on the other side of the table versus writing an e-mail message and waiting until the other person has time to reply. Often e-mail threads introduce more confusion than initially existed. Globally distributed development, where project team members work more anonymously and in a more isolated way, need wise project organization to overcome these challenges. We'll take a closer look at this topic in Part 3 of this book.

One technique, which is out of the ordinary but extremely powerful, is that the development team is allowed to work only when the business analysts are present in the room. Part-time and casual assignments immediately bounce back to the business as an impediment.

Product Owner

Scrum has a different view with regard to the business representation as well. Instead of requirements being written and clarified by team members, they are written by the product owner. This person is a highly visible figure in a scrum project and in the organization. The product owner is primarily responsible for the project's success. The product owner is also responsible for planning each release and works on the specifications for and refinement of the features for the team to develop.

The product owner sits in the driver's seat in terms of authority and prioritization of features. This role is the primary go-to person from a project portfolio management perspective, but it is also the point of contact for the entire project team when questions about the features of the current sprint emerge.

Project Team

Especially for Scrum projects, the team itself takes over many project management activities we know from traditional projects. A self-organized and empowered project team plans the work and assigns work to themselves. If the team prefers to work in pairs, team members sign up and form pairs on their own.

From a reporting perspective, the project team members derive the metrics of the project from their own daily activities, and they broadcast the metrics among the team, product owner, scrum master, and other external project stakeholders. That mechanism keeps the metrics and reports unfiltered and unmassaged.

Responsibilities

The following tasks are typically performed by an agile project manager during or in be-tween iterations, or they are co-performed by an agile project manager and other project team members, such as business analysts, developers, or sponsors. Most commonly the team and business analyst work hand-in-hand with the agile project manager.

Removing Impediments

Every project usually has plenty of impediments—small, unforeseen issues here and there, major problems, and organizational obstacles. Even worse, they can pop up anytime, most commonly at the worst moment. I've seen plenty of teams that have had difficulties getting started because of unknown passwords, insufficient server rights, lack of software licenses, lack of access to rooms, and other internal administrative procedures. Official escalation procedures are commonly used to resolve these issues, but even those procedures can take weeks and sometimes months to clear the issue.

In addition to administrative issues, challenges related to technologies and requirements commonly arise. There are two mechanisms in agile projects that deal with these impediments. First, the daily stand-up meeting, where issues are expressed and captured for resolution, and second, the role of the project manager (scrum master), who is responsible for tackling issues that impede team progress. Therefore, the agile project manager must be willing to go the extra mile within the organization and serve the team. You can see here that the role of a project manager can be quite different from a development role. An introverted brilliant test engineer might not like becoming an agile project manager.

During the daily meetings, the team repeatedly expresses an issue until it is resolved. In return, the project manager reports progress on resolving impediments back to the team. So everyone should have at least a little progress to report on—the team reports development activities, and the project manager reports about impediments.

If other stakeholders participate occasionally in one of the daily stand-up meetings, everyone should sense the urgency and importance of certain open issues. Just to be clear, paving the path for a project and removing impediments could be a full-time job in itself.

Iteration Planning

Iterations are usually between 2 and 6 weeks long. The shorter the better, especially in the early stages of the project. Many times, I've been asked if the iteration length can vary. In my experience, fixed-length iterations throughout the entire project work best. I have seen projects in which project managers started with two 4-week iterations and then switched to a 2-week rhythm. There are several good reasons why this can be a good idea. One reason is that it can reduce the pressure of a 2-week iteration for new agile teams. Once the team gets more familiar with iterative-incremental development, a reduction to shorter iterations might be beneficial. Changing the length of iterations (for example, 2, 3, 4, 2, and then 5 weeks) based on the intensity of the planned stories is, however, not recommended and not needed. There are great books available that assist you with assigning requirements (stories, use cases, and nonfunctional requirements) to iterations instead of the other way around. Stories documented on index cards are common among agile developers, as are the techniques for iteration planning.

If an agile project uses use cases instead of stories, the procedure of iteration planning remains similar. A use case represents a collection of start-to-end business scenarios. Some of them are common and typical; other scenarios might be alternatives or exceptional cases and less frequently executed. The challenge with use cases is that some of them are long and complex, whereas others are easier. In addition, dependencies exist between them. If you look closer at use cases, you'll notice that they usually consist of an abundance of scenarios. Therefore, instead of tackling the entire use case, the team must focus on individual scenarios. With that approach, even dependencies between the scenarios can be resolved. A positive aspect of documenting requirements with use cases is that identifying and documenting these scenarios in this format flows naturally with the work that business analysts perform regularly. Figure 3-4 (which abbreviates *use case* as *UC*) shows how the implementation of a use case is done incrementally, scenario by scenario.

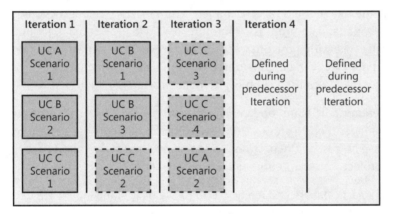

FIGURE 3-4 Iteration plan with use-case (UC) scenarios

Although a rough outline and the high-priority requirements are determined by the customer, the project manager facilitates the iteration planning session with the rest of the team. That way, dependencies between requirements can be considered and the best possible plan for the upcoming iteration can be assembled, according to the wish list of the customer.

In the second part of this book, when I outline the agile portfolio management approach, you'll see how essential iteration planning is. We will then apply the practice of iterative development to the organizational level and get the entire organization into a rhythm.

Retrospectives

Retrospectives are not lessons learned. They are much more. Traditional *lessons-learned sessions* are scheduled at the end of a project. Not only is it too late at that point for the team to rectify behavior and remember all the "lessons," it is also challenging to get all the people at a table together when the project is over. Agile teams perform *retrospectives* in between iterations. The project manager facilitates the retrospective, which includes iteration review and iteration planning (preview). Psychologically, the term *lessons learned* also implies that there was something to learn. That is not always the case and can lead to a negative impression that something else could have been done instead by changing the project and the process.

Estimation

There are two famous questions that customers ask project managers: "How long will the project take?" and "How much will the project cost?" Especially at the beginning of a project, these questions are extremely difficult, if not impossible, to answer. If you ask a team to estimate the answers to these questions based on a few index cards or use-case scenarios, the likelihood of getting a good estimate turned around is higher. If you ask a team after a few iterations to estimate the time and cost of completing tasks on a few new cards, the accuracy of the estimate gets better and better. Why?

With every retrospective, the team reflects on the past iteration. Some requirements might have been underestimated; others might have been overestimated. The team's estimate of upcoming requirements takes the experience from previous estimations into consideration.

Traditional project managers, who have usually been transitioned from an engineering role to a project manager role, tend to produce estimates themselves or influence the estimation of others. This heroic attitude of "I could get it done in two days instead of four" does not really help if team members cannot get it done in two days. There is also no proof that the manager could get it done anyway. This kind of assistance does not add any value to the team. Sometimes project managers influence the team through a backdoor approach such as, "Do you agree that this task takes about two days?" Do estimation practices like that really help your project, your customer, and the expectations?

To prevent this issue, agile project managers stay out of the estimation exercise unless they play both roles on the team. In agile projects, the development team, and only the development team, produces the estimates. The agile project manager captures and tracks the estimation results and, of course, the actual results. Remember, the project manager should "lead" the project and connect with the customer and sponsors, rather than micromanaging people. The selected estimation technique should be easy and quick to adopt—for example, a Wide-Band-Delphi (discussed in Chapter 5, "Metrics and Reporting"). Another effective method is having team members hold up a certain number of fingers for estimated efforts and size and then averaging the results.

For example, a project team gets together and publicly estimates the effort. Everybody's input has been heard, a quick average is taken, and the process is continued for the next estimation. Even if a story was underestimated or overestimated, it will balance out over time, just like the calls from umpires in baseball. An alternative, but more time-consuming, method is to collect the estimate from the team members anonymously. That reduces the chances that, especially during early estimating sessions, team members are unduly influenced by their colleagues.

By the way, the planning poker game (which you can learn more about at *http://www. planningpoker.com*) is a variation of the Wide-Band-Delphi estimation technique.

Reporting

As with estimating, the quality of the reporting gets better over the course of the iterations. An agile project manager has extremely powerful tools to report status almost in real time. But to keep the team focused on its deliverables, the exchange of these metrics is suggested in between iterations only. Considering that the iterations are only 2–6 weeks long, it is still a very frequent exchange of reliable information. Reporting in agile projects is extremely powerful because teams can always share internally and externally the requirements that have been completed (stories), the progress (size of stories) of the project, and the quality (defects) of the system. When asked, the project manager can accurately answer the following questions: "What has been done?" "How are we doing ?" and "How good is the system?" This is enough information to judge whether the past iteration was a success.

Remember, all the data is naturally created by the agile developers and business analysts while they are working. No extra effort is necessary to generate the data.

Daily Stand-Up Meeting

The agile project manager facilitates the daily stand-up meeting, ensures that the meeting starts on time, and ensures that it is conducted in a timely manner, usually no longer than 15 minutes. If the team is geographically dispersed, the meeting time needs to be synchronized and resources need to be synchronized and prepared. Facilitation of this meeting includes ensuring that team members report status to each other in a collegial way and side discussions are eliminated. Impediments that might be expressed during the meeting are captured as a to-do list for the project manager. The challenges of this activity are to keep the team on track and the meeting on time. To simplify the logistics of this meeting, it is usually conducted at the same time each day and within the team room. Because the daily stand-up meeting is open to the public, bystanders can receive additional ad hoc status updates from the project team.

Leading

During the iteration, leadership skills are needed to keep the team moving. Typical issues within the team are that trivial or very challenging defects have not been tackled, a build broke and no developer took ownership to resolve the issue, two developers pair up too much and need to mix more with the rest of the team, and requirements need to be negotiated. The agile project manager reminds team members to get things done, asks for status updates for critical items throughout the day, and captures completion.

The agile project manager also represents the team to the outside world and also protects the team from the outside world. Too much interference can distract the team from its goals. Agile project managers report to the executive manager and portfolio managers, as we will see in the second part of this book.

Summary

This chapter introduced the roles and responsibilities of an agile project manager, and it explained how they differ from traditional project management. We explored typical tasks of an agile project manager—in particular, the tasks of estimating, reporting, planning, performing retrospectives, and performing day-to-day activities such as removing impediments.

Part II
Defining, Planning, and Measuring Portfolios

In the first part of this book, I detailed the common understanding of agile development and management throughout the industry. I also defined some critical business drivers for agility and the motivations behind this software development process.

Now, during this second part, I'll elevate the agile principles to the business and executive levels, which are typically sponsoring these IT projects. For that reason, you'll need to establish a new mechanism for sharing and exchanging information between the IT department and the business or management entity. Although I've already covered in the first part of this book what agile teams do and produce, I still need to establish for you a clear definition of an agile portfolio, its practices, and its links within the organization.

Throughout Part 2 (Chapters 4 through 10), I'll provide a detailed description of agile portfolio management, which orchestrates the collaboration between executives, the business, and the agile IT projects. Here are the chapter topics:

- Chapter 4, "Foundation," covers the fundamentals of portfolio management and the organizational models.

- Chapter 5, "Metrics," defines a set of metrics that will help executives assess the status of an agile project.

- Chapter 6, "Return on Investment," is dedicated to the financial decisions that are made when projects are kicked off or evaluated.

- Chapter 7, "Project Portfolio Management," outlines the tactical and strategic options when agile projects are selected and the entire project portfolio is evaluated against the corporate strategy. We will also discuss how proposals are submitted and managed through the concept of a funnel.

- Chapter 8, "Resource Portfolio Management," describes how project resources are managed in an agile portfolio. The chapter includes details about managing financial, human, and technological resources.

- Chapter 9, "Asset Portfolio Management," presents the last of the three portfolios in this book. The asset portfolio contains the materialized vision, projects, and systems that have been completed in the past. After these projects are completed, the vision of an organization does not stop evolving. For that reason, even completed projects will feed the project portfolio with new project proposals. Retiring, enhancing, or replacing operational systems is the topic of this chapter.

- Chapter 10, "Portfolios in Action," provides an example of how these portfolios interact, integrate, and harmonize. I chose a fictional scenario-driven approach to illustrate the evolution of the portfolio dashboard in an agile enterprise. The dashboard provides at any given moment a snapshot view of the evolution of the portfolio.

Chapter 4
Foundation

To promote agility in the enterprise and apply agile principles throughout its projects, you'll need to recognize the organizational structure that's in place. Even though every organization has perhaps a slightly different spin in terms of hierarchies and structures, it usually fits into one of the three categories: functional, projectized, or matrix. I'll describe how these structures work with agile development. Furthermore, I'll define projects, programs, portfolios, and their relationship within the rest of the organization and its project management office.

Facts

Before we take a deep dive into agile portfolio management, let's get a statistical feel for the size of the information technology (IT) portfolio management market in general.

Gartner, the world's leading information technology research and advisory company, reported in 2007 that the revenue for portfolio management software products increased over 7 percent, reaching nearly $7.2 billion in total software sales by 2006. The forecasts for the upcoming years include a two-digit percentage increase, which means that yearly portfolio management revenue will break the $1 billion mark by 2009.

Why is there such a big demand for portfolio management tools? Research shows that 40 percent of the IT investments in the US fail to deliver the intended results. Considering that more than $2.3 trillion is invested in IT projects in the U.S. every year, it is understandable that executives try to keep an eye on their IT projects. This transparency enables them to make a true and fair assessment of a project and its progress.

Gartner suggests that 40 percent of all IT organizations rely on manually harvested project metrics, which *"...is labor intensive and error-prone."* Portfolio management software products create a platform for exchanging deliverables and look like a quick fix for the problem of manually creating project metrics. The products, however, embrace the existing process and often deal with maintenance projects inside the portfolio rather than with innovative new projects. According to the META Group (an information technology market assessment firm that was acquired by Gartner in 2005), a staggering 84 percent of all organizations do not create business cases for their projects at all, or they do it just for a few key projects. Additionally, 89 percent of all organizations have no metrics in place and have literally no clear view into their projects. When you consider all the unused potential of project resources (human and financial) combined with the lack of business value, it is not surprising that chief information officers (CIOs) have the shortest tenure among all executives.

Running parallel to these trends in portfolio management are the eye-opening trends and developments within the agile community. For example, attendance at the annual agile conference rose from 675 in 2005 to 1100 in 2006 to a sold-out event with 1600 attendees in 2007. Although agile development typically grows from the bottom up in organizations, project managers, business analysts, and executive managers are now getting more and more involved, and they have very good reasons to do so.

VersionOne, for example, conducted the second "State of Agile" survey in 2007, which suggested that 90 percent of agile adopters realize increased productivity. Furthermore, 83 percent of adopters materialized at least 10 percent acceleration in time-to-market de-livery and 66 percent decreased their costs by at least 10 percent. With all the focus on in-creasing the pace of delivery and reducing costs, you might think that the quality might be lacking. The opposite is actually the case: 85 percent of the same agile adopters indicate that their defects were reduced.

When asked what their motivations were for adopting agile processes, many of those responding indicated that the root cause was the need to improve portfolio management. Twelve percent wanted to increase project visibility, 24 percent were interested in accelerat-ing time-to-market delivery, and 30 percent had the goal of better coping with changing business priorities.

Agile development claims only a very small fraction of the overall worldwide IT budget, but that number is steadily increasing. Based on the facts outlined in the *State of Agile* sur-vey, this trend is likely to continue. Agile projects have proven that they return the amount invested in them and consistently live up to their promise. So what are the obstacles that prevent agile from flourishing in organizations? Thirty-six percent of those participating in the survey responded that there was a general resistance to change, 24 percent blame lack of management support, and another 25 percent blame their current existing organizational boundaries.

There is a trend in the IT industry to accommodate two key needs demonstrated by the statistics introduced in this section. An increasing agile workforce will make these needs even more relevant.

First, agile project teams need a simple and effective mechanism for exchanging project information with their stakeholders. In addition, the agile project team needs to be prepared to realize a vision that might not be captured in a business case. Second, executive manage-ment needs to see into the operations and steer projects so that they provide their expected value. The ability of executive management to lead instead of manage a project, combined with the benefits of agile development practices, will increase productivity, quality, morale, time-to-market delivery, and the ability to react to change.

The link and collaboration between the business and the agile development teams is described as *agile portfolio management*.

Organization

Every organization has a structure and culture. Each organizational culture is unique and is a combination of all individuals' skills, practices, and social behavior. The culture comes in so many variations and flavors that it needs to be assessed on a case-by-case basis. How to assess corporate culture is not a topic covered in this book. Although organizational structures are also very diverse, they can usually be generalized as belonging to one of three distinct types: functional, projectized, or matrix. A blend of these models is also possible and is referred to as a *composite*. It is important to understand the structure of an organization, particularly how it affects the interaction and collaboration between departments and individuals, before we lay out an agile portfolio management strategy.

Functional Organization

In a functional organization, departments are organized in silos. Figure 4-1 illustrates how an organization is divided into silos of functionality—for example, having human resources (HR), accounting, marketing, and IT all report to the CEO. The larger the organization, the greater the chances are that you'll find subhierarchies with specialized functionality inside the silos. The managers of the subhierarchies report upward in the chain, with the information eventually being reported to the CEO.

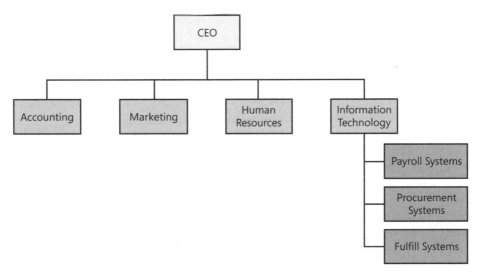

FIGURE 4-1 Functional organization

Two advantages found in a functional organization are the simplicity of communication and the presence of a project sponsor who has a vested interest in every endeavor of the project. Aside from the advantages of clear communication channels and a dedicated sponsor, the functional organization provides little of value for agile portfolio management because of its command-and-control environment. For example, the functional structure has the following negative affects on agile portfolio management:

- Functional structures restrict the ability of team members to cross organizational boundaries, making it difficult for them to collaborate on requirements and an overall project strategy.

- The project team has little authority compared with their managers, who are in charge of the line of business (also known as line managers) as well as career development.

- Line managers become project managers, making the project manager role overloaded with political considerations.

- Communication goes through one channel—that is, up and down the chain of command through the line manager.

- There is little room for creativity because of the lengthy bureaucratic approval process.

- There is a greater degree of subjectivity when corporate strategies are defined.

Functional organizations find it very challenging to adopt agile portfolio management as well as agile software development. The longer the structure has been in place, the harder it is to change the behavior of the employees from the top down. Because of organizational policies and the lack of exposure people have to other people and processes outside their own silo, implementing a bottom-up approach is also significantly more challenging than in other structures. Existing procedures and policies result in bottom-up changes being rare. This structure is ideal for companies that manufacture consumer products. These repetitive production cycles are less dependent on innovation or creativity.

Projectized Organization

In contrast with the silos in the functional organization, the projectized organization consists exclusively of projects rather than being organized around functionality. Every project has a project manager who is fully authorized for the duration of the project. (See Figure 4-2.)

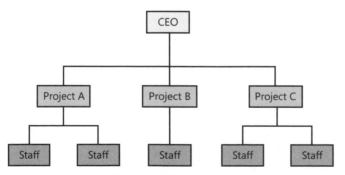

FIGURE 4-2 Projectized organization

The advantage is not only that the project team is in charge of and responsible for its actions but also that the projectized organization changes dynamically with the implementation of each project. Other positive factors that this structure holds for agile portfolio management are as follows:

- It's easy to hire external consultants, even ones who are geographically distributed.

- Teams are empowered and on the radar screen of the organization.

- The organization has a project-oriented culture.

- It's easy to manage resources from an organizational perspective.

- Team members are not distracted by operational work.

- It's easy to assign work to consultants and third parties, including giving them full responsibility for parts of the project.

A side effect of this project-focused structure is that project team members need to have a personal vision and career path that extends beyond each project. This structure is the most modern of the three presented and is a very good candidate for accommodating agile portfolio management.

This organizational model is especially appropriate for companies that constantly schedule numerous projects. Organizations that focus more on operational aspects are, as a general rule, better served with the functional or matrix form.

Matrix Organization

The matrix organization adds a new dimension to the functional organization—in our case, a hierarchy for project management that is parallel to the existing departments (human resources, accounting, or marketing). This organizational form is useful for businesses that need departments for the operational activities to keep the business going but that also need to be able to smoothly instantiate new projects. Figure 4-3 demonstrates that project management becomes divided among project managers who crosscut vertically through the silos of the functional departments.

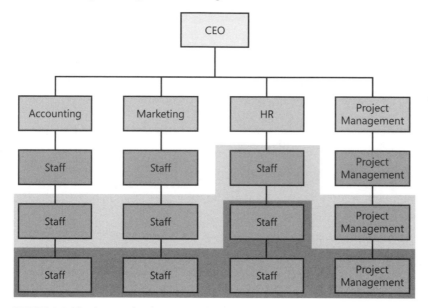

FIGURE 4-3 Matrix organization

For example, suppose a project is needed to develop a new component for the payroll system. A team is assembled from members of the IT organization as well as from human resources. In this type of structure, the supervisory roles and authorities are the same as in the functional silos, but for the duration of the project the project manager is authorized to build a team across the silos. Advantages for agile projects inside the matrix organization are these:

- Team members will always have a home, even after the completion of the project.

- Achieving dedication to projects by sharing best practices of project management is its own branch of the organizational chart.

- It's relatively easy to assemble project teams.

- There is broad stakeholder involvement.

The one big disadvantage of this organization is that competing functional managers have different political agendas. They might not assign resources in the best interest of the organization or project. The individuals on the team are challenged when communicating their accomplishments through the channels. Conflict of interest is created when team members do not know who the target audience is for project reporting (especially the bad news) or how reports might affect career improvement. The reporting structure within the project itself can also create problems. That is the case if a team of junior and senior team members from different departments are mixed to form a project team. It is also not uncommon that the individuals in a matrix organization become confused about their roles, especially for longer projects when team members report to the project manager more frequently than to the manager of the department. The longer these projects last, the further an employee may drift away from the department.

The matrix is probably the best next step for a functional organization that is interested in agile portfolio management. The matrix allows for the inclusion of stakeholders from a variety of departments and already includes the notion of *projects*. Ideally, for the duration of the project, the resources from all departments are 100 percent committed to the project. However, in reality, that is often not feasible. That level of commitment is particularly a problem during the daily stand-up meetings, when team members decide to participate based on their personal schedules. Those schedules might be affected by their duties in other lines of business.

As mentioned earlier, the three structures defined in this section do not always fit these definitions exactly. The matrix structure in particular comes in different flavors, which are called weak, balanced, and strong. The project manager in the weak matrix oversees the project but has little authority. In the balanced matrix, the project manager shares the authority with the line manager, and the project manager in the strong matrix has full authority. Because authority is not a strong characteristic for agile project teams, any of the flavors would work. The success of agile projects is much more dependent on how the agile project manager collaborates with the line manager on a day-to-day basis and keeps team members protected from having to perform operational duties.

Composite Structure

Many organizations have a variety of these structures in place—as a matter of fact, they often have parallel implementations. For example, a functional model might be applied to the operational work (assembly line, procurement) and very critical projects are executed through a projectized model (for example, the research department). For that reason, a variety of rules and reporting structures might be in place depending on the part of the organization your project finds itself in.

Project Management Office

To successfully share and communicate good project management practices across an organization, a project management office (PMO) is usually established. This is particularly true for large organizations, where many projects can benefit from the services of a PMO. The PMO is a common unit in projectized and matrix organizations, where the members report to the executive level of the organization or to the project management branch. Figure 4-4 shows common options for structuring a PMO in a matrix organization.

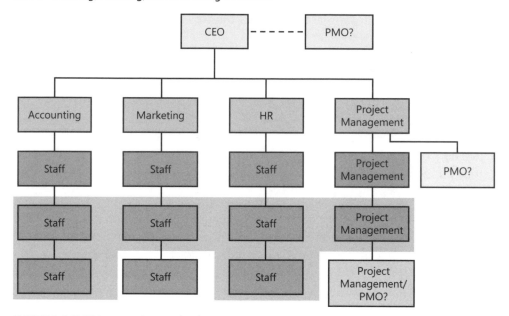

FIGURE 4-4 PMO in a matrix organization

In a strong project-focused matrix organization, where alignment of the overall strategy with the portfolio is essential, the PMO takes an advisory role with direct connection to the chief executives or upper management. Alternatively, the PMO can also report to the head of project management. That way, the PMO works hand in hand with its line of business and shares in good project management practices.

In a more loosely connected way, the PMO can also be a resource pool of project managers who take on responsibilities as the project leader or mentor in a project. That way, the harvested best practices from and for the PMO are the most realistic ones. In this scenario, the metrics and reporting structures have to be extremely lean and agile to be effective so that PMO personnel serving as project managers aren't burdened with other commitments.

In a projectized organization, the PMO has two reporting channels: one to the executive level to align the mission of the PMO with the rest of the organization and one to each project within the organization. The latter channel results in the PMO distributing and communicating successful practices across all other projects in the organization.

In some cases, the PMO plays an advisory role for the top-level executives; in others, it is actively participating in active projects. Part 3 covers the role of a PMO in an agile organization.

Terms and Definitions

By no means should this section be considered an in-depth introduction to project management. It is designed, instead, to provide you with common definitions of project management terms. Let's walk through them quickly. Additional reading material is listed in the bibliography section at the back of this book.

Project

According to the Project Management Institute (PMI), *"A project is a temporary endeavor undertaken to create a unique product, service, or result."*

This definition contains several key words that make it particularly accurate. *Temporary* indicates that a project has a boundary of time. The initial start and the forecasted end date provide the time frame. We know from our agile discussions that this boundary might be initially loosely defined, but the project still is given expected start and completion dates. Therefore, projects are not activities that are part of daily ongoing operations.

The second important word is *unique*. A project must introduce some level of newness to the organization. That uniqueness, however, introduces risks, because the newness of the project makes it difficult to guarantee that the goal will be reached within the set time frame. Figure 4-5 illustrates the important characteristics of a project and highlights that the uniqueness of a project comes with risks.

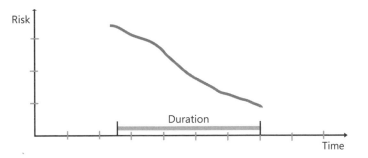

FIGURE 4-5 Project characteristics

Agile practices such as test-driven development, continuous integration, and iterative-incremental development have one goal in mind: reducing various risks while the project is in progress. Agile processes can be applied to initiate projects for a variety of industries—for example, product development. But "a project" could also mean an effort to transform an organization that uses traditional project methodologies into one that adopts agile development.

The "Big Dig" in Boston is a great example of a project. In addition to having an initial start and end date, it was also the biggest engineering effort in the history of the United States.

The project involved creating a very large underground tunnel system to relieve the city of Boston from downtown traffic jams. A project of this magnitude definitely justifies calling it a unique endeavor. Although the project was eventually completed, it was not completed on the originally planned end date. Therefore, the project compromised the original time and cost estimates, but the planned outcome was achieved. To distinguish between project success and failure, organizations must specify goals that projects will be measured against.

For agile projects, the goals cannot always be clearly defined when the project is being kicked off because of the lack of requirements. Keep in mind that this is not necessarily a weakness. The entire team and management will revisit the goals while the project is in the early iterations.

Program

When projects become really large, as did the "Big Dig," they are commonly broken down into smaller projects. These smaller projects then have project managers assigned to them individually, and demonstrating the agile spirit, the project teams take responsibility for the projects. The overall effort is coordinated by a program manager. Programs are large in size and often span many organizational boundaries. Therefore, programs often require larger investments, and the managers who manage such large endeavors are *program managers*.

It is important, however, that each project within the program serve the common goal of the program. Therefore, the projects have relationships and dependencies with one another. A change of direction of one project has to be in sync with the vision of the program, and it can affect the goals of the neighboring projects.

Because of the size of programs and the necessary resource allocation, programs are planned in phases, where a few projects are higher in priority than others. Similar to allocating features to iterations, projects are planned so that the dependencies are resolved and priorities are considered.

Even though agile project teams test, build, and integrate often, the integration of projects within a program requires even more attention and effort from the participants. For example, in a program comprising six projects, perhaps only three of the six projects are instantiated while the other three are placed on the back burner until resources are available. Each project could also be very large as well, perhaps requiring every one of them to be organized and broken down into several agile teams.

In this scenario, not only is every team responsible for executing its tests and producing builds, the teams also need to plan periodic integration points with other participating projects. For example, each team working on the three active projects executes its own daily stand-up meeting. In addition, the three project managers meet to resolve impediments related to the integration of the projects. Last but not least, also periodically, the project managers of all three projects and the overall program manager meet and share reports of their progress and discuss impediments they might have created for one another. After resources have been identified, one of the three future projects can be kicked off and included in the program management process.

Portfolio

Each portfolio is like a collection of assets and investments, and every organization might decide to split these assets into three common portfolios in the IT organization: project, resource, and asset. That way, members of the IT organization will have access to concentrated information about the assets and investments. Even better, the overall dashboard can provide synergies between these portfolios. Chapter 11 will take a closer look at the dashboard view. Using all of these portfolios, or a combination of them, is the most effective way to conduct portfolio management. This book has dedicated chapters for each view as it relates to agile management practices. The important point here is that using all three portfolios together increases the focus on projects, personnel, and existing systems. It provides flexibility in starting and stopping projects and reduces redundancies of work within the organization. Using all three portfolios reduces organizational waste and the burden associated with project and product management inside organizations.

Through *asset portfolio management*, executives monitor the spending related to IT systems currently in operation. That budget includes ongoing operational costs such as hardware, upgrades, and service center fees. It might also include costs for staff to keep the system well maintained.

Project portfolio management is a view on projects that are currently in development. Therefore, upon delivery, a project transitions out of the project portfolio into the application portfolio. Application and project portfolios will both be covered in dedicated chapters.

Resource portfolio management is related to managing the talent pool in an organization. It keeps track of available and needed resources for future IT projects. Within the resource portfolio chapter, we'll take a close look at the specifics of this kind of portfolio.

Basically, a portfolio can be compared with a watch list or grouping. An agile project portfolio, for example, contains individual projects and sometimes programs. Programs can be treated in three different ways:

- Every project that is part of the program will be tracked as an individual project.

- The program is tracked only at its highest level—the program metrics themselves.

- The dependencies among the projects within the program are also tracked.

In organizations where a program plays a crucial role, it is also not uncommon to have a separate portfolio for the program itself. In this case, the program manager also plays the role of a portfolio manager. In a separate activity, the program portfolio is synchronized with the entire project portfolio of the organization.

Stakeholders

Every role within an organization looks at portfolio management from a different angle. For example, each member of the finance or accounting department might look at the portfolio to get information about potential audits or financial resources. The CEO wants to see the current and planned value to inform other stakeholders, including the shareholders, about it. The technician compares projects in the portfolio in terms of innovation, complexity, and technical strategy.

There is, of course, no complete list of potential portfolio stakeholders because every organization has a unique culture. If you are in charge of a portfolio, keep in mind that everyone has different expectations of the information gathered in the portfolio.

Goals

There can be many different reasons why an organization decides to implement portfolio management. Three of the most popular ones are high-level goals that motivate executive management to invest in portfolio management:

- Maximizing value of the entire organization
- Achieving a balance between investment and return
- Linking the strategy of the portfolio with goals of the organization

In practice, striving for all of the goals at the same time is extremely challenging. Organizations struggling with such a challenge usually show one or more of the following symptoms:

- Too many projects are under way at the same time.
- Projects rarely get terminated, even when they should be.
- Not enough resources are available for the project.
- There is a lack of metrics for the project.
- There is no vision for the project.

Let's take a look at these symptoms before we illustrate how agile practices will respond to these challenges and prevent an organization from suffering from these symptoms.

Too Many Projects

Every active project added to the portfolio consumes project team resources and also requires more resources to be dedicated to administering the portfolio itself. If, for example, a team of executives comes together once every other week to assess and evaluate portfolios, a portfolio of 50 projects is easier to assess than one with 100 active projects.

In addition, when there are too many projects on the radar, the organization can hardly keep up with spreading good project management practices within the organization. A project management office (PMO), which is an organizational unit with an advisory and control function, then needs to be created. Further, even though there are common practices in place, the procedures for project initiation and reporting might not be consistently followed. That is related to the communication effort of the PMO to other units within the organization by sharing best practices across the enterprise or harvesting metrics from the projects. Subsequently, the execution of project tasks and phases will turn chaotic, and internal costs will spiral upward. Reducing the number of projects will therefore have a positive impact on the PMO. It can focus on the most important projects in the organization and share practices and techniques in a coordinated fashion.

In Chapter 7, "Project Portfolio Management," we review the various options for initiating and executing agile projects. That chapter introduces techniques to reduce both the number of projects in the portfolio and internal costs. In addition, Part 3 of this book takes a fresh look at the PMO and its role in an agile organization.

Projects Rarely Get Terminated

Terminating or canceling projects is often seen as an organizational weakness. But it is also a weakness if an organization never, ever terminates a project. The difficulty in terminating a project can be traced back to the time when the project was kicked off. If a project has to be canceled, the person who gave the thumbs-up for it must admit to being wrong. From the definition of *project*, we know that every project has to live with uncertainties and has a specific time frame. When project risks are high, the project's potential payoffs are also high. Not taking on risky projects out of fear of having to cancel them later might not be good decision making in the long run.

Consider a project for building a new system using a new but highly promising technology. After three months, the executive team realizes that the time was not right for that technology and cancels the project. Two years later, the technology becomes the standard in the industry. Resources and support are easy to find, and the project is far less risky to get started now. On the flip side, the potential payoffs of the project are much lower. We realize that the time frame of the project has a significant impact on risk assessment.

What we need is a mechanism to address the risks and situations while the project is in flight in an iterative rhythm. That way we are able to abandon the project if necessary. From an organizational point of view, canceling a project could be good thing. Consider a project that takes on a life of its own and competes for resources in the organization without ever being officially initiated. These projects simply start and continue consuming resources, while nobody revisits their purpose. More important projects might starve for attention because of these rogue projects.

To treat this symptom of too few projects being terminated, we'll need to perform a periodic check of the projects inside the project and within the portfolio. Sounds like the end of an iteration, right? Not only do we have a checkpoint after each iteration, we also know the progress (increment). Based on this information, go/no-go decisions can be made. Chapter 7 outlines a different approach and demonstrates how agile projects provide more options when projects are being selected and iteratively reapproved.

Not Enough Resources Are Available

Many large IT organizations have a tremendous resource pool, but you still hear in meetings that a project does not have enough people. Even though the human resources budget might be large, sometimes too many projects need to consume more resources than are available. When the resource pool works at full capacity, with no other options for adding capacity, a request from projects to add more people to the project's staff is most often resolved by splitting the time of existing personnel between assignments. That solution gives the impression that every project is moving along. The opposite is the case.

Task switching has its internal price tag and makes matters worse. The root cause of insufficient human resources is the lack of an overall portfolio management strategy. The reason why resources are sparse could be that too many people are working on lower-priority projects. Instead of resources being spread and split across the entire portfolio, proper prioritization and alignment of projects with the corporate strategy will identify the most important project. Once it is identified, resources are focused on the most important project only, and team members can make progress on that project without being distracted. Other projects that cannot attract sufficient resources have to be placed on the back burner. If additional financial resources become available, projects can be outsourced to consultants.

Agile projects require a full-time commitment, which reduces the task-splitting penalty and keeps the team focused. In daily stand-up meetings, team members have one audience to report progress to: their one and only team. By using trend indicators unique to agile project management, resources can be better planned, scheduled, and coordinated within the organization. Chapter 8, "Resource Portfolio Management," discusses these opportunities in depth.

Lack of Metrics

In meetings with members of the project management offices and executive managers, I often witness the same frustration. These higher-ups don't know what is really going on inside the active projects. Yes, managers have their reporting channels and status reports, but if you have, for example, 500 active projects in an organization, it is impossible to digest all the textual, often unstructured, information and draw conclusions from it. Even worse, the project status might be reported at different intervals and in different formats. Instead of making the right decisions about strategy, managers spend valuable time filtering, condensing, and evaluating information.

What is needed is a channel of transparent project information. We know from the discussion of agile development practices in Part 1 that agile projects produce a very powerful set of progress and quality metrics. We do not want to put an additional burden on the team to produce more status information. We'll discuss the opportunities these metrics provide for portfolio management in the following chapter, "Metrics." That chapter describes how agile metrics are interpreted and how these metrics help to assess even very large project portfolios in a timely fashion. Without metrics, portfolio management is dependent on emotions and politics.

No Vision

Organizations without portfolio management rarely have a real strategy implemented in their portfolios. That means the business goals do not map to the active items in the portfolio. Even if there is a strategy, it is often different for the short term and the longer term. In addition, the portfolio can be evaluated according to risk factors. That allows planning a more aggressive strategy with a moderate back-up plan in case the criteria change. Because some larger projects run longer and some strategies change, projects that were once strategic might become less strategic than you initially thought.

Based on my own experience in many small and large-scale projects, even if there is a business vision in a non-agile environment, it seldom gets communicated clearly or at all to the project teams. As a result, project teams rewrite the vision to understand the motivations and draw requirements from it. Without proper validation of the requirements and the interpretation of them, a project can detour significantly from its set route.

Agile projects, conversely, are evaluated in an iterative approach, not only against their progress but also against how they adhere to the vision of the portfolio. Especially in early iterations, the agile team collects feedback from a broad variety of stakeholders. That way, the vision is translated directly into the project, but project metrics about progress, quality, and morale are fed back from the team to the portfolio. The newly gathered information, collected in an iterative rhythm, can be used by executive management to reevaluate the overall vision. The feedback loop has closed.

Chapters 7, 8, and 9 give examples of how the vision is translated into each individual portfolio and also show how agile projects influence executive decisions by reporting on features, progress, and quality in an iterative rhythm. Chapter 10 brings these three portfolios together into an executive portfolio dashboard.

Summary

The foundation of successful portfolio management is formed by understanding the organizational structures and strategic goals. For that reason, we have looked at the functional, projectized, and matrix organizational models. We have clarified the terminology for the projects, programs, and portfolios and examined how these aspects relate to one another. These definitions will facilitate the discussions throughout the book.

The foundation also addresses the three common goals of implementing a portfolio management strategy: maximizing value of the entire organization, achieving a balance between investment and return, and linking it all to a portfolio strategy that is consistent with the goals of the organization. On the other hand, the symptoms of ineffective portfolio management are a lack of vision, which is characterized by projects rarely being terminated; projects having insufficient resources; projects having a lack of effective metrics; and the organization or project team having no vision for the project. I hope that the statistical information about portfolio management and agile development that I provided at the start of the chapter helps you to make a strong case for agile transformation projects within your organization.

Chapter 5
Metrics

Projects do not operate in isolation. Measuring the value and progress of an agile project requires reliable data and a consistent yet simple form of project reporting. The larger the portfolio of a development organization, the more challenging it is to measure the progress and quality of a system as well as the team's morale. To achieve accurate measurement, reporting metrics need to be reduced to the most essential elements.

This chapter introduces key metrics to use when establishing an interface between an agile portfolio and its projects. In the spirit of agile development, one goal is to prevent any additional effort from being required to build new metrics; instead, it is preferable to reuse what has already been produced by the team and is currently available. Therefore, all the parameters are directly derived from agile development and are easily reused from your project to the portfolios.

Let's explore the parameters the agile projects report on and how we can analyze them. These project metrics will be the basis for the project selection process, which we will cover in the following chapter.

Metrics

One important purpose of using reporting metrics in an organization is to give a meaningful periodic update on the project's health to the external stakeholders, typically the project sponsor and executive management. Keep in mind that a project is their investment in the future of the organization; it is quite understandable that investors want to see how their investment is doing. As we do with the financial stock market, we interpret certain parameters and form our conclusions based on the most up-to-date information. For example, the most frequently examined parameters of a publicly traded company are the stock price, trading volume, and fluctuations in those items. Likewise, certain metrics are used to keep a project team focused and to create a common vocabulary among team members.

Agile project teams therefore try to determine which metrics summarize the project status most effectively. Team members then use those metrics to measure their progress as well as to report to external entities. Often the project manager provides additional status information in prose style, primarily information about the impact of the previous iteration on the overall project. We can compare the project manager's written report with the elaborate quarterly or year-end publication of a public company that is used to keep shareholders informed. That is where the analogy to financial reporting ends, because information technology (IT) projects have their own characteristics. We'll investigate the three cornerstones (shown in Figure 5-1) for agile project reporting: progress, quality, and team morale.

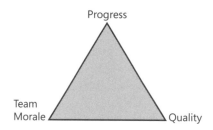

FIGURE 5-1 Reporting metrics parameters: Triangle of key metrics for agile portfolio management

The triangle in Figure 5-1 shows the three parameters for agile reporting. The lines between the parameters symbolize the dependencies between them. If you move one parameter, you affect others.

Progress (Velocity)

Measuring progress means comparing the plan with the actual value. In this context, the *plan* is the estimated effort for a requirement and the *actual value* is the effort that was necessary to convert the requirement into working software. The project team reflects on the progress at the end of each iteration and refines its estimates for upcoming requirements accordingly. That is an extremely powerful mechanism in agile projects, because not only will future estimates get better, but so will the progress reporting itself. The longer the project, and therefore the greater the number of iterations, the better the accuracy of those estimates will be.

When you track the progress of agile projects objectively, you need to look at the estimation method. Two major and commonly used methods are story points and use-case points.

Story Points

Let's assume a project is on a semimonthly iteration rhythm. At the end of each iteration, the team reports how many user stories they have converted into working software. Story points are an arbitrary, but consistent, number used by the team to size every story (also referred to as a "user story"). Remember that a user story is used by the team to capture requirements for a system. For example, a story estimated as two story points is double the size of a user story with one story point. With a point system in place, the project team can avoid having to use person-days or dollar values to estimate the size of a task. Every documented user story is estimated by assigning a point value to it either at the beginning of the iteration or before the story is tackled. Not every story has the same complexity, risk, or size, so story points are a better measure of these things than real person-day estimates. Person-day estimates are problematic because estimators often picture their own productivity when estimating size or complexity. In reality however, someone other than the estimator often performs the actual work.

Story points, on the other hand, focus on size instead of duration. You can see story points as the currency in the agile project. To be consistent with the agile spirit, you should avoid trying to come up with a complicated point system. For example, let's start our project with three levels of story sizes (small, medium, and large). Then we can assign points to each of these levels (for example, small=5, medium=10, large=20) or estimate each story card independently.

The same user stories are used by the team for requirements work as well as the estimation process. In addition, once the team completes a story, the initially estimated story points have been burned down. After the iteration is completed, the team can reflect on the amount of story points planned versus the amount burned down and adjust their efforts accordingly.

The estimation and the progress reporting have exactly the same basis: the user story. I have seen projects experiment without a use case point system and go back to the initial use of estimated person-days. Forming such an estimate using person-days distracts from the challenge: estimating the size of a requirement rather than the duration of a task. Every project team can basically determine its own story point system. This system must only be consistent, for example estimating and assigning 2 points for one story instead of 1. If a different project team assigns 20 points instead of 10 the story will represent double the effort. For example, two user stories estimated at 1 and 2 points have the same relative value if they are estimated at 10 and 20 points, respectively. One story requires twice the effort as the other. Once an agile project team establishes a good definition of *low*, *medium*, and *high*, the team can quickly build piles of cards that fit into the defined categories. The point system also has a huge psychological impact on the team during the development of the story. Stories that turn out to be more complicated than initially anticipated are not as demoralizing when the number of work hours needed to complete the story is replaced with a simple point system.

The point system is extremely powerful for agile portfolio management because of its simplicity and quick execution. Project teams and stakeholders can compare the iteration plan with the actual result after each iteration as proposed in Figure 5-2.

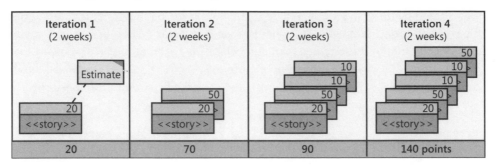

FIGURE 5-2 Example of story burndown

For example, project team A has five members and they decided to sign up for 18 points. After the iteration, they realized that they delivered 19 points. Team B with eight members decided to sign up for 25 points and delivered 20. Even though the points should not be used to compare teams, they will give portfolio managers a sense of how much progress each team has made. Remember, we will not know if 1 story point from project A is the same size as 1 story point in project B. What we will know, however, is that team A slightly beat its own expectation, whereas team B was below its own set expectation. Without any historic project metrics, however, these parameters can disguise a different error. For example, project A might not have allocated enough story points to the previous iteration. Although project A reported 19 story points, the real story point amount for each iteration to finish the project on target should have been 25. A project trend like this one that persists after a few iterations will make the issue obvious.

Comparing project A with project B is almost impossible because both projects have their own interpretations of small, medium, and large.

At a glance, you can see that team B has underdelivered according to its own forecast and team A has three fewer team members. It looks as if team B slacked off and team A is much more productive, right? Not necessarily. With agile portfolio management, you need to look at the entire picture of the project—progress is only one part of the picture. You'll see later in this chapter why an isolated view that focuses on progress metrics can lead you to the wrong conclusions.

The important fact for the experienced agile portfolio manager is that the portfolio of projects (projects A and B) has 39 points more value now than before the iteration started. The projects in a portfolio gained value based on delivered functionality.

Story point estimation also has another big benefit for agile portfolio management. All the forecasting comes straight from the source: the development team itself. In agile development, it is the team, not the project manager, that estimates the user stories commonly documented on 3-by-5 index cards. This is a huge paradigm shift from more traditional project management techniques, where the project manager often estimates or influences the effort and directs the team members to stay on schedule. To take a negative example of traditional project management to an extreme, if the original estimates prove to be inaccurate, the results are often manipulated to make the project look good. That is relatively easy to do, by declaring things done that are only 90 percent done. Successful agile portfolio management is built on trust and honesty among all teams. Passing the metrics already developed by each agile team on to executive management is the foundation for a successful agile portfolio.

As a byproduct of the story point system, the progress in one iteration allows you to draw conclusions about future iterations, including the overall schedule of the project. This technique is a measure of *velocity*. Velocity can be described as the speed of the team. For example, consider a project team that burns 20 points in a two-week iteration when the rough estimate is that the entire project scope (size) is 200 points. After the second week (when the iteration is over), the project manager forecasts that the project can be completed after 10 iterations, or 20 weeks, based on historical data. During the next iteration, the team completes 30 points and realizes that the initial estimated burndown rate for each iteration was conservative. The new schedule trend would like this:

180 (initial project size – burned stories from first iteration) / 30 (new burndown rate) = 6 more iterations needed (or 12 weeks)

Compared with the original schedule, the project would be completed six weeks early.

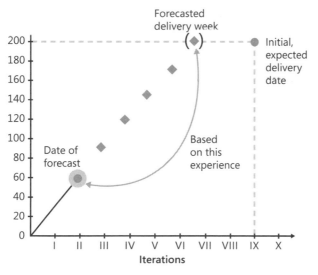

FIGURE 5-3 New schedule based on the velocity trend

This is a significant departure from traditional portfolio management, where projects use a color scale to indicate the state of the project—with green signifying "on time and within budget," yellow signifying "caution," and red signifying "critical." With progress and schedule reporting using story points, the project manager can predict at the end of each iteration the delivery status of the project (early, on time, or late) and also when the project is expected to be completed. (See Figure 5-3.) Because the project team will learn more iteration by iteration, the historical information will get more and more reliable over time. I guarantee that every manager will like this increased accuracy in forecasting.

Use-Case Points

Although story points have become popular in recent years, many organizations instead choose to document their project requirements with use cases. Use cases are a suitable form of documenting business processes from start to finish. As with story points, business analysts and object-oriented software developers find this technique to be very intuitive.

Use cases are commonly larger than stories and can cross a variety of architectural (business or technical) boundaries. From a planning perspective, larger use cases can also span multiple iterations. For that reason, a use case is documented as a collection of scenarios. These scenarios are a more reasonable portion of requirements to be tackled in one iteration. The following iterations can tackle other scenarios from the same use case.

The use-case point-estimation technique is a multistep process. Please do not get discouraged by the following calculations—one spreadsheet application can quickly generate the values based on changing parameters.

Three values—the product of Unadjusted Use Case Points (UUCP), Technical Complexity Factor (TCF), and Environment Complexity Factor (ECF)—result in Use Case Points (UCP). (These three values are derived by calculating certain other values, as explained in the sections devoted to each of them.) If you look at the three values feeding the UCP, you'll notice functionality multiplied by two factors: one for technology and the other for the project environment. Let's look at each value in more detail.

Unadjusted Use Case Points

To create the UUCP, the project team adds two values: Unadjusted Use-Case Weight (UUCW) and Unadjusted Actors Weight (UAW). Both values are determined by assessing the use cases and the use-case diagram against a set of categories. Unadjusted means, that only the functionality of the system was evaluated, not the project or technical environment yet. That will occur in the subsequent calculations. This estimation method assumes that the use-case diagram and use scenarios were already captured by business analysts, for example.

To produce the UUCW, every use case is evaluated by the team and categorized as simple, average, or complex. Each category carries a weight: 5, 10, and 20, respectively. The classifications are based on the number of *steps* in each use-case scenario and occur usually in an initial team meeting (for example, a project kickoff meeting). A counted step is an action that causes a system to respond. For example, a user action to print a document causes the system to perform the actual printing procedure. The simple category is defined as a scenario with a maximum of three steps. The average category is a scenario that has from four to seven steps, and a complex scenario is a scenario that contains more than seven steps. For each use case, steps are counted, a classification is assigned, and the total UUCW created.

UAW is created using a similar system. A use-case diagram illustrates use cases, actors and the system boundary. We have already covered the use cases, which leaves us with the actors and the boundary. The boundary of the system is indicated by a box. Everything within the boundary is inside the system scope. Everything outside the boundary is outside the scope and is something the project team will rely on to exist. This could be an already existing external system or interface, which must be functioning when the system under design will be released. The considerations are essential when using this estimation method because it will have significant impact on the scope of the system. Using external systems, the estimated scope will shift from building functionality to building an interface to access functionality.

Similar to the use cases before, every actor in a use-case model is also evaluated and grouped by the project team by using the simple, average, and complex categories. Actors in a use-case model will fill a role in using the future system. An actor could be an administrator or s user of a system but in reality could be the same person. The weight is 1, 2, or 3, respectively, for simple, average or complex. This time, we are not categorizing the weight by steps, but are defining whether the actor is a human actor or a nonhuman actor and whether the interface between the actors is defined or not. The values are assigned based on a simple voting exercise among the project team members.

Both sums (the UUCW and UAW) together give you UUCP. The UUCP represents the estimate to build the functionality of the system. In the following step, the project team will adjust the use-case points and include effort for the chosen technology and the project environment.

Technical Complexity Factor

To assess the technical complexity of the overall system, the project team evaluates the complexity based on 13 complexity factors. This assessment is done by using a standard template. Using a checklist of the items, the project team walks through them and assesses their complexity. The perceived complexity is a value from 0 (zero) to 5. When in doubt, you should assign 3 as an initial value.

TABLE 5-1 Sample Template for Technical Complexity Factors

Factor	Description	Weight	Perceived Complexity (0-5)	Calculated Complexity Factor
T1	Distributed system	2	3	6
T2	Performance	1	0	0
T3	End-user efficiency	1	2	2
T4	Complex internal processing	1		
T5	Reusability	1		
T6	Easy to install	0.5		
T7	Easy to use	0.5		
T8	Portability	2		
T9	Easy to change	1		
T10	Concurrency	1		
T11	Special security features	1		
T12	Provides direct access for third parties	1		
T13	Special user training facilities are required	1		
Total Calculated Technical Complexity Factor				e.g. 20

The total calculated technical complexity factor, which is the result of the sum of all individual factors (in our example, 20), will be needed to calculate the TCF. The formula for the TCF is

*TCF = 0.6 + (.01 * Total Calculated Technical Complexity Factor)*

Similar to the TCF, the ECF is calculated by assessing six environmental factors for the experience of the project team in its organization.

TABLE 5-2 Sample Template for Environment Complexity Factors

Factor	Description	Weight	Perceived Complexity (0-5)	Calculated Complexity Factor
E1	Familiarity with UML	1.5	2	3
E2	Part-time workers	-1	0	0
E3	Analyst capability	0.5	3	1.5
E4	Application experience	0.5		
E5	Object-oriented experience	1		

Factor	Description	Weight	Perceived Complexity (0-5)	Calculated Complexity Factor
E6	Motivation	1		
E7	Difficult programming language	-1		
E8	Stable requirements	2		
Total Calculated Environment Complexity Factor				15

The following formula is used for calculating the ECF

ECF = 1.4 + (-0.03 * Total Calculated Environmental Complexity Factor)

UCP

After the UUCP, TCF, and ECF have been calculated, you can derive the overall use-case points by using the following formula:

UCP = UUCP * TCF * ECF

The total use-case points will give the team a first clue about the size of the initial project scope. If a project team will need to communicate the effort to executive management to allocate project resources, it can convert the use-case points to work hours, which are then called the total estimate. To convert the estimate from points to effort, a performance factor is used.

Although the performance factor is a unique value, which needs to be determine for each organization individually, a default value should lie between 15 and 30. Because the performance factor translates a use-case point into effort measured in hours, it means that an average team will need, for example, 20 hours to "build" a use point. A more efficient team might apply a smaller value as its performance index and build the same functionality in less time. An organization that has its own historic performance values from past projects can create its own organizational performance index. It basically traces back to previous projects within the organization and translates how many hours of work were necessary to convert a use-case point to working software. The formula for the PF is

PF= total project hours / UCP

If you do not have any historical data, you should take, for example, 20 to begin with.

Total Estimate

After all the calculations and assessments, the total initial estimate of your project is calculated by multiplying the UCP by the PF. The result is the overall work-hour effort of your project. Both values give executive managers an initial feeling of the size and length of the project. But please remember that this method is applied based on the initial scope and will most likely change while the project is being executed. Therefore, the size and length of the project cannot be set in stone and must be reported in such a way to executives.

Experiences with the Application of the Use-Case Point Estimation

Use-case point estimation is a good technique for agile projects that build systems with a use-case driven approach because it is a multistep estimation approach. Many organizations depend on guidelines for estimating size and effort, and the technical and environmental factors provide great input.

However, the technique has its challenges. Many of the factors do not necessarily map to the needs of an agile project—for example, the *visual modeling with UML* or *stable requirements* factors listed as environmental factors. The importance of visual modeling has been devalued in agile projects, and unstable requirements are assumed when agile projects kick off. Therefore, the factors themselves need to be revisited when agile projects are being estimated using this method. Also, the performance factor is estimated at the beginning of the project, whereas agile teams will gain momentum over the course of the iterations. Therefore, the performance value will ideally decrease over the course of the project.

A big challenge for use-case estimation is that counting the steps within the scenario requires that the use cases be written out in the beginning of the project. That is not the case in agile projects.

Changing and revisiting this estimation with every iteration also does not seem effective. So where does this technique come in handy? I see primarily two areas for its use. First and foremost, it can be used to get a rough initial estimate for a project when the team is asking for funds. Second, by calculating only subsections or estimating use cases individually, instead of calculating the entire UCP of the complete system, you can determine the size of a use case and the performance factor, which will tell you if the use case will fit into an iteration.

Ideally, on an organizational level, the PMO will adjust the environmental and technical factors and tweak the list of these technical complexity factors to its own needs. I decided to present this technique not as a method to be applied blindly for every potential project but to provide an alternative estimation method. I do strongly believe that either the environmental or technical complexity factor should be revisited or dropped entirely by the PMO or the project team before agile projects are estimated.

Other Estimation Techniques

The following techniques are typical approaches for performing project estimates in the IT industry, even for non-agile projects. Let's walk through them briefly and discuss the relevance when applied in an agile context and how they complement the previously introduced popular estimation methods.

Expert Method

The expert method is simply a method of asking an experienced person in the organization for his or her opinion regarding the effort required to complete a project or task. The problem with this technique is that the person often answers as if she would perform the work herself. As a result, the estimates are completely subjective to that person and usually on the lower end of the range of likely time or effort to complete. It is challenging for the expert to adjust the estimate so that it applies to less experienced team members. The estimation process is, however, very quick. Another problem with the expert method is that the result is often the effort measured in days instead of size (use-case or story points). Size is, however, the measure for progress and velocity and therefore the more important measure.

Both estimation techniques discussed previously (use-case points and story points) have a flavor of the expert method included. However, with use-case points and story points, instead of the project manager asking only one expert, the entire team is invited to give their estimates. You will receive more opinions from more experts in slightly more time.

Bottom-Up Method

This estimation technique is connected with work breakdown structures and traditional project management. Work items are broken down by the project manager at the beginning of the project to a level where an expert or project team member can estimate the work. Once one level in the work-breakdown structure is completely estimated, all the values are accumulated and delegated by the project manager to the next highest level and so forth.

Work is commonly not broken down into smaller and smaller tasks in agile projects. Work is also not outlined as a set of tasks but as a set of stories or use cases. Therefore, this estimation technique plays no significant role for agile projects. When use-case scenarios or stories are too large to be tackled, they can be split into smaller units. That is important to be able to complete entire stories or use-case scenarios during an iteration and report progress on it. Remember that the goal of agile projects is to complete stories, so their size must fit the timeframe of an iteration. When stories are too large, they have to be broken down. Although story cards can be split, the cards are not structured in a hierarchy and estimates are not merged back together at higher levels. Breaking story cards down into smaller stories still requires you to perform a series of software engineering activities for each story, whereas traditional projects break the engineering activities (instead of the requirements) into smaller units.

Analogous

Analogous estimation is a technique of comparing the scope of a project with other similar systems developed in the past. For example, if project A is similar to a new proposed project B and project A was 500 story points in size, project B must also be 500 story points in size.

This technique is challenged by the fact that agile projects do not start off with a set of requirements. Often the teams start with a few high-level objectives that are hard to compare. Where this technique is applied in the agile context is between iterations. If a project team digested 10 story points in the past iteration, it will attempt to do the same in the following iteration.

Cocomo (COnstructive COst Model)

The Cocomo estimation method is based on historical project data. Initially, the values that Cocomo measures were derived from mainframe systems with waterfall projects. The size was measured in terms of lines of code, which presents a problem for agile projects. Agile projects develop features from a very basic interpretation of requirements to a more complex one. Stakeholders decide when the decoration of features is enough. In other words, a feature might be delivered with very few lines of code, which has no relationship to the size of the feature.

Therefore, the Cocomo method has little or no value for agile projects. In short, the project parameters do not line up with the historical data captured by the Cocomo method. The lack of agile historical data and the availability of more modern technologies that do not map to the Cocomo parameters make this technique obsolete for agile projects.

Function Points

Although use-case point estimation is influenced by the function point technique, a pure function point estimation has been criticized in the agile industry. This is because it adds little value when the scope of a project changes, resource constraints appear, and reprioritizing affects the project. As we know, these situations are almost the norm in agile projects. For existing systems in an application portfolio, however, function points could be used to derive maintenance costs and the cost of common enhancement projects for an existing system.

Wide-Band-Delphi

Asking the entire project team to assess a story card is a good start to what is known as the Wide-Band-Delphi method. It is also a modified version of the expert method; instead of asking one expert and taking her word for granted, the Wide-Band-Delphi method interviews a group of experts. Here is how it works.

In a facilitated workshop, the project team is invited to estimate a specific requirement, story, or use case. Every team member reads the story and estimates the size individually. In addition, every estimator captures a reason why he thinks the estimate is justified. Every team member will capture not only the estimate value but also a range from the lowest to highest possible estimates. This should not take longer than a minute for each card.

After every team member has estimated the card, the facilitator will ask each team member to publicly share the lowest, most likely, and highest estimates, as well as the team member's reasons for those estimates. The facilitator usually illustrates the results either as text or graphically.

Now each team member has seen the other estimates and ranges and has heard the opinions of other team members. The facilitator now repeats the same steps. Every team member can reconsider the initial estimate, taking into account everyone else's opinion. The facilitator will repeat the steps until the ranges narrow down to a workable level.

This technique is a quick way to build consensus among all team members, and it even works for larger use-case estimates where only a few more rounds are needed to get the metrics narrowed down. As a side effect, by using the lowest to highest range, this technique is especially interesting for very early estimates where the project team is not comfortable releasing one final number.

Quality

The quality of a system can be easily measured by looking at the number of open defects. The project team, which applied the agile principles of test-driven development and continuous integration of newly introduced software code, will objectively expose the defects. That will subsequently lead to usable metrics about the quality of a system.

For example, building unit tests before the actual component is built guarantees that test cases will exist when components are released. Automating the execution of these test cases through a continuous build process ensures that the system is tested again and again with every iteration to follow. Therefore, all software components are incrementally tested, which will create confidence and demonstrate among the team members the quality of the system, even if those components have not been completed.

The evolution of a system through a series of successful builds allows the agile team to look back any time to the last good build that passed the success parameters. That said, every failed build exposes one or more defects, which are then captured for the team. Depending on the severity of a defect, the person who caused the build to fail will likely be in charge of resolving the issue. If the defect is critical, nothing will have a higher priority than fixing the defect immediately. If the impact is low, the defect might be recorded and tackled some other time.

Do you remember our two project teams, A and B, where B achieved only 10 story points more than B although they had three more team members? Team B did not progress at the rate initially planned and might be less productive in terms of the actual progress of its project, but the team might have had a stronger focus on quality during that iteration.

This is a perfect example why an isolated focus on progress does not convey the real story of a project and why other parameters are needed. A project team might have fixed a tremendous amount of defects and created a stable project code base again. Fixing defects did not earn them any progress, but it increased the quality. The reason why defects should not earn points is that the story (the one that introduced the defect) has already earned the points.

Earning points for defects would disguise the velocity trend. Here is why. Suppose an estimated easy story earned the team 10 points in the previous iteration. Now, with new code added to the code base, a defect pops up that is related to the 10-point story. If the team earns points for correcting the defect, let's say 5 points to illustrate this, the team would have made progress on paper without burning requirements. Fixing the defect constitutes effort, but it amounts to no additional progress.

It is quite normal that the activity of testing is connected with the discovery of new defects. So what if a project does decide against test-driven development and reduces the unit tests to a bare minimum? Remember, the defects will pop up sooner or later. I recommend finding them sooner. In situations like these, pick a quality metric that includes the total number of tests or a ratio between test cases and open defects. Please keep in mind that a successful regression testing strategy also includes graphical user interfaces and functional tests.

Quality Metrics

This section discusses quality metrics that are relatively easy to automatically produce and quality metrics that can be derived manually.

Automated Quality Metrics

The following examples of project metrics can be used for agile project reporting between the project and the portfolio. More is not always better, so sometimes selecting one metric on a corporate level is sufficient. The four approaches I will cover here are as follows:

- Total number of defects
- Ratio of total number of test cases to open defects
- Unit-test code coverage
- Total number of unit tests

If you asked me to select one of the four metrics, I would use the ratio of test cases to open defects. Other ideas about quality metrics that are not listed here include the following:

- Cyclomatic dependencies
- Average lines of code in each method
- Percentage of code covered with test cases
- Estimation accuracy
- Percentage of automated test cases versus manual test cases

Total Number of Defects

Consider the following example. After the first iteration, the project team reported 18 defects. The second iteration ended with 27 defects, and the third iteration ended with 38 open defects. (See Figure 5-4.) Let's assume that the team immediately resolves all critical defects and that the defects left at each iteration have a low or medium impact. However, the analysis of this metric, which may include the number, severity and therefore priority of each defect, reveals clues about the future quality of the system. In our example, the number of defects hase constantly increased over the duration of only three iterations. Assuming that the number of critical defects rises according to the total number of defects, the system will eventually be lower in quality and the project team will need to remove the defects, which will consume more time and resources. Based on a trend derived from Figure 5-4, the project team would be well advised to dedicate time and start removing existing defects as early as iteration 4.

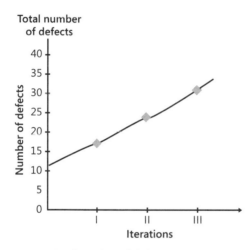

FIGURE 5-4 Total number of defects

Ratio Between Total Number of Test Cases and Open Defects

After the first iteration, a project reports a ratio of 13.3 percent (135 tests with 18 open defects). At the end of the second iteration, the ratio is 19 percent (142 tests and 27 open defects), and by the third iteration the ratio is 24.5 percent (155 tests and 38 open defects). These numbers are charted in Figure 5-5.

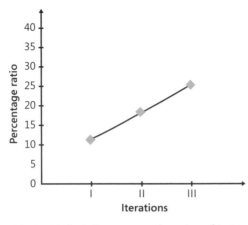

FIGURE 5-5 Ratio between total number of test cases and open defects

As compared with the total number of defects approach, this metric provides much more information about the quality of the system. Not only did the number of open defects rise, but the number of test cases was almost stagnant. Something new must have been added to the system that caused it to break. Most likely, the team did make progress, but it probably violated the practice of test-driven development by not generating new test cases. And defects continue to pour in.

This metric is powerful when you put the various parameters into context. If our assumption is correct and a great burn-down rate should have been reported, the portfolio manager needs to get involved. Remember, writing all the missed unit tests later and decreasing the number of defects will consume resources later in this project. And at that point, the expected progress will not be made.

Unit-Test Code Coverage

Suppose you want to know how much of your entire project code is executed and scheduled through unit tests. To illustrate how to do this, let's take a simple pseudocode *if* statement:

```
If amount > 10
then doThis()
else doThat()
```

In terms of code coverage, *doThis()* and *doThat()* are protected by the *if* guard. If we have a unit test covering only the case if the amount is larger than 10, the code nested inside *doThat()* will never be executed. That is a ticking time bomb waiting to explode. The unit-test code coverage metric reports on exactly this type of quality. In a perfect world, this coverage would be 100 percent. However, aiming to have everything higher than 90 percent seems more realistic and can still be considered successful with the code coverage tools currently on the market. (See Figure 5-6.)

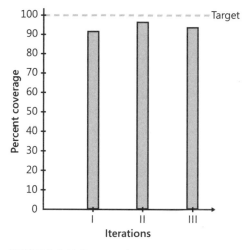

FIGURE 5-6 Unit-test code coverage

Total Number of Unit Tests

The total number of unit tests is a good indicator for measuring whether the project team puts the same amount of quality into the development of unit tests (quality) as in the progress of the project. (See Figure 5-7.) If the total number of unit tests develops at the same rate as the velocity, the project has most likely developed a healthy balance.

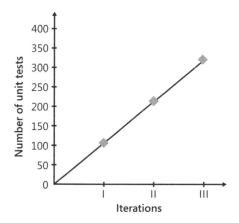

FIGURE 5-7 Total number of unit tests

Manual Quality Metrics

The following three metrics are interesting parameters for a project manager to have handy, even though they put an extra burden on the team because the metrics are difficult to automate. However, they provide great insight not only into the quality of the system, but also into the team focus on quality

Time to Resolve a Defect

This metric measures how focused a team is and how fast (in days) the team deals with removing open defects. The average time to resolve a defect shows two things. It shows the quality of the thinking of the project team, and it also shows how flexible the system is at incorporating the changes. Tracking this parameter is almost an incentive to the team to remove open defects as soon as they appear. The project manager can either build this metric on an ongoing basis throughout the project (as shown in Figure 5-8) or build it for each individual iteration.

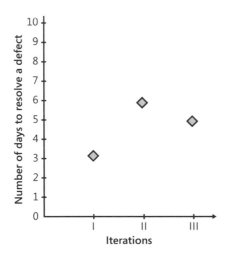

FIGURE 5-8 Number of days to resolve a defect

Defects per Story

This metric takes the defect and relates it to the actual requirement story. Some stories might be too ambiguous or poorly written and cause new functionality surrounding a story to constantly introduce new defects. Associating each defect with a story helps the team identify bottlenecks in the requirements area. On the downside, this metric requires a relatively high level of manual effort or use of tooling. Tools, however, do need to be paid for, installed, and integrated, and they might require a bigger effort than manually capturing this metric.

Impediments

In addition to using the quality metrics related to actual code, use of this method shows the quality of agile project management by reporting on the total number of impediments. This metric is relatively easy to compile when agile teams reveal issues and problems during the daily stand-up meetings. Although a typical tendency is that more impediments are identified early in the project, this metric shows how effective the project leader is at removing them.

Team Morale

I remember Extreme Programming being one of the first methodologies that actively targeted the issue of overtime work and the negative impact of it on team morale. That does not mean that a team is not willing to work overtime occasionally; instead, the issue is that the stress level usually increases in an agile project toward the end of each iteration. The stress level is especially high at the end of an iteration because this is when the final build is produced the demonstration about the progress to the stakeholders takes place, and outstanding defects are removed. During the iteration, there are sometimes technical issues with the technical project environment, which prevent the team from making the anticipated progress. All this affects the morale of each individual and the team as a whole.

The Morale Barometer

Especially on longer projects, you should not underestimate the significance of team morale. A high turnover rate early in the project will have a negative impact later in the project. There is no better way of finding out about morale than by asking team members directly. In one of my more recent agile projects, an anonymous vote was taken during the retrospective. Each member wrote down a number from 1 through 10, with 10 representing total happiness and 1 indicating that the person would like to get off the project. Figure 5-9 shows a graph that I refer to as a *morale barometer*.

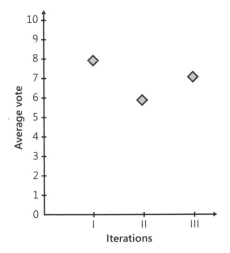

FIGURE 5-9 Morale barometer

When you establish an agile portfolio management process, please do not underestimate this third cornerstone of the metrics: the social aspect of software development. Team morale is seen as something soft, and sometimes it might be difficult to explain fluctuation in the graph. But at the end of the day, the team has the chance to assess its own experience during the iteration and how they felt about being part of it.

If you have another effective mechanism of measuring the morale of your team, please continue to use it. If not, think about adding team morale metrics to your status reports. A team's morale is commonly seen as healthy when it scores 6 or higher on a scale from 1 through 10, with 10 being the highest.

Although this technique is an extremely quick way to capture the mood of the project between iterations, it lacks more granular feedback. For example, suppose the agile project manager is confronted with decreasing morale after every iteration. The project manager cannot fix the situation if the root cause is not known. That is true, but how could the project manager not know? I believe every good project manager can sense the issues at the daily stand-up meeting and learn what they are by observing how the team collaborates on a day-to-day basis. It is often obvious whether the issue is a one-time thing (for example, something that occurs at the extreme peak of tensions at the end of an iteration) or an ongoing problem (such as personal disagreements among team members). The morale barometer should capture such differences of severity. A few random breakouts in the morale barometer would indicate a problem with a specific iteration, rather than with the project, as long as team morale recovers again. If the morale of a team has a constant trend downward, the project manager must take effective steps and tackle the root cause of the problem.

I also do not recommend overinvestigating every tiny development in this chart. The graph could simply be showing a reaction to a new team member, a planned vacation, or changes in the psychological state of team members unrelated to project activities—for example, less exuberance during winter months.

Team Survey

In a more elaborate fashion, the organization could develop and provide a questionnaire at the end of each iteration for every team member. The feedback would then also be more anonymous. Common team morale-related attributes could be measured by the team members' answers to standard questions. Every team member would answer a series of questions about the following categories:

- Job satisfaction
- Team success
- Education

The results from the questions to these categories can then be related to facts about the project itself:

- Length of team existence
- Size of the team

- Professional experience in years
- Turnover rate of the project

Studies indicate that there is a strong relationship between the individual's morale and the team's morale and the long-term performance of a team within a project. Statistics also indicate that the longer the team works together, the higher its morale is and, therefore, the better its performance is. Assessing the team's fitness through a quick survey between iterations is also a useful metric to get short-term (iteration-to-iteration) and long-term career paths of individuals in sync.

Reporting

By using metrics, we know how we can condense certain information. Let's take a look at the status report and how the information in it can be broadcast most effectively. Subsequently, we want to take the perspective of the portfolio manager, who needs to interpret the reports quickly and consistently and come to the most accurate conclusions for the benefit of the organization.

Status Report

With the completion of an iteration, the project team reports its status upwards based on the requirements of the portfolio manager, the PMO, or executives. Although many of these metrics could be automated, the exchange between the project and the portfolio is very manual. Most likely, a status report is involved to share the metrics consistently.

An agile portfolio management process includes the three cornerstones of project metrics mentioned earlier in the chapter: progress, quality, and team morale. A common mistake with project metrics is that the project teams report metrics that are too detailed and report too many metrics at the same time. Often, all metrics are reported without specifying who the target audience is. This omission pollutes the status report with information that is irrelevant to the decision makers. On the other hand, senior executives are also often interested in performance-related information about each individual rather than focusing on a team. This tendency is clearly a violation of the agile spirit, where teams and pairs of developers deliver as a group. Therefore, the metrics should be team-focused and contain at least one component about progress, quality, and team morale.

As a next step, the agile project manager assembles the written status report, which should be a short and meaningful report of the status of the project and, in particular, the past iteration. In addition to the actual metric portion, the status report can include a variety of sections. Here are some ideas to consider.

Schedule

This section should contain a brief summary of the impact of the past iteration on the schedule of the overall project. At a minimum, it should state the general project status: ontime, ahead of schedule, or behind schedule. If the velocity metric is based on enough information, the project manager can also provide the expected end date based on the trend. Because the velocity can fluctuate to a greater degree in early iterations than in later ones, organizations might not require a trend to be declared until after a certain time period has passed—for example, after the first four 2-week iterations.

Key Issues

A status report can also include a summary of the key issues the project team faces based on the past iteration. These might even be issues carried over from earlier iterations. The project manager can also share with the stakeholder the planned action for each issue.

Requirements

A status report can include a list of stories, use cases, or other documented requirements that have been completed in the past iteration. With this information, stakeholders can relate the progress metric (velocity) to the actual stories. Other stakeholders—for example, the marketing department—can learn about the features implemented in the system and can plan their related efforts.

Risks

Every project contains a lot of risks. Agile projects are no different in that regard. An updated risk list can demonstrate which mitigation strategies the team attempted and whether they were successful. Ideally, the list of risks will shrink over the course of the project, especially in terms of risk probability and risk severity. The risk list can be a status report appendix. Remember, project risks are issues that have not materialized yet. They are different from the issues reported earlier.

Change Control

The status report can outline when and how long the change control board met during the past iteration. It can be a short outline of the decisions made, including the impact of the decision. For example, this section of the status report can indicate the agreement to remove a story card (reduce the project scope) and replace the card (and the effort it would have entailed) with a new card that the business analyst finds more useful.

Comments

Every status report should have a comment section, where the project manager can capture some important information about the past iteration that does not fit into one of the other categories—for example, information about training courses or conferences that team members attended during the time frame of the iteration.

Technical Information

Some project teams might include information about and the location of the last good build, which will be demonstrated to the stakeholders after the iteration. If the release of the iteration might be of interest to a broader audience in the organization, instructions about how to access the partial system can be included. For example, an Internet or intranet application might require a password and a URL that stakeholders can use to follow the progress of the project.

Interpretation

The following scenario demonstrates how a simple status report, which consists only of metrics, could be interpreted by project outsiders. Keep in mind that even if some of the metrics are inconclusive there are alternative ways of learning about project status—for example, attending the daily stand-up meetings or participating in the retrospective. The goal of the following scenario is to evaluate many projects in a short period of time.

The scenario uses a status report that contains, exclusively, the following metrics:

- Velocity
- Defects versus number of test cases
- Morale barometer

Equipped with an understanding of what these metrics mean, let's take a quick journey through the first three iterations of a project. Let's analyze the status of this project in an iterative fashion.

Iteration 1 produces the following results:

- Progress:
    - Estimated: 30
    - Actual burn-down: 35
- Quality:
    - Ratio of defects to test cases: 5%

- Morale:
    - Morale barometer: 8.5
- Our assessment:

    The project is new and might even be the very first agile project the team or organiza-tion has attempted. It is therefore not surprising that the morale of the project starts out quite high. The team achieved a higher burn-down than expected, which indi-cates that more progress was achieved than anticipated. The low number of defects in relationship to the number of test cases also indicates a high level of quality for the software released after the first iteration.

Iteration 2 produces the following results:

- Progress:
    - Estimated: 35
    - Actual burn-down: 25
- Quality:
    - Ratio of defects to test cases: 12%
- Morale:
    - Morale barometer: 5.8
- Our assessment:

    The team estimated that it could burn down the same number of points as in the previous iteration and fell short. Most likely, the team had to focus on controlling the damage of the defects because the percentage of defects increased significantly. The team's morale is lower, most likely because the velocity goal was not reached and the number of defects spiked. This is a very typical situation for new agile teams when the integration of newly introduced functionality messes up test cases from previous iterations. Builds broke, the defect rate increased, and time was used for things other than making progress.

Iteration 3 produces the following results:

- Progress:
    - Estimated: 30
    - Actual burn-down: 25
- Quality:
    - Ratio of defects to test cases: 7%

- Morale:

  - Morale barometer: 5.6

- Our assessment:

  To keep the project on schedule, the velocity of 30 was reduced from the velocity expected in the previous iteration. The team exceeded the original number (35) only during the first iteration, and it fell behind in both the second and third iterations. The team might have realized at some point in this iteration that the project will be delivered late because the goal of burning down 30 points was not accomplished. It seems more realistic, then, to calculate the new schedule using 25 points as the average iteration velocity. Although the defect ratio recovered slightly, the team's morale is still almost the same as in the previous iteration. As a portfolio manager, I would visit the daily stand-up meetings of the team and learn more about its day-to-day issues.

Summary

This chapter introduced typical agile project metrics. Although they all provide important information about the progress, quality, or morale of the project, a combination of the three categories is what provides a more complete picture. The metrics also allow portfolio managers to assess projects in the portfolio quickly and consistently. The good news for agile teams is that all the data is a natural byproduct of the software development process and the team retrospectives after each iteration.

In larger organizations, status reports are commonly formalized to consistently share the same data across multiple projects. The final section of this chapter provided examples of the input for these reports and analyzed the metrics from the first three iterations of one sample project.

Chapter 6
Return on Investment

Every portfolio reflects the vision of an organization, and each item (project, resource, or asset) inside the portfolio is a specific investment supporting that vision. As with financial portfolios, investors expect that, upon completion, projects will generate cash flow and profits. If the gains from a project exceed the investment made in the project, the return on investment is positive. Although profits are not the only parameter for measuring the success of a project, a positive return on investment is always a good indicator. A long-term, financially balanced, and profitable IT portfolio is the backbone of your development environment. Equipped with the reliable metrics introduced in the previous chapter, let's look at individual projects from a different perspective, the financial aspect.

Goals and Objectives

Visionary companies have goals, and these goals should directly translate into a series of projects. These goals can be either qualitative (that is, they strengthen the brand of a company) or quantitative (that is, they increase sales by a specific amount in a certain amount of time). However, with additional business analysis, many of the qualitative goals might become quantifiable, which makes it easier for portfolio managers to break them down into projects. For example, the goal "strengthen the brand" could be quantified as "1 out of 10,000 random people in the United States will recognize the brand" (compared with 1 out of 100,000 prior to the project). Even though we can make these qualitative goals measurable, their soft (or imprecise) nature cannot be entirely eliminated. And even after the goals are identified, it is still not easy to translate a business goal directly into a technical project, which the following example illustrates.

An airline's goal is to increase the number of yearly reservations by five percent. This goal can be translated into three totally different projects:

- Marketing Project (a TV and print media advertisement campaign)
- Financial Project (offering better pricing than the competition)
- IT Project (developing a super-saver Web site that sells nonrefundable tickets)

Even though there is no guarantee that any of these projects will produce the desired increase in reservations, they are investments that might possibly satisfy the stated goal, even if a combination of them must be used.

Let's assume that we use the third option and build a low-fare Web site that sells last-minute, nonrefundable tickets. We can derive the initial high-level features of the vision statement for our project directly from the project goals. Business analysts can start defining more detailed requirements for the first iteration.

Keep in mind that some of these goals might be contradictory. If the airline in the example had a second goal called, "Increase profit by five percent in the new calendar year," the type of project selected to increase the number of reservations might change. The low-fare reservation system might increase the number of overall reservations, but it might also lead to less profit because of the lower fares. The airline would need to launch a new project to compensate for potential profit sacrifices caused by the low-fare system.

Connecting these business objectives with individual projects is extremely challenging. We face the challenge of defining two imprecise variables: the goals and objectives, and the development effort. (See Figure 6-1.)

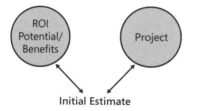

FIGURE 6-1 Two estimation variables

Each estimate comes from two different sources. There is a product team, which might feel bullish about the project and its potential, and there is the development team, which sees the size and scope through different eyes.

Then there are projects that have no ROI potential, or very little, but still need to be evaluated. The Y2K initiatives or compliance projects are good examples of such projects. These initiatives are often related to systems that are already rolled out in organizations on a large scale. In cases like this, not investing in the projects could have a negative impact and the indirect impact of causing a decline in revenue the system is currently providing. Or in other words, the project itself does not promise any additional revenue stream or benefits, but not executing it would have a negative impact.

The Increment

Agile software projects deliver the system in increments, which represent the value added to the system. That value could represent newly implemented features, removed defects, or an improved user experience. The value to the business traces through the project to individual requirements (for example, stories). In many situations, the story represents some sort of benefit to the user. To illustrate this with an actual example of how the features can be linked to the goals of a project, one iteration ago an end user of the flight reservation Web site could not recommend a cheap flight to a friend because an automated feature for doing that was unavailable. Now, after the iteration is completed, the feature has been implemented and the user can actually do that. The feature has been implemented, can be demonstrated, and is measurable. Value has therefore been added to the system and therefore indirectly to the organization. (See Figure 6-2.)

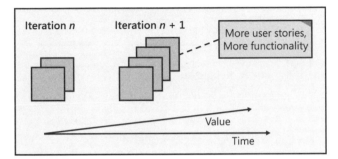

FIGURE 6-2 Value and stories

The increment in which the feature "recommending a flight to a friend" has been implemented is linked to a goal of the project—in our case, "increasing the number of reservations." However, because many goals are coarse and requirements are more granular, multiple stories often are bundled together to serve a larger project goal. These are known as *epics* and *themes*. These epics and themes are also documented as stories but meet higher-level project goals.

In other situations, one story might serve multiple goals. The feature "recommend a flight to a friend" might increase the number of reservations, but it also helps increase the brand recognition. The beauty of agile development is that the practice of continuous integration allows the project team to demonstrate the latest release to stakeholders. As a positive side effect, the code is potentially ready to ship (internally or externally) anytime. The newly added value is real.

The project team can demonstrate the progress to the business group during the iteration retrospective, and the business group can re-assess the ROI potential. That is an extremely powerful and unique characteristic of agile projects and one that is impossible for traditionally managed projects to match. Keep in mind that not every increment could or should be delivered, but there are opportunities to do so. That's what counts when you assess your project portfolio.

With waterfall-phased development, the system is delivered only once, at the end, and often with a lot of surprises. Because there are no builds available, the only one left for the team to look at is the one at the very end of the project.

Let's take a look at Figure 6-3.

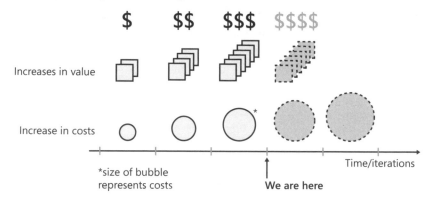

FIGURE 6-3 Incremental project cost-value evolution

Frequently, project costs increase cumulatively, iteration by iteration, by the amount of resources dedicated to the project. In parallel, the value of the project to the organization, which is realized incrementally, also increases. Based on trends, executives can then make decisions about the cost-benefit ratio of upcoming planned iterations. In the previous chapter, we saw how velocity can be used to outline a progress trend for the upcoming iterations. The velocity is tightly connected to the requirements stories, which are associated with one or more goals. Therefore, we can derive the delivered business potential from these goals and associate them with the progress of the project. After each iteration, project sponsors can re-evaluate whether the costs still match the potential (actual and trend) and whether the estimated potential has changed. Keep in mind that our assessment is based purely on estimates as well as a trend based on the performance of past iterations. The only hard fact is the actual project value at one given moment, expressed by the previous increment. Assessing the projects iteratively will yield better results than not performing such assessments. But please keep in mind that the earlier we assess the project, the more subjective these metrics are, because they are based on estimates. The longer the project proceeds, however, the more predictability we will gain. This is adaptive and agile.

At the halfway point of the project, for example, executives might even decide to deploy a version of the system into operations and materialize the expected revenue potential. Both estimates—the one for revenue potential and the effort for implementing it—have hit reality and will be tested in a live environment. The only unpredictable variable left is the timing of the release. The potential has been assessed and evaluated at a different time than the project will be launched. The context and the environment might have changed since the assessment was performed. The actual metrics (cost, velocity) collected throughout the previous iterations of the project will help the team to project the final delivery date, and the anticipated revenue potential is verified within the real marketplace. All these steps enable a new model for executives: gaining return on investment in an iterative but also incremental fashion. Therefore, we are departing from a one-time funding, development, and delivery model, which is typical for waterfall development, and moving toward an iterative-incremental financial assessment of agile projects.

In summary, to realize the financial benefits in an agile project, we will to need to evaluate the investment from two different angles:

- The potential of projects prior to selection

- The potential of the materialized (iteratively and incrementally) goals

The following section introduces models that can be used to perform a financial analysis from either angle listed above. They can be used separately or in combination.

Financial Models

Similar to the various estimation methods (for example, Wide-Band Delphi), different financial methods are available to measure the effectiveness and potential of projects. We will discuss and assess the appropriateness of each method for agile projects. Let's start with a very popular method, the payback period.

Payback Period

The payback period is probably the most straightforward method. It is a very common but effective method of evaluating the potential of a project. Its simplicity is striking, but the payback period approach ignores the time value of money. In other words, this technique ignores the fact that the money possessed today has a different value when the system is completed. The payback period can be used to evaluate the risk of a project, but it can also be used to make a case for a project financially. Within this section, we will focus on the latter. Let's illustrate this with a fictional scenario using the payback period technique. Here are the project parameters:

- **Project:** Super-Saver Airline Seats

- **Initial Project Cost Estimate:** $1 million

- **Size:** 500 story points; estimated velocity 50 story points/month

- **Estimated Duration:** 10 months

- **Estimated Potential:** $200,000 per month

In traditional development, the payback period is five months. This means that after five months in operation the system's benefits will pay back the costs to develop it. (See Figure 6-4.) We are assuming in this scenario, of course, that everything went well and the system was delivered after a total of 10 months with its originally planned capacity. The payback period for the project illustrated in Figure 6-4 is identical for an agile project that has been deployed after completion and for a similar project following a waterfall process. The idea behind this example is that we are outlining the similarities before we focus on the differences, which follow directly after.

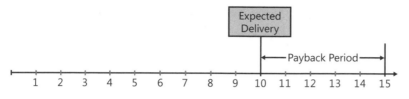

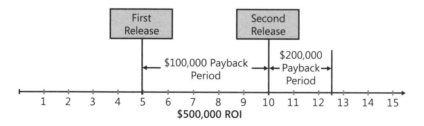

FIGURE 6-4 Payback period with one increment

Traditional projects do not allow earlier deliverables than the final deployment after 10 months. Agile projects, however, do. Let's take a look at the following, more detailed, options.

Let's tackle the same project using an agile approach. And let's say that the first meaningful release opportunity is after five months and that we're using a two-week iteration pattern. Prior to the five-month mark, the releases are only for internal use. For simplification, let's also assume that half the system will deliver half the profits. Now you'll see that agile methods speed up the return on investment.

Let's analyze the financial opportunities presented by using the agile approach, which are illustrated in Figure 6-5.

FIGURE 6-5 Payback period with two increments

The same project with the same requirement scope, financial forecasts, and estimate would see an increase in the payback period to 7.5 months, and the payback is complete only 2.5 months after the system has been fully delivered. What is even more impressive, the system already begins delivering a return on investment while still in development ($500,000 for the final five months in development).

To take this example even further, assume that every increment evenly pays back $20,000, peaking at an estimated total of $200,000 after the project is completed (after 10 months). As in our preceding step, we deploy the system for the first time after the fifth iteration, but we then release the system in monthly iterations, as shown in Figure 6-6.

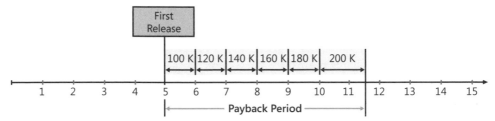

FIGURE 6-6 Payback period with iterative increments

In this case, the payback period is shortened because the returns (incremental cash flow) earned after the final deployment are earned in steps, with incremental deliveries between the fifth month and the tenth month. Therefore, the payback period is now 6.5 months. But again, the same system has paid back 3.5 months earlier than the traditional project simply because we changed the planning and development style to agile.

Just imagine—by finding ways to release the system incrementally every month, we can start releasing the system even more quickly than in 5 months and earn $20,000 a month in early payback. (See Figure 6-7.)

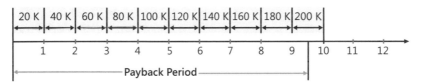

FIGURE 6-7 Payback period with monthly increments

You might already be able to guess what will happen next, but let's spell it out. Because of the low payback in early increments, the payback period is now the longest of the three approaches discussed, with payback occurring over 9.5 months. But as you can see, the entire payback period runs parallel with the project development. Half a month before the project is completed, the project has paid itself back already. With the final release of the system, we have already earned $100,000 more than it had cost.

If you had taken a loan (internally in your organization or externally through a bank) to build the system, you would have 5.5 fewer months of interest to pay, which would be about $32,000 if you use a 7 percent interest rate. If you had used your own internal funds, you could have reinvested your $1 million in a new business after 9.5 months instead of waiting an additional 5.5 months, as you would have done with the traditional method.

I know this is a textbook example, and in reality it is difficult to attach a specific ROI to each increment because of the missing factor of the time value of money. It shows, however, that even a few additional releases will speed up the payback period tremendously. The traditional method seemed impressive with its five-month payback period, but we saw that we could do much better. Also, remember that the earlier the payback period is completed, the earlier the capital will be available to be reinvested in other new projects waiting in your portfolio. With frequent ROI realization, the funding of your portfolio travels in the express lane.

Without a doubt, all payback examples that use an agile approach make a much better ROI justification for including the project in your portfolio. The agile approach gives you more options for selling projects and ideas in your organization and also for how you tackle your competition. I realize, though, that for competitive reasons you might not want to release the software even though you could. There are situations where an organization does not want to release features too early and thereby reveal too much of the overall product strategy. These incremental releases are not always desirable. But that is something we will examine in more detail in a later chapter.

Net Present Value (NPV)

The *present value* of a system or feature that is being considered as a project refers to the amount of money that is needed today to realize a desired amount of money at a specific point in time in the future. The Net Present Value method considers the time value of money, which is a factor missing in the previous payback period method, and it carries a strong risk factor that arises from the uncertainty of whether the profit can be realized between the present time and the deadline. Some investments are guaranteed (such as a savings account), and others are much more risky (such as stocks). Let's assume that your goal is that you will have $100,000 one year from now. To be able to meet this goal, you must translate future amounts into the present value, which is called discounting.

One solution would be to take $98,039 (at present value) and put it into a savings account for one year with an interest rate of 2 percent. One year later, you would have a total of $100,000. You can also look at projects as investments in the future of an organization. Because there is no fixed interest rate for projects, organizations need to determine their opportunity costs, which is a percentage value based on the gains realized in previous projects. Even though all projects are assessed using the same opportunity costs, it is important to point out that funding project A will take away financial resources from project B. That requires you to prioritize projects and project proposals in terms of innovation and marketability in parallel with the financial analysis. In other words, resources are limited, and projects need to compete for them. Financial methods help assess the profitability of each project, but they must include a comparison between the projects as well.

What is interesting about this method for agile projects is the fact that it allows investments to be assessed yearly, quarterly, monthly, or even on a shorter basis. Therefore, we can map the schedule of iterative-incremental development projects directly to the NPV. Because the NPV is a powerful method for comparing one investment (that is, project) with another investment (that is, project), it represents a great technique to use for a project selection process.

As a general rule, if the NPV is greater than 0, taking on the project is a good idea. If financial resources are sparse, however, the NPV decision is not as straightforward, because project managers will need to understand the broader context of how this investment will be made. For example, project A has a calculated NPV of $40,000, and project B has a calculated NPV of $45,000. At a glance, project B looks like the better choice for the organization. In a full assessment, however, you might realize that project A requires $100,000 in investments, whereas project B has $500,000 in development costs. At decision points like these, you need to know whether the funding will be allocated from within the organization or through a line of credit and outside investors. We know that projects carry many risks, and in this case, project B might be much less risky. As a result, investing into project B might not be a bad decision at all, even though the financial parameters are inconclusive or seem less attractive at first glance.

Last but not least, you need to investigate the timing of the investment. Do the investments need to be made at the start, middle, or end of the project? The answer to this question determines when the investment will be made, when funds are allocated, and when interest payments are due.

Another interesting aspect of this method is that the NPV can be applied to each feature of an IT system instead of at the project level only. Because certain features of a system might be more profitable and less risky than others, NPV can help you realize additional benefits by applying the NPV on a feature level instead of for projects only. A feature that requires a high level of investment up front can be dropped, and other, less resource-intensive, features with promising returns can be considered instead. Mike Cohn, in his book *Agile Estimating and Planning*, discusses this approach in the context of themes of stories and how they could become subject to financial assessment, including the NPV.

Figure 6-8 illustrates that a project might start with a negative NPV in the first two iterations because of project setup costs followed by positive NPVs and lucrative iterations when value has been added to the organization. Because the NPV calculation considers costs when they occur and is not spread evenly across the duration of the project, high up-front costs will affect the NPV even more. These up-front costs could be, for example, one-time costs such as computer equipment that occur at the beginning of the project. This calculation might even result in a negative NPV in early iterations.

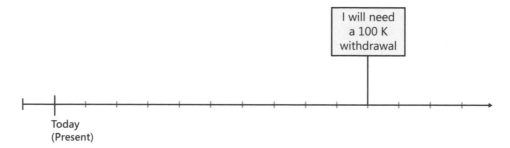

FIGURE 6-8 Iterative NPV assessment

Internal Rate of Return

Unlike NPV, which indicates a monetary value, the Internal Rate of Return (IRR) is an indicator expressed as a percentage. For example, when you go to the bank to open a savings account, the interest rate your savings will earn (given as a percentage) is the IRR. To use this approach for development projects, which are all unique, you create this IRR for each project and use it to compare them. Therefore, the return required to justify taking on the project is a level of cash flow that makes the NPV equal to 0. In other words, if the IRR is greater than the required return, taking on the project is a good decision.

Although the IRR uses the present value, the formula also distinguishes between initial project start-up costs and ongoing project expenses. The result is expressed as a percentage, which indicates how good of an investment the project will be for the development organization. For example, a project with an IRR of 5 percent is a better investment than a project with an IRR of 4 percent. But is it good enough to warrant initiating the project?

Project A in Figure 6-8 has five cash flows (one in each iteration): the first two are negative, and the last three are positive. Assume that accumulating these individual cash flows after each iteration will result in a total of $100,000 after the duration of the project (5 months). For a net-present-day value of $90,600, the internal rate would be 12 percent. If the organization could get funding for the project at an 8 percent interest rate, the project would be considered profitable.

Without the proper formulas, calculating the IRR is complex and cumbersome. In the back of this book, you will find references to the applications and formulas for calculating IRR, as well as examples of how to do it. If you attempt to apply the IRR method to multiple agile projects, building the parameters for IRR and figuring it can be very time consuming. In addition, agile projects can potentially return actual values in money because every increment results in working software, whereas waterfall projects often have, in early phases of the project, only paper to show. Recalculating the IRR in an iterative fashion will make the IRR even more challenging and time consuming. But without a doubt, the IRR percentage values provide extremely valuable metrics for making project comparisons.

Cost-Benefit Analysis

The cost-benefit analysis is a straightforward comparison of all the costs of a taking on a project and the benefits the project will produce. This method includes all costs—including marketing costs (internal and external), production costs (for example, cost for the system media), development costs, rent, personnel costs, maintenance costs, and so forth. However, it does not include the time value of money. When organizations try to lower development costs by producing a system in a globally distributed marketplace, the cost-benefit analysis also includes costs that are unique to this offsite approach, including costs to set up a global development center, increased travel expenses, and online collaboration licenses, as well as very granular and detailed items such as long-distance calls. For many of these fixed costs, the organization's accountants can break down costs to a project or team member level. The method is sometimes applied prior to project selection, so many costs are estimates, and the accuracy of the figures might be low.

When estimated project costs are lower than the estimated project benefits, taking on the project is a good decision. For agile projects, the cost-benefit analysis provides some great advantages. First, there is the striking simplicity of accumulating all costs and comparing them with the potential benefits. Second, this method produces more reliable cost data because the actual cost figures that are derived from the project retrospectives can positively influence the next estimation made by the project team. Based on what we learned from the previous iteration, our next estimate will be adjusted. As a project team, we have learned things about the project and its environment that we had not considered before. As a matter of fact, the project itself can be challenged after each iteration if the portfolio manager asks the executives, "Knowing the cost structure of the project today, was it a good idea to approve it x months ago?" If the answer is no, it might be a good idea to change direction or cut losses. If the answer is yes, you've learned that the initial estimates were reliable.

Benefits Provided by Projects

Many items in a supermarket are marked with an expiration date. The closer the product gets to the expiration date listed on the product, the more the value of the product is diminished. If the product reaches or passes that date, it becomes basically worthless.

Requirements, especially the ones for an IT project, promise to provide benefits to the organization. Similar to supermarket items, many of these benefits have an expiration date. If, for example, a project team develops a new software product unique to the marketplace, the value of this requirement is tightly linked to the date that competitors release similar or alternative services. This is where the analogy to the supermarket items ends, because we will not know this expiration date up front as we do for perishable goods.

If we calculate the overall projected returns and apply the financial models when we compare the investments, we also need to include the potential diminishing returns caused by the environment. Therefore, the return on investment is highly dependent on the time window of the benefits.

Within this time period, the benefits might increase, decrease, or abruptly end when a deadline is reached.

Decreasing Benefits

Today's cars are all equipped with airbags. The situation was quite different when airbags were invented and first began to be used in cars. Back then, cars had many more expensive features than an airbag, but marketing campaigns of the companies that were the first to include airbags in their vehicles emphasized the greater safety that this feature provided. When other manufacturers caught up with the technology and also included airbags in their vehicles, consumers seemed to lose their fascination with the feature. But did they really?

Imagine if an auto manufacturer released a car today without airbags. It's likely that hardly anybody would be interested in the product unless some better safety mechanism had been introduced. In other words, the airbag still provides benefits to automakers, but the value of the feature decreased significantly. The same is true for retail banks that do not offer online banking, retail stores without an online sales channel, airlines without frequent flyer programs, and so forth. Figure 6-9 illustrates that the value of benefits decreases over time but usually does not hit an actual end date. The window stretches over a long period of time, even if the benefits taper off.

FIGURE 6-9 Decreasing benefits of a system feature

We can clearly see that the benefits are at their highest point early on. The organization that is the innovator defines the timeline and is most likely in front of it. Organizations that are the followers need to decide whether they want (and can) grab a piece of the revenue pie—and if they decide they can, they must release a similar feature or product as soon as possible.

Not only can innovative and visionary companies develop systems in an iterative-incremental way, they can surprise the market with early and frequent releases. With a clear vision beyond the initial innovation, the company can continue to stay one step ahead of the followers. And agile development can help organizations that are the followers catch up with the innovators. Agile development can therefore stimulate the marketplace by helping organizations launch their new products earlier in a window of opportunity. Organizations using agile methods can exploit the earlier pockets of higher benefits. A positive side effect is that consumers receive long-awaited features much sooner.

Benefits Deadline

In contrast with the decreasing-benefits scenario, a scenario in which there is a significant deadline abruptly stops the benefits, often in just one day. A deadline is often caused by laws, regulations, and other fixed variables. For example, a marketing department of an on-line retail shop might require that promotional and discount codes be added to its shopping cart. This feature might be useful throughout the entire year, but if this feature is not delivered by, say, November 15 to track, support, and stimulate holiday shopping, it might not be beneficial. (See Figure 6-10.)

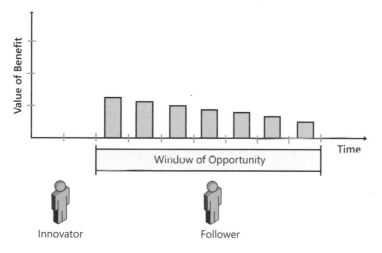

FIGURE 6-10 Benefits deadline

Tax software applications, for example, have a well-defined window of opportunity. By the beginning of the tax season, the system has to be developed to a point where it can correctly interpret the tax rules, and it has to be as user friendly as possible. All the features that are completed before the deadline can be included in the new version of the application. Features that are not ready by the deadline might lose their window of opportunity entirely. They might find their way into the next year's version, or because of tax law changes and other factors, they might be lost forever.

Increasing Benefits

As you might have already guessed, increasing benefits react opposite to decreasing benefits. These benefits might increase their value over time within the window of opportunity. They can constantly grow without a deadline at all or peak toward a certain date.

Increasing benefits are associated with features that are needed to build other features. For example, a professional organization might express a desire to have a feature to renew yearly memberships automatically if the professional has not canceled the membership four weeks prior to the end of the existing subscription. Although the real benefit of this automatic renewal is that more people will stay subscribed, some of the benefits are gained only because of the original subscription. That means that what was initially a good feature to review active subscriptions is now the foundation of another feature. That basis needs to be credited accordingly. If that feature had not been implemented earlier, it would need to be included in the financial calculation of the automatic renewal feature.

Increasing benefits should also be included in the financial calculations of the methods introduced earlier. Increasing benefits have not been considered in all of the previous calculations. However, if organizations are aware of a benefit window, managers can make a much stronger case to include the feature early on when making up the priority list.

Risks

So far, our financial methods assumed that all projects will be executed without interruption as they progress toward the set goals. In reality, that is rarely ever the case. From a sponsor's perspective, each project (investment) carries risks. Risks are problems that have not materialized yet.

Think about your own personal financial details, and apply that perspective to the organization you work for. You could put money into a checking or savings account. The interest rate is guaranteed, and you can therefore easily calculate the profit that results after a certain period of time. You could also take the same financial resources and put them into the stock market. Instead of having a guaranteed interest rate, you now carry the risks of the stock market. The higher volatility of the stock market also offers the possibility of higher profits. Unfortunately, it also raises the possibility of large and unpredictable losses.

Every organization has its own financial market as well. Let's take a company interested in profit maximization instead of a nonprofit organization. The company's capital could be invested in a savings account, the stock market, or the possibility that is relevant to this book—IT projects.

If you put yourself in the shoes of the person who makes these investment decisions (for example, the CEO, CIO, CFO, and so forth), wouldn't you compare the risks of the investments, not only between the projects but also between IT projects and other investment opportunities?

An even more important consideration arises if the company has all its available funds invested in other projects. In this situation, the company would need to borrow money from external sources to execute a project. That is dangerous territory to wander into if a project is not planned right. It is pretty much the same thing as when individuals take a loan to invest into home renovation or the stock market. Nobody knows up front whether the home improvement project will increase the value of the house enough to warrant the expense of the loan or whether the stock market will yield the necessary profit. Although you can estimate returns based on past experiences, the important points are that the rate of return is not guaranteed and allocating funds to a project that were acquired from outside sources introduces additional risks and costs.

Although every agile project tackles risks early and iteratively and reduces them with different risk-response strategies, project teams can't eliminate risks entirely. The risk trigger, however, which is a specific event in the project, could be released any time.

What if executives compared investments (in stock markets or IT projects) using different methods? Using the cost-benefit method, the stock market has a relatively low cost (broker fees, fund maintenance, and so forth) compared with project costs (personnel, facilities, equipment, and so forth). The benefits of investing in the stock market are purely financial, whereas new IT projects might contribute to the organization's effectiveness (for example, business process optimization) or safety (for example, monitoring and controlling hazardous situations). This can save money and even lives in the future.

The payback period focuses on project investment risks. Using this method, investors learn how fast an investment pays its investment entirely back. IT projects are especially good at returning the investments made in a project. This is because computer systems can automate so many labor-intensive processes—for example, routine administrative tasks. The payback period is often more lucrative for technology projects because of this large savings in personnel costs. For minor up-front costs, high cost savings can be achieved.

I've been involved in projects where these calculations were based on average labor costs. In these cases, the payback period method was especially meaningful, because certain features were directly linked to cost savings in the organization. That association allowed me to make a strong case during the project selection process, as well as during the proposal selection process (which we will cover in the next chapter).

In some instances, actual personnel were affected to the extent that they were replaced within the organization. Using the payback period method, a quick assessment of the project's potential and the associated risks clearly showed that the changes were needed. You might think that this is a cruel view of human resources, and I agree that it does not sound nice. But the reality is that organizations will constantly need to streamline to stay competitive. And remember that a person who is released from one duty can be repositioned to take on new responsibilities.

In other situations, especially in manufacturing, robots and computers can increase the quality of life for many workers, not to mention the added benefit in hazardous work environments of reducing risks to worker health and the potential lawsuits related to such hazards. The negative results (financial and other) of not executing certain projects and not introducing associated changes (such as personnel cuts) might also create risks to other projects across other parts of the organization.

Let's consider the example of an executive using the discounted cash flow method. She would look at a $1 million initial investment we proposed and identify what the money would be worth if invested somewhere else (for example, in bonds). Assuming a 12 percent interest rate, the $1 million would be worth $1.1 million. In contrast, our project promises higher returns (a $200,000 return for 12 months, amounting to $2.4 million) than the bond market. (Note that the return from the bond market is available immediately, but the project does not realize its full value until the payback period is completed.) However, the keyword here is "promises." Our project's estimated return on investment does not guarantee anything, whereas the investment in bonds does. In the worst-case scenario for our project, the entire capital invested could be lost if the benefits do not materialize at all.

If you put yourself in the shoes of the project sponsor, how would you decide in certain situations when high-risk projects should be taken on rather than lower-risk financial investments?

When I say a "project," I don't necessarily mean a very long project. However, some projects go on for a few years, and as the length of a project increases so does the nervousness of the investors. In a traditional (waterfall) project, the funds are committed for an entire project. Every month, a certain amount of resources is burned. This is an all-or-nothing strategy, and I admit I would be nervous as well. Usually, non-agile organizations try to minimize this issue by creating more detailed requirements documents, which results in the exact opposite effect. Even more resources are spent up front without working software being produced, and therefore potential ROI is delayed.

In addition, agile projects deliver great advantages in terms of project risk assessment. Instead of subjecting you to a 10-month waiting period (until the project is delivered) before being able to compare the revenue expectations with reality (as traditional methods do), agile projects provide more frequent opportunities for assessment, depending on the length of the iteration. Assume that after one month, an agile project has consumed $100,000 and has $20,000 in potential revenue. Doesn't this make it easier to decide whether to continue moving forward?

In this chapter, we have primarily discussed the financial risks. However, there are also risks related to technology and day-to-day project activities. In the same way that agile teams try to remove high-risk requirements and issues in early iterations, the portfolio manager can attack business and financial risks in early incremental assessments. We'll pick up this topic in the next chapter, when we discuss the agile project selection process.

I remember a situation with a company in the infancy of the dot-com phenomenon. The company adopted a very interesting approach early on to cope with business risks and investments. The company made customers believe that they were ordering certain products online, but in reality everything behind the site was 100 percent manual. In fact, employees used telephones to order what customers could have done themselves using their telephones. The company could not wait until the entire shopping cart solution was developed and wanted to be in the online market and benefiting from the increase in e-commerce as quickly as possible. A full-store solution, including an accounting and secure payment system, would have delayed the project, and therefore ROI, significantly. The company's solution provided for an extremely fast return on investment, which decreased the financial risks. At the same time, however, the race was on in the business community to build online applications that would streamline and change the e-commerce business forever. Agile projects in your portfolio can be used to release a system feature by feature in an incremental approach, which allows you to respond to your competitors or set the standards for the future of your marketplace.

Technology

We frequently use the term "IT" projects without realizing that the "T" stands for technology. The challenge with technology is that it constantly changes, like anything else in life. I have seen many so-called "strategic" systems, platforms, and frameworks developed. But often they disappeared from the organization's IT landscape much faster than originally anticipated. Although a system that is in place might still do its job somehow, it might be outdated technology-wise compared with its neighboring systems. Of course, IT managers should not constantly follow the mood swings of the industry they are operating in, but sometimes the replacement of a system cannot be ignored any longer. Every system has a life expectancy that is based on the industry an organization is in and the expectations of the customer base. In my opinion, the best way to treat a system replacement is to learn from the original but welcome and use changes wherever possible. For example, whenever I hear people say, "I want this but new," it turns out they most likely want something just a bit different. They like a system as they have it, but they want it with additional features. A pure rewrite would be excessive and might not give them the features they are really looking for.

Not only do benefits have an expiration date and return on investment, but the entire system does. Eventually all IT systems will be retired, rewritten, or abandoned. But herein lies the chance to increase ROI again, using newer technology and making that new technology work to your advantage.

Think about how inventions and implementations such as the bar code, global positioning systems, the Internet, and e-mail have changed our lives by using new technologies. These inventions have also had an impact on organizational processes. On a smaller scale, the newly invented technologies can be used inside organizations to gain an additional advantage and influence on your ROI—for example, sales terminal software, which reads bar codes on products, or electronic document-archiving systems based on new ways of electronic communication. All these inventions will outdate existing systems or generate ideas to build new ones. But even if it seems totally unforeseeable today, these technologies will be challenged by newer, emerging technologies in the future.

Summary

Agile projects provide significant benefits to the overall organization. They yield faster payback for projects, which can then be reinvested faster in future projects.

Agile projects can be compared by using a cost-benefit analysis, net present value analysis, or internal rate of revenue analysis. Using agile methods, organizations and portfolio managers within those organizations can take on projects in smaller steps, reducing the financial risks and increasing the frequency with which systems are deployed. That is particularly true for projects with expiring benefits. During this chapter, we have evaluated one project at a time. In the following chapters, we will look at all projects in the portfolio and cover the agile project selection process for a project, resource, and application portfolio.

Chapter 7
Project Portfolio Management

To make sound decisions about projects or about selecting one project over another, managers need reliable metrics to compare the plan with the actual results. The return on investment (ROI) estimate, corporate vision, and technical feasibility will drive the long-term selection process of your portfolio. In addition to having a portfolio strategy, agile projects have a tactical plan for upcoming iterations, and this plan is refined throughout the increments. The actual accomplishments are captured at the end of the iteration, and metrics summarize the overall health of the project in a statistical form. We have covered all these fundamental topics in the two previous chapters.

In this chapter, we will focus on the project portfolio and learn why this type of portfolio is often the most popular portfolio in organizations compared with the other portfolios introduced in Chapters 8 and 9. A project portfolio provides quick and noticeable changes to organizations that are implementing a portfolio management strategy. A project portfolio is formed by three major needs: selecting and initiating projects, linking the portfolio to the corporate strategy, and maximizing the value of the project portfolio. These needs trace back to one of the biggest challenges for portfolio managers, *maintaining a balance of projects*. To achieve a balance, the project selection process is a crucial piece of the overall portfolio management strategy, and it will dominate the discussion in this chapter. When we discuss the project selection process, we need to look at the proposal management as well and review how project proposals will eventually turn into real projects.

Balancing the Project Portfolio

In Chapter 4, "Foundation," I noted that one of the three major challenges in portfolio management is to achieve and maintain a balanced project portfolio. Although the definition of "balance" is something that needs to be defined on a case-by-case basis, an unbalanced portfolio has one or more of the following symptoms:

- Too many active projects
- An incorrect mix of risk and reward projects
- A lack of visionary projects
- An emphasis on small projects

Let's get to the root causes of these symptoms before we discuss how agile projects tackle the imbalance. Each of the following subsections is dedicated to one of these symptoms.

Avoid Pursuing Too Many Projects at Once

The following sections detail the problems that arise when an organization pursues too many projects at once. An organization that responds to these problems by dividing limited resources among simultaneous projects actually increases the costs of the projects while decreasing efficiency. As you will see, better approaches are available to portfolio managers and other managers in an organization.

Understanding the Productivity Costs of Having Too Many Projects

Many organizations just have more active projects on their radar screen than the workforce can handle. Hiring new talent increases the cost structure and challenges the internal organizational logistics as well as office environment. Therefore, increasing the staff to handle all ongoing and future projects is often not an option. Having too many projects can also be an indication that the organization has no proper project selection process. As a result, every idea turns into a project. Mitigating this lack of a project selection process simply by increasing staffing makes the situation even worse.

The next bad choice is to assign people to multiple projects. In other words, the resources work on more than one project at a time. Project switching is expensive and similar to task switching, where people constantly bounce between different projects. The organization in need often searches for a *multitasker*, which is a bad idea. Tom DeMarco, in his book *Slack* (Broadway Books, 2002), states that a minimum 15 percent productivity penalty is associated with task switching. This balancing act among projects might seem impressive to outsiders because it gives a sense of parallel progress. In reality, the activities are still performed in sequence. The sequence is, then, a series of very short cycles.

As a matter of fact, humans cannot really multitask at all; our brains can focus on only one thing at a time. The productivity penalty is a result of individuals switching back and forth from one project to another. Tom De Marco's penalty estimate is based on activity switching in general; switching across different projects adds a level of complexity to the switch and causes the penalty to be much higher. For example, when the project context is switched, the social and physical boundaries change as well. Figure 7-1 illustrates the productivity penalty based on the schedules of two projects following a two-week iteration rhythm. Keep in mind that this is purely an example to illustrate the impact of the penalty on both project schedules. In reality, the penalty is often nested in individual assignments and not as easily identifiable.

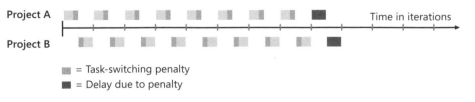

FIGURE 7-1 Project switching penalty

Even if we consider only a moderate 15 percent penalty, both projects would extend their schedules by almost a month. Gerald Weinberg, in his book *Quality Software Management: System Thinking*, uses software engineering tasks as a basis for determining the productivity penalty and believes the number is much higher. The context switch from one system to another is what makes the figure even higher. A software developer must memorize large pieces of the systems to understand dependencies and relationships. The switch between projects requires, therefore, a more than trivial shift in the developer's mental pictures.

Weinberg predicts 20 percent waste as a result of switching between simultaneous projects. The penalty increases even further if we add to the equation a third project (up to 40 percent) or a fourth project (up to 60 percent). A 60 percent task-switching penalty means that each project ends up with 10 percent productivity because only 40 percent of productivity is left, which is split among the four projects.

Although our example in Figure 7-1 indicates that we are planning on switching projects after iterations, it will be nearly impossible to separate e-mail messages, phone calls, or meetings that define and protect the boundaries of each iteration. As a rule of thumb, avoid project switching as long as possible and tackle the root cause of the need for it by reducing the number of active projects in the portfolio. This recommendation also applies to agile projects that provide an option to switch tasks after every iteration. The context of iterations is too short and the scope too small to justify a switch between projects after every iteration. In addition, continuity and ongoing progress keep team morale elevated and allow individuals to identify with their group, their peers, and the project itself.

For these reasons, project switching in agile projects decreases the velocity of both projects. Although this is generally true, later in this chapter we'll see when a switch of projects might be appropriate and the penalty justified.

Reducing the Administrative Overhead Caused by Multiple Active Projects

In addition to creating a productivity penalty for projects, an inordinate number of simultaneous projects also affects the portfolio management practice itself. Many initiatives listed in project portfolios are, by definition, *projects* (that is, they are unique and temporary). The more projects that are contained in the portfolio, however, the higher the internal administrative efforts are of managing that portfolio.

Tracking and collecting metrics, initiating and selecting projects, prioritizing, and closing out projects take energy out of the portfolio management team. The effort of administering an abundance of small projects distracts from the more important challenge for portfolio managers, linking the portfolio to a strategy. Deciding which of the many small projects are the important ones, and figuring out their dependencies, is a task that is very time consuming.

Instead of managing all projects as multiple related small projects, why not group them into one larger project effort under one umbrella? The dependencies and relationships between the formerly isolated mini-projects are then handled by one project team. Combining many small, separate projects from the portfolio and making one project out of them decreases the number of active projects in the portfolio. Such a strategy also defines a new, larger project boundary (scope) that is much easier to place into an overall strategy.

Finding Closure; Avoiding Gold-Plating

Projects are a temporary endeavor, which means they have a start date and an end date. Agile projects are commonly less strict about the end date because the focus is on balancing stakeholder needs rather than accomplishing an on-time delivery of all that is initially requested. Some agile project managers might argue that the end date of a project is meaningless if the right system cannot be delivered. However, nothing changes the fact that even agile projects will stop at some point.

When that final date approaches, projects often do not appropriately close out. That means that some projects stay officially alive. A phenomenon called *gold-plating* is a reason why projects do not disappear from the list of active projects. That means that small enhancement requests or unwanted features are implemented that the customer never actually articulated a need for.

Gold-plating is often performed to impress customers by giving them more for their money than they asked for. In reality, the customer pays for it one way or the other. Either the funding stops when the customer indicates it is satisfied or the project team has extra time to work on these additional features. In the worst-case scenario, gold-plating introduces defects and unwanted or false business logic to a previously good system. Having the project manager signal the project end and transition the team to a new project prevents the team from unnecessarily consuming additional project resources and forces the organization to close out the active project from the project portfolio. That, in return, reduces the number of active projects.

Balance Your Portfolio with Risky and Rewarding Projects

Every organization should have a bird's-eye view of the overall list of its active projects. A portfolio manager provides such a view by creating a diagram like the one shown in Figure 7-2.

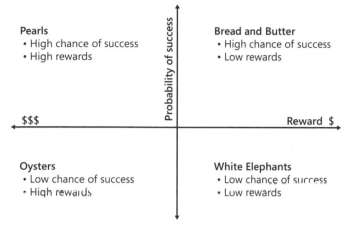

FIGURE 7-2 Risk-reward diagram

A diagram like this one, which categorizes projects in terms of risk and reward, can condense information about the vision, risk, and potential return of investment. This approach has the benefit of enhancing the project selection process. The lack of accessible and digestible information is often a reason why executives cannot properly select projects. Every organization might label each axis differently, but regardless of what parameters an organization chooses to measure, a risk-reward diagram is an extremely powerful tool.

Each active project is assessed by executives and assigned to one of the quadrants of the diagram. The upper-left corner contains the potential stars (such as new systems or complete overhauls of systems) of the organizations, which represent the organization's strategic projects (pearls). From Figure 7-2, you can see that these projects are placed at the top of the success axis and on the higher end (the left side) of the reward axis. The speculative projects (in the lower-left quadrant) also promise significant reward (oysters), but they are much more risky (for example, projects aiming for some type of breakthrough development).

Both quadrants on the right side of the diagram, however, will reward the organization much less. The Bread and Butter projects in the upper-right corner are projects that will have a very high success rate (for example, small enhancement projects), but the financial benefit of these projects is small. Having a high concentration of projects and resources in the upper-right corner represents a moderate approach, with low risk and a conservative vision. The White Elephants on the lower-right side should be removed from consideration because they represent a combination of a low chance of success and low reward.

> **Note** Please keep in mind that every organization needs to define the thresholds for each quadrant in a separate exercise. Whether or not the IT organization needs to invent and introduce breakthrough systems (those that would appear in the upper-left quadrant of a bubble diagram) depends on the company profile. A market research, competitive analysis, or SWOT (Strength, Weakness, Opportunity, and Thread) analysis can be used to define the meaning of the quadrants for each organization.

A *bubble diagram* is one of the most popular diagrams for facilitating the project selection process. The advantage of using a bubble diagram is that it can illustrate more than two project parameters in the same picture. In addition to signifying the risks and rewards by using quadrants, you can signify the amount of resources each project will require by using bubbles. Larger bubbles indicate that a project requires a greater amount of resources. (See Figure 7-3.)

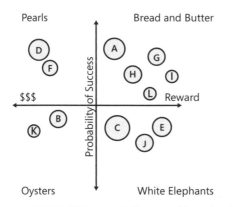

FIGURE 7-3 Risk-reward diagram with project bubbles

By analyzing the portfolio shown in Figure 7-3, you'll notice a concentration of projects on the right side of the diagram, which indicates low reward. In addition, the projects in the White Elephants section in the lower-right quadrant consume a large amount of resources, as indicated by the size of the bubbles. The failure of these large projects (which are in the high-risk quadrant) would affect the organization's bottom line more than the failure of the smaller ones; therefore, the diagram is illustrating an organization that has an especially costly or risky mix of IT projects lined up. The portfolio shown in this example is also not very visionary, as indicated by a lack of reasonably sized projects on the left side of the diagram, primarily in the upper-left quadrant.

Large organizations can also increase the readability of the risk-reward diagram by adding shades or colors to the bubbles. In this way, each project bubble can be clearly allocated to a line of business or technology, thereby increasing the diagram's detail without adversely affecting its readability.

In general, a well-balanced project portfolio shows significant activity in the upper-left quadrant. In addition, these projects should also be of significant size, which means that a solid portion of the resources are spent on low-risk, high-reward projects. Experience shows that the upper-left quadrant is often the most difficult to fill, because projects in this quadrant are innovative and leading-edge projects. Launching these kinds of projects requires a broader vision and a commitment to change an organization. To free resources for the left side of the diagram, portfolio managers must constantly try to remove projects from the right side, especially from the lower-right quadrant. That way, the resources allocated to the White Elephants section are more wisely used on promising projects.

Managing the Evolution of an Agile Portfolio from a Risk-Reward Perspective

Figure 7-4 illustrates the evolution of an agile portfolio in a risk-reward bubble diagram over a period of time—for example, four iterations of four weeks' time. Each iteration improves on the mix of projects in the portfolio.

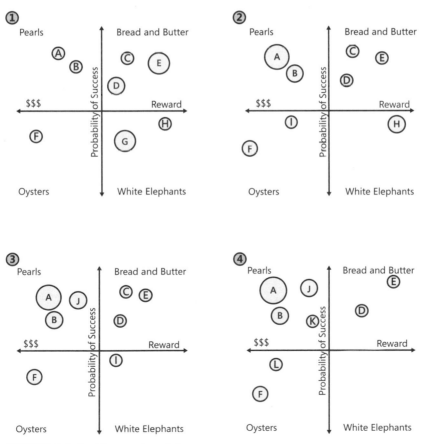

FIGURE 7-4 Agile risk-reward evolution

Following is a description of the elements shown in Figure 7-4:

- **Iteration 1**   The portfolio is unbalanced, with a drift toward the quadrants on the right side. Compared with the other projects in the diagram, projects G and H in the White Elephants section consume too many resources. Projects A, B, and F are the only ones that promise high returns, but the risks are also high, especially for Project F. This portfolio has little vision.

- **Iteration 2**   Changes were made to the project portfolio. Project G was closed out, which made a large amount of resources available for other projects. Although projects D and E were not stopped, the resources were drastically reduced. These resources were shifted to the Pearls, projects A and B. Because management now has access to more resources, it was able to initiate a new, small speculative project, project I. Project F has been reassessed and found more profitable than anticipated an iteration ago.

- **Iteration 3**   It turns out that the investment in the speculative project I was not a good decision. An executive assessment revealed that after only one iteration the project should be moved into the lower-right corner. One reason for such a transition might have been that the business team evaluated and downgraded the potential ROI. More cleanup work in the lower-right corner has been done, and project H was closed out. The resources from that project were moved to a new project, project J, that was categorized as a future star project.

- **Iteration 4**   After the fourth iteration, you can see that projects I and C were removed from the portfolio. That made resources available for an additional future Pearls project (K). The organization was also very bullish about project A and increased the resources accordingly. After the organization had no luck with project I during the previous iteration, it was canceled, and the organization launched a new speculative, Oysters project (L). After only four iterations, the organization moved resources from low-reward projects to visionary high-reward projects. You can see this shift illustrated by the concentration of projects in the two left quadrants.

Executives who are creating a risk-reward diagram for the first time are often surprised when they see which quadrant the large projects are located in. Also, as in our example, there is commonly a strong concentration of projects on the right side of the diagram. Other very aggressive development shops have a concentration of projects in the lower-left quadrant, without a balance of more conservative projects. Sometimes smaller organizations concentrate all their efforts on one project, which might be extremely speculative. One organization comes to my mind that had about 90 percent of all resources in a project situated in the Oysters quadrant. The organization was not a risk-taking organization by nature, but the risk-reward diagram gave a totally different impression. It looked like the organization was adopting a strategy equivalent to playing roulette in a casino, and unfortunately this project eventually took the company close to bankruptcy.

Evaluating the Costs of Project Switching

If we look at projects A and B for potential project-switching penalties, the risk-reward diagram also reveals interesting information, especially when adding return on investment to the equation. As an example, suppose project A adds an estimated ROI of $20,000 with every iteration (and $160,000 by completion), while project B adds $30,000 per iteration (and $240,000 by completion). Both projects together will return about $400,000 on investment during the development period of eight months. Also assume that, because of task switching, the development period has increased from eight months to approximately nine months in length and no additional ROI can be achieved.

From an organizational perspective, both projects together will incrementally add $50,000 of benefits every calendar month (two 2-week iterations). Was our project selection a good decision? Before we explore the alternatives, let's take a look at the impact of this scenario, which is illustrated in Figure 7-5.

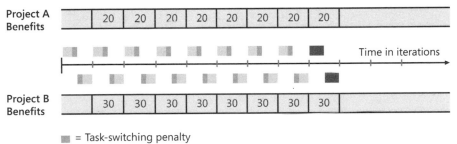

■ = Task-switching penalty
■ = Delay due to penalty

FIGURE 7-5 Task-switching penalty using iterations

After nine months (which includes the one-month task-switching penalty) of running both projects, the value of the organization increased by roughly $350,000. The exact number will depend on the exact amount of the penalty over a period of time. We also assumed that the value increases in equal increments (amounts) over the entire period. This is not likely to happen in any real-world situations because not every feature will have equal weight in terms of value.

Now let's remove the productivity penalty and align the projects sequentially. Doing this requires that the amount of active projects in the portfolio be reduced to the capacity the organization can handle without penalties. In other words, every person works on one project only. With the possible benefits being slightly higher for project B ($30,000 instead of $20,000), why don't we first eliminate the task-switching penalty for that project and take a fresh look at the impact it has on the benefits? (See Figure 7-6.)

To make things even more interesting, assume that the benefits for both projects will eventually expire. The benefits of project A will expire after one year, while project B's benefits will last for one year longer.

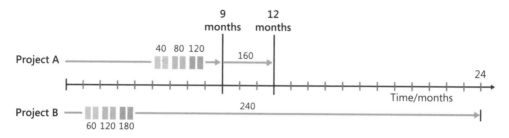

FIGURE 7-6 No task-switching penalty, and benefit expiration factored in

Now let's see if the situation has changed and if selecting project B over A was a good decision. First, the development time of both projects is now eight months instead of nine months. We won this one month back because we removed the productivity penalty. In the long term, that will lead to higher returns being gained earlier from the more profitable project B. Second, project B will return investment for a longer time because it will be completed after four months and will continue to provide a return on investment for another 20 months.

The diagram makes it easier for us to see that the time to harvest ROI from project A is relatively short. Four months, to be precise. This brings up the question of whether it was a good idea to tackle project A at all. Or should we have lined up project A prior to B? Let's compare the facts. If we had started A prior to B, our overall predicted return on both projects would be $5.7 million after 24 months. If we scheduled project B prior to A, our overall revenue would be only slightly higher—in this example, $6 million. If the estimated ROI for project A increased only slightly, selecting project A prior to project B would yield more rewards.

We can see from this scenario that the promised rewards of a project are directly connected to the rewards of each feature, and the estimation is related to the overall rewards of the project. That reward will determine which position of the risk-reward diagram the project will be located in. The expiration of benefits as well as the penalty for project switching, however, has a crucial impact on the selection process. That means that the potential stars of an organization prevent productivity penalties due to project switching. In addition, potential stars are characterized by late-expiring benefits. A portfolio with only two projects, as shown in Figure 7-6, is extremely uncharacteristic, and these two sample projects were smaller than most in terms of duration and resources.

Balance a Portfolio with Visionary Projects

I have seen large IT organizations across many industries that were constantly trying to catch up with the latest business drivers and technologies rather than incorporating new ideas and technologies into a portion of their portfolio.

The result is that the project teams *react* to new situations but hardly ever *act*. Introducing change is easier when an organization is profitable and growing rather than struggling financially. Thriving organizations seem to be more experimental with their resources. Organizations with tight budgets, on the other hand, are usually less tempted to take on additional risks. This defensive approach is quite natural and understandable. On the flip side, however, projects in the upper-left corner of the risk-reward diagram are the ones that have the potential to turn the organization's economic situation around again.

Based on my experience, introducing new project ideas is often a one-way street. The business segment of an organization tells the IT department what it needs, and IT delivers the needed applications. The situation is hardly ever reversed. Agile development practices transformed the actual development process by keeping the business segment constantly involved and creating more of a dialogue between IT and the business groups. There is no question that this concept was revolutionary in the industry and that it has proved to be successful.

With agile project management, the introduction of visionary projects (those in the upper-left quadrant of a risk-reward diagram) is not limited to only business products and services. Projects introduced through the IT department might be equally important. New features of the latest technology releases are commonly something that members of the IT department are aware of first, and they are also most likely to see how such features can benefit the organization. By the time the business users and end users become aware of new technology, the "cool factor" of the technology has often disappeared. A technology's "cool factor" often helps to make a strong case for marketing departments to invest in certain projects. Although the benefits of these projects are often short, and therefore less lucrative, from a financial perspective, they can create a positive image for a brand.

Remember that information technology has transformed many businesses—for example, the invention of the Internet has transformed the entertainment industry and retail business. Although many business visions exist (in the form of documents), they are often not visionary at all from the perspective of technical innovation. These business cases describe what the stakeholder will expect, based on what they know today. But instead of describing the issues of today's business, a vision should tackle the issues of tomorrow! That means that a vision needs to make assumptions about the time between today and the date the system will be released in its environment. Those are the assumptions that make a business case visionary.

Avoid Small Projects That Limit Vision and Impede Development

Earlier in this chapter, we discussed the problem associated with too many projects in a portfolio. Whenever there are too many projects in a portfolio, there is also a likelihood that the projects themselves are small in size. If so, it is likely that we can't see the forest for the trees. When we have only small projects, we tend to estimate and prioritize small projects instead of stepping back and reevaluating the overall situation and strategy. An emphasis on small projects is a major drawback for an organization. Let's see why.

Road construction is a good example. It is performed every spring to fill potholes caused by the stresses of the winter season. A year later, the roads are in similarly bad shape, and often they are in worse condition. Not only did the water get into the cracks, but it got between the patch and the road. At the next freezing point, the melted water caused by the application of salt gets in between the cracks, expands, and has no room to go. It breaks up the road even more. More patching has to be done the following year until there is no good repair strategy. Sooner or later, the entire road must be repaved or replaced. If our resources are all allocated to patchwork tasks in tiny projects, how can we plan and apply a corporate strategy? And remember, patching will work for a little while, but sooner or later a major change will need to happen.

Small projects usually do not have the visionary direction that larger and more fundamental projects have. It is quite understandable, but a one-week or two-week project does not have the scope and foundation to influence the direction of an entire organization. A large, substantial project influences the organization more deeply. Of course, many small projects together might replace one large project, but the coordination and administration of these projects on a portfolio level requires a large amount of effort. As discussed earlier, bundling the smaller efforts together into a larger project provides many benefits—for example, the possibility of detecting additional synergies among the projects through daily team communication.

Therefore, an emphasis on small projects in a portfolio is directly linked to a lack of vision in the project portfolio and to an organization having too many projects.

Testing the Waters by Starting Small

Agile project management with its iterative-incremental development approach introduces a different perspective we need to investigate. Many great ideas begin as small ones. Agile projects usually start small—for example, they focus on the outcome of the first iteration. By decreasing the project resources required at the beginning, a new project can test the water before future resource commitments are made.

Increasing or adding scope over time is easily done for agile projects. That way, a small project can prove its value on a small stage before additional resources are added. That reduces the risk assumed by the organization, as other elements of the project are placed on the back burner. By doing this, portfolio managers ensure that the portfolio is less crowded and convoluted and easier to manage. Agile management teaches that while it's great to start small, it's not great to stay small.

Initiating a Project

An imbalance in a project portfolio might start as early as the point of initiation of new projects. That is the time period when the best possible projects are selected according to the company's strategy. Therefore, it is important to discuss the project initiation process, which can minimize the imbalance quickly or help you avoid it to begin with.

First we'll discuss how an agile project could be initiated based on a rough idea or business case. Figure 7-7 shows the typical process of how an idea is transformed into a funded project. Let's take a closer look at each of these steps.

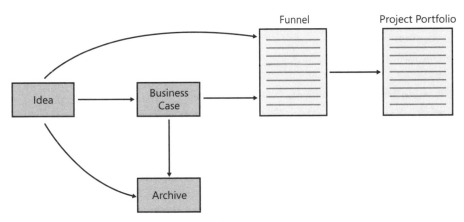

FIGURE 7-7 Transforming an idea into a project

Implementing a Process for Collecting Ideas

The various ways that ideas can be transformed into a project are as diverse as you can imagine. For example, ideas can be submitted directly to a project management office (PMO), or, in smaller organizations without a PMO, the ideas can be sent informally via e-mail directly to the top executives, who will then evaluate the suggestions.

Intranets are also an excellent medium for submitting ideas, and one that doesn't even require employees to leave their chairs. Large organizations might want to use sophisticated submission forms so that the proposed idea will be submitted directly to the most appropriate department or contact. Using an electronic submission system, the organization (PMO, CTO, and so forth) can be proactive and offer a public voting page. If you include a comments section on the voting page, employees who do not have the time to actively submit ideas can at least share their opinions about the ideas submitted by others. This feature would be especially useful when conflicting ideas are submitted and the decision maker wants to collect additional opinions, such as by asking, "Would you prefer A over B or B over A?" Keep in mind that majority votes are often suboptimal and might not reflect the perspective of the organization's executives. The Agile Alliance used this approach to collect and evaluate session proposals for the Agile 2008 conference in Toronto. It's easy to see how using something similar on an organizational level could lead to many ideas for improvement.

If groups within an organization or the entire organization work under one roof, a physical drop box similar to a mailbox might be just as appropriate. Placed strategically at the main entrance, in the cafeteria, or in another common area, the box is a highly visible daily reminder for every employee entering and leaving that area.

In addition to a title and short description of the idea, you should also ask for at least a short reason for the idea from the submitter. Many times, ideas and suggestions seem like a wonderful idea to the submitter, but the reader might not realize the idea's business potential. Because the submitter might see the potential from a different angle, have the submitter estimate and describe it. Capturing the name and contact detail of the submitter allows you to clarify the idea's potential in a one-on-one conversation.

Also, an organization should consider offering a bonus or some form of employee recognition for each idea that turns into a project. Some might argue that every employee should have an interest in improving the organization and should not gain additional financial rewards for contributing in that way; others believe that monetary rewards will keep people alert to shortcomings in the organization and make them proactive in removing those shortcomings.

Once submitted, the ideas need to be assessed for their potential and feasibility by executive management and project sponsors. Ideas that are small and easy to accommodate should go straight into the project funnel, which we cover later in this chapter.

Sometimes, ideas that are found to be useful but are not defined well enough to receive project funding need to go through an extra step. These ideas might need someone to make a stronger case for them, which is commonly referred to as a business case.

Presenting the Business Case

A business case is typically a document that captures the information about the market demographics, financial justification, and perhaps even a few high-level requirements for an idea. Ideally, as the name indicates, this document should be used by the business group to make a case to executive managers (sponsors) to invest in the project idea. Therefore, this document is used to get the idea proposal refined and to determine its scope before an investment is made. Many organizations I have worked with, however, turn the business case into something much more elaborate, often with a too-detailed view of individual requirements. Detailed requirements do not necessarily present a problem, but they are often simply not needed. In such cases, time and money have been spent to build a business case for an idea that might be dropped anyway.

I completely understand executives who get nervous about investing a large amount of money in an IT project based on a brief business case. That is particularly true for traditional projects, where all requirements are specified up front. With agile projects, however, building a business case can be quite a different experience. Let's see why.

Agile projects provide a milestone for reevaluating the project after each iteration. All the initial business case needs to do is provide enough information and justification to get the first, and perhaps second or third, iteration funded. After these initial iterations, the organization and portfolio manager not only have a much better understanding of the depth of the idea, they already have working software. Instead of funding the creation of the business case document, the organization simply invests in the initial iterations. Once the case has been made and the initial iteration has been completed, the project might receive additional funding for the rest of the application by applying iterative-incremental development techniques.

If some group or individual in the organization has spent a lot of time and money creating a business case document, it becomes very difficult to say, "No more. We must stop here and go no further!" Keep in mind that through the many meetings, revisions, and conversations needed to devise a detailed business case, other members of the organization might falsely assume that the project is already under way. And so many resources have been used that the business case feels like a real project already. That is exactly where the dilemma begins in a traditional funding model, where projects need to be so carefully defined in the beginning that a fixed amount of funds is dedicated to a project.

On one hand, detailed business cases are needed to allocate proper funding within the organization, especially to secure large sums of money. But on the other hand, building such a business case is expensive in itself. Also, innovation is very difficult to plan on paper, and more ideas surface after the initial iterations. I'm sure nobody sat down and wrote a business case about electric light and the potential of lightbulbs prior to their invention. These inventions were the result of experimental entrepreneurship. The business analysts and the developers together need to dive into the core of the issue and not labor over the high-level requirements at the start. They need only a little time and money to isolate the technical challenges and start driving the overall progress. After that, a better decision can be made. Again, that all sounds like an iteration, doesn't it?

Just to illustrate the dilemma for executives one more time: Imagine you are the person making the decision (and therefore, the person responsible for the IT strategy) in a traditionally managed organization and none of your projects are executed using agile principles. What would your answer be if someone asked you to allocate a very large piece of your budget to one project? It sounds like a big risk to me. You will have to wait months or years for the delivered system until you can see tangible progress and review the effectiveness of the final system in its environment. Wouldn't you rather have a team making the case for a system in much smaller cycles? Smaller cycles, of course, mean less financial commitment. I think the answer is clear.

Being at ease with inaccuracy and a lack of details in business cases is a characteristic of agile development practices. Because of this and other benefits of agile practices, I can see that in the future many organizations will use agile portfolio practices to experiment with larger ideas in smaller steps. Many of these ideas might get canceled after initial iterations, which is actually a good thing if you think about the damage that pursuing a bad solution can cause. I prefer finding this out earlier rather than later.

Even if a final decision about a business case or an idea cannot be made after one iteration, after a few iterations the potential of the case shapes up. But unlike an unlaunched project awaiting a fully specified business case, the agile project has already delivered value in the form of working software. Challenge your own organization sometime by taking a business case from a system that has been already completed. Read the business case document and compare it with the actual system documentation. You will see that the original vision was probably not delivered, but the system might still have provided value.

You can argue that stakeholders should know up front what they will get and what they are paying for. In a perfect world, that would definitely be something we would like to achieve. In reality, the time needed to write a business case is a very soft and gray area. Because of the lack of tangible outcomes, which are verified in the form of increments of the system, the business case might be as unstable as the requirements. Agile development and project management can tackle and resolve this problem. Because the entire business case is not spelled out up front and evolves over time in the early iterations of the project, constant face-to-face stakeholder involvement is recognized as essential to clarifying questions for the project team on an ad hoc basis.

Another issue with business cases is that they are often too positive. It is natural to be excited about new ideas and potential projects. Unfortunately, the positive energy might influence the content and writing style of the business case itself. For example, instead of noting the threats and risks, analysts document the economic and technical potential of the project. If nobody tries to poke holes in the business case and play devil's advocate, the business case might not be a true assessment of the situation. Even if the business group feels very positive about an idea and gives the IT department an overwhelmingly optimistic business case to work with, reality will sink in shortly afterward. Agile development will manage the expectations realistically, which might involve dealing with some negative outcome early in the project.

Assessing a Business Case

In an agile portfolio, the business case can be handled in two different ways. In the first approach, the business case is an improved version of the idea, with background information, an analysis of the business impact, and an analysis about the potential, stakeholders them-selves. Rough revenue or cost-saving estimates and some high-level requirements round off the first draft of this document. Based on this input, the project team produces a high-level estimate. If the business group can still make its case after this assessment, the business case will be included in the project funnel, which we will discuss in more depth shortly.

In the second approach, the idea—instead of the business case document—is handed over to a development team, which receives initial funding. This way, the project team feels as if the project has started, with one huge difference. The funding is limited for a few initial itera-tions. After that, the business case is made by the business group after the initial iterations or the idea is allowed to die. This internal milestone is extremely important because the organi-zation did not approve the large-scale project, perhaps because of a weak business case. The organization gives the team a chance to work toward a high-level result. Once the milestone is reached, a decision about the project is made. If the revised business case does not deliver the support necessary to warrant further investment in the idea, the case will be closed and archived. If the business case still sounds like a good idea, it will be placed in the funnel of proposals waiting and competing for resources in the organization.

Collecting and Managing Proposals

Portfolio managers should keep in mind that maintaining a good balance of proposals is as important as maintaining a good balance of projects in the project portfolio. Proposals are ideas that include market research, the benefits of the features and their related estimates, a visionary statement, and suggestions about which stakeholders should be targeted. Like projects, proposals need to be assessed and constantly revisited. The mechanism for accept-ing and promoting proposals, referred to as a *funnel*, is more loosely defined, and proposals can drip in and drop out more casually. Calling it a funnel, therefore, is quite appropriate.

Creative and forward-thinking organizations manage a constantly filled funnel. Some argue that proposal management is more important than the project portfolio itself. If you have nothing valuable lined up, what do you select as your next project? We also know that starting too many projects at the same time is not a good idea. The answer is, therefore, that we need a well-prepared proposal funnel that can challenge the value of projects already in the project portfolio. (See Figure 7-8.)

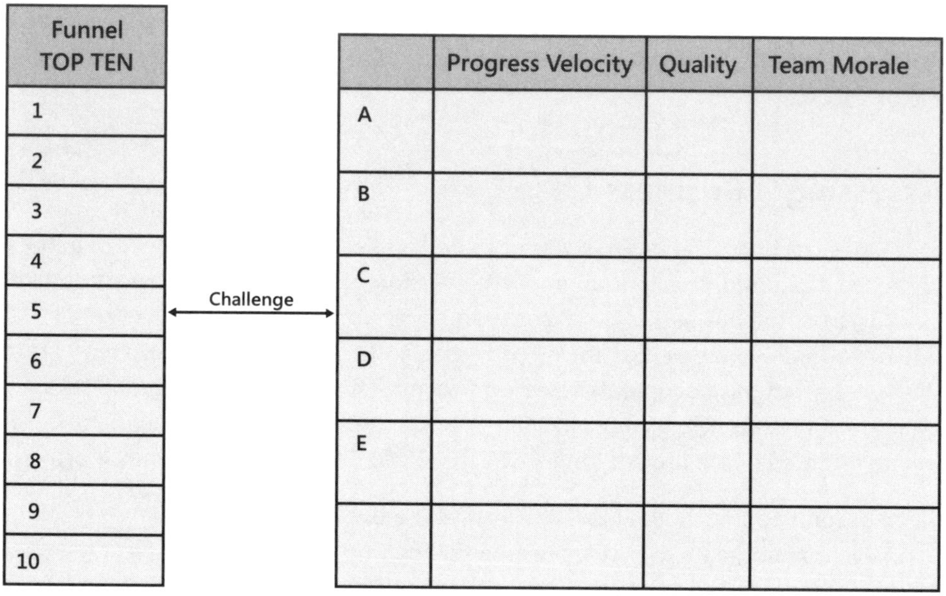

Funnel TOP TEN		Progress Velocity	Quality	Team Morale
1	A			
2				
3	B			
4				
5	C			
6	D			
7				
8	E			
9				
10				

(← Challenge →)

FIGURE 7-8 Top 10 proposal funnel items

Challenging every active project with all of the proposals, however, is time-consuming. How can we reduce the time that portfolio managers spend on the proposal selection process to create a healthy balance?

Ideas are sometimes submitted to the funnel in an unorganized and random way. To prevent chaos in the actual project portfolio, portfolio managers need to manage and prepare the ideas in the funnel so that existing projects are challenged only with better ideas from the funnel. Ideally, the portfolio is revisited in between iterations of a project. Otherwise, assessing a large portfolio and an even larger funnel might just be too time-consuming. We also want to focus on challenging the projects that fall into the right side of the risk-reward diagram. Challenging every project at every iteration would not be beneficial for business continuity or team morale. Some consistency is needed and useful. Even projects that might drift slowly from the left to the right side of the risk-reward diagram should not be challenged. Sometimes, there are reasons to continue with or finish a project even though the trend is not as positive as it was at the beginning of the project.

One useful approach, similar to music charts that track the most popular or best-selling songs, is to keep a top-10 list of funnel entries. You can recompile the entire list of proposals many times during the iteration, but use only the best 10 proposals in the organization to challenge the active projects between iterations. The funnel can be extremely volatile and dynamic, but the low performers in the project portfolio are challenged only by the 10 most promising funnel items.

If an idea has not worked its way into the top-10 charts by the end of an iteration, it stays in the funnel for at least another iteration. Therefore, whoever is behind the ideas and business cases needs to make the strongest possible submission to reach the top 10 and finally compete with active projects in the portfolio. The number 10, by the way, is arbitrary; you can adjust this number (up or down) depending on your enterprise and the size of your portfolio.

After being submitted into this funnel, the proposals are evaluated by business analysts. Common tasks for an initial proposal review include the following:

- Is the proposal large enough to become a project?
- Has a similar proposal been rejected in the past, and why?
- Is the proposal a duplicate?
- Is the proposal currently covered by another project?

Decision makers can answer these questions more easily if they know the origin of the proposal. For example, end users usually identify bottlenecks, defects, and labor-intensive routine work that could be automated. These proposals are often small and do not always justify being turned into a project. Remember, one issue of an unhealthy portfolio balance is having too many small projects. Therefore, bundle the proposals together, and build a group of them into a project—for example, creating a new version of an existing system. A stronger case can then be made for pursuing the group of proposals rather than making a case to pursue each of them individually. As a group, they will also present stronger strategic value to the organization.

Just because a similar proposal been rejected in the past does not mean that the new proposal should be thrown out too. The situation might have changed, and what was not a good idea in the past might be a good idea now.

Sometimes a submitted proposal is similar to a proposal that turned into an active project. Some submitters might not have the benefit of seeing the entire project portfolio when submitting proposals. Instead of simply removing the duplicate proposal, you should review, compare, and evaluate the proposals. They might be similar but not identical.

If the proposal survives these basic questions, the idea can be added to the funnel. Usually, business analysts evaluate the funnel and present the proposals to the next stage, where executives and business analysts together prioritize the proposals. Once the proposals are prioritized, they can compete for resources with already active low-performing projects.

Competitive Projects: May the Best Project Win

Visionary organizations might actually address the same problem with more than one project. As a matter of fact, they might start multiple projects in parallel with the same goal in mind.

Executing projects in parallel often happens without the project teams knowing about it because one team is working internally and one is working externally. External vendors can perform in this model very well, because they are typically used to providing a quick turnaround time with their services.

The idea of parallel execution is straightforward: more than one agile project team receives the same business case and enough funding for the first initial iterations. With traditional processes, executives would have to pay three times the full sum and wait until the projects were completed. Agile development changes that formula. Instead of paying twice or three times for the very same system, the iterative-incremental approach allows executives to test all projects competing for the best implementation. A decision about which direction is best for the project can usually be made after a few iterations. Especially in the finance industry, where the benefits of new products delivered faster often quickly compensate for the extra expenses, competitive projects are a very good idea.

Here is another approach. Consider a business case that offers three different implementation technologies to reach a business goal. That would mean one business case that could be implemented using three different technologies. That one business case would then result in three projects. Instead of conducting three proof-of-technologies (POT) in sequence, why not begin with three projects in parallel? The POT is an incomplete increment. The POT could demonstrate that a chosen technology proves to be appropriate for a specific problem. The outcome might, however, be an incomplete user scenario or just a framework. The delivery after a true increment can be linked to a specific user story or use case. Three project teams will work on the same iteration timeline, on different projects, and using different technologies. The project sponsor, who is the person or business unit who funds the projects, expects two of the three projects will be stopped once the best approach is identified. Upon first glance, this approach might sound like a waste of resources, but let's look at the following example.

The business predicts an ROI of $300,000 for the next 24 months. Project A will have costs of $200,000 per month, project B's costs will be $150,000 per month, and project C's costs will be $175,000 per month. Without competition, project A would have been chosen and the system would have been expected to be delivered after 12 months.

After only one month (two iterations), project B was dropped because of technical performance issues. After an additional two months, we eliminated the next candidate—in this case, project A. Project C's technology proves that the team can deliver the system in 8 months (at a cost of $1.4 million) instead of in project A's time frame of 12 months (at a cost of $2.1 million). Let's take a new look at the costs for the scenario in Figure 7-9.

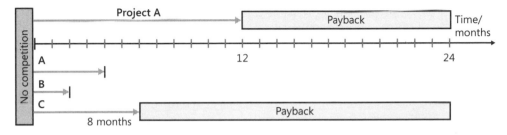

FIGURE 7-9 Competing projects

The costs for each project are as follows:

- Project A: $600,000

- Project B: $150,000

- Project C: $1.4 million

- Total costs: $2.2 million

The critical point in this example is actually not only the development costs but the return on investment calculated here using the payback period. Because project C can deliver the system so much faster, not only are the total development costs lower, but the project will create an additional four months of estimated payback. That is an additional $1.2 million difference. Especially in industries where time-to-market makes a difference, using competing agile projects might work to your advantage. Especially for speculative (oysters) and potential star projects (pearls), the additional costs for using competing projects might be justified by the high returns that are gained, for example, by providing the organization with a competitive advantage in its industry.

Launching new versions of your system with every increment might sound very appealing. The ROI potential, customer satisfaction, and frequent feedback all speak in favor of adopting this approach.

In some situations, though, using the competitive projects approach might not be a good idea. This is especially true when you deploy a system to a public marketplace—in which case, you might want to look at other options. Consider a car manufacturer. It hides newly developed models until the car is presented at a car show or marketed to increase visibility and create a shock-and-awe effect. New cars are even kept secret during test drives, when they are camouflaged. The same is true for software functionality. With every release, you reveal a piece of a strategy. You might even divulge clues about your future plans and strategy. In other words, rethink your public deployment strategy and review your competitive advantage. You could steadily provide more and more features or shock the market and competition by unveiling major improvements all at once. Internal, nonpublic releases might also benefit at times from bigger releases when you factor in the training and communication efforts.

Alternatively, instead of creating a competitive environment, an organization can explore a variety of alternative solutions in parallel. After evaluating all the options, the best ideas and approaches can be selected to build the final system.

Selecting a Project

Funneling ideas as well as business cases and converting them from proposals to an active project is only one side of the story. Once they have entered the project portfolio, they are on the radar screen, and the development team needs to demonstrate the proposed value of the project. As with air-traffic control, we need to review and evaluate the status of active projects to avoid collisions and offer detours when necessary. In the agile spirit, this can be done with quick status assessments, focusing on key performance indicators based on common metrics. (See Chapter 5, "Metrics," for more information.) Traditionally managed projects indicate status based on milestones in a master plan, which is commonly laid out entirely at the beginning of the project. Agile projects, however, have a significant, powerful advantage compared with the traditional approach. First, agile projects can report status based on a short iterative rhythm, and they can release software. Let's review when and how we can influence the portfolio and what the options are.

Go/No-Go

Every project selection process requires go/no-go decision points. These are the points where management evaluates the status and progress of a project. In addition, the potential of the active project is reassessed. The agile approach does not change this fact at all. Agile project teams are different in the sense that they can provide much different feedback than traditional project teams. First their metrics are linked to tested and integrated software, which is a tremendous detour from nonagile projects. Second, the system can be potentially deployed.

Traditional portfolio managers, who have only a go/no-go decision point, often see the cancellation of a project as something negative. Cancellation is also seen as failure. Agile projects, however, are evaluated differently, and those working on agile projects see cancellations differently. In addition, agile projects allow a more subtle interpretation of the project status at the go/no-go decision point by providing more alternatives than continuing or canceling. We will discuss these alternatives in this section. This go-/no-go checkpoint is typically aligned with the iterative rhythm of the projects. Therefore, the project teams do not need to report status additionally; instead, they use the checkpoint already used for project reporting, in between iterations.

Just before the agile project team reaches its retrospective between the iterations, the metrics (for example, progress, quality, and team morale) are compiled and added to the portfolio. In the best-case scenario, the various projects are on a similar iteration rhythm to allow portfolio managers to take a snapshot of the portfolio, including an overall decision point.

Figure 7-10 illustrates three projects with three different iteration lengths: project A with four-week iterations, project B with two-week iterations, and project C with six-week iterations.

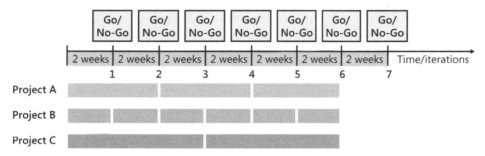

FIGURE 7-10 A project with different iteration lengths

Although it would be more ideal to have consistent iteration rhythms across the organization's projects, at least all the projects provide a synchronized checkpoint every quarter. If project C could decrease the iteration length to at least four weeks, the entire portfolio could be evaluated every month. The result after each checkpoint is either "go," which means that the project will go forward for at least one more iteration, or "no-go," which means the project will be eliminated from the portfolio. In the latter case, the resources are released from the project and made available to other projects. The issue with canceling a project is that we need to remove the negative stigma and realize the organizational benefits that a cancellation provides.

Consider a long-running project that has received the "go" signal over many iterations. At the end of a large—and therefore, long—project, the project might run out of steam. There might be changes to resources, a customer might have changed, and even the requirements might become diminished in terms of team energy and benefits to the organization. In other words, even though the project was extremely important to begin with, the team has covered the critical functionality of the system already. The less important requirements no longer provide any drastic benefits to the organization, and there are more exciting ideas waiting in the funnel. Agile projects can be cut short, making room for other important projects, and still be considered a success and materialize the most important benefits.

Next, consider a large project that gets canceled after only two iterations. It is not uncommon that a large project begins in the speculative quadrant of the risk-reward diagram and then makes a transition to the no-go quadrant (white elephants). Large projects in this quadrant especially need attention because they consume many resources. Canceling such a project is also positive. First, it's positive for the organization, which initially sponsored the project. But it's also positive for the project team, which was working in a no-win situation.

Keep in mind that in both scenarios agile development made a more granular decision possible. In the first scenario, we achieved a great return on investment and delivered all the necessary functionality. In the second scenario, canceling the project prevented further losses.

How many large-scale traditional projects are killed during the requirements, analysis, or design phase? Rarely any. Even when we do cancel these projects, there is little to no software available at all.

The early cancellation scenario just described can also apply to a few initial iterations of a business case that was taken beyond its initial paper version. After two or three short iterations, for example, the project can be canceled because of the organization's lack of interest. Again, remember that the situation could be much worse. A project team could have pursued the project and realized its lack of potential after years of development effort.

Pausing a Project

A third option beyond Go and No-Go is Pause. Because of the iterative rhythm of agile projects and the agile development practice of continuous integration, there is always an integrated and tested system available. When the project reaches a checkpoint and there are more important projects demanding resources, a project can be *paused* for a few iterations. Figure 7-11 illustrates how project A is put on hold, work is completed on project B, and resources are returned to project A later.

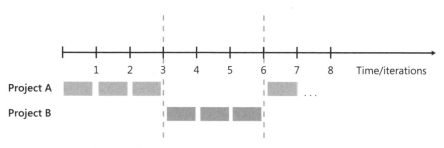

FIGURE 7-11 Pausing a project

As with project switching and task switching, pausing comes with a productivity penalty. The difference, however, is that the pausing is a longer context switch, which means the penalty should affect the team only twice: when they transition out to a new project and again when they transition back to the original work after the other project is completed.

If the company does not want to return to the project later, the paused project will be canceled and closed out to remove the project from the portfolio.

Accelerating a Project

Imagine a large project in the future-stars (upper-left) quadrant of the risk-reward diagram. The project does make the expected progress, but the promised benefits are very high. In other words, the system's completion is eagerly anticipated, but incremental delivery of finished pieces of the system might not be an option. In this situation, a fourth option, acceleration, is available.

Traditional project management commonly uses two techniques to accelerate a project. They are called *fast-tracking* and *crashing*. First let's take a quick look at these techniques so that we can see how they are different from accelerating an agile project.

Remember when we discussed the issues related to the critical path in Chapter 5? When two critical-path tasks are lined up in sequence, they can potentially be executed in parallel. That is called fast-tracking. That, of course, assumes that either different resources were initially assigned to each activity or new personnel were assigned later. In addition to increasing project costs, fast-tracking also increases the project risks, because two activities on the critical path have to be managed in parallel. A delay of one task delays all tasks on the path. An additional risk with fast-tracking is that because two tasks on the critical path have been compressed, a brand-new critical path might have been created. Tasks previously not on the critical path might be now. For example, two 3-day long activities are performed in parallel instead of sequentially. The duration of these activities is now 3 days in total, instead of 6 days. If there was an additional separate 4-day activity in the project plan that ran parallel to the two 3-day long activities, the 4-day activity had a 2-day buffer. Now, after the schedule has been compressed, the 4-day activity turns out to be on the critical path and the two 3-day activities have a buffer of one day.

Crashing a project compresses the schedule by adding resources to critical path activities or reducing scope from critical path activities. As you can see, there is no magic formula for accelerating traditional projects.

Many experienced project managers know that adding resources to a project does not always speed things up. Fred Brooks, in his book *The Mythical Man Month*, states that adding resources to a late project makes it later. Project tasks are not always easy to separate or possible to delegate. Let's see if there is a way to speed agile projects up.

In an earlier chapter, we saw that there is no critical path per se in agile projects, but rather iterations that either failed or succeeded. The tasks inside the iteration are organized by the team and appear to be executed in parallel.

Adding resources to an iteration works only if it comes with an immediate penalty in productivity and cost. It also increases the team size, which creates another concern. Scrum, for example, recommends a team size of seven, give or take two. If the team size grows beyond this number, the communication effort becomes too expensive compared with the outcome. In this case, two teams working in parallel that have meetings to synchronize their efforts is the better choice.

Here is another idea for acceleration. If a large amount of work needs to go into the express lane, pausing one project and releasing its resources to another project might be an option. In this case, an entire subcomponent of a project could be handled by a separate team that was pulled from a paused project to expedite the higher-priority features of the second project. The communication channels work properly because the team members know each other from previous project work. They are also self-organized, and they have a clearly defined scope for their next iteration, which is a specific feature set. Two iteration plans for two different teams now exist for the same project. That is truly a unique agile acceleration technique because the teams can work largely independently of each other and synchronize their work through quick daily integration meetings. The retrospectives between the iterations can intensify the exchange even further.

Canceling a project and releasing the personnel is another valid acceleration option.

Another acceleration method is built into the agile development process itself, the burn-down, or velocity, measurement. If a team burns an average of 20 story points each iteration and starts to increase the burn-down over the later iterations to 24, the productivity curve shows an upward trend. As is typical for agile projects, the later iterations contain items that have a lower priority, are less risky, and are less architecturally significant. Therefore, it is very likely that the progress (measured as velocity) will increase and peak toward the end of the project's iterations. Therefore, a trend of 20 story points in the earlier iterations, where fundamental architectural work might not allow higher burn-down rates of story points, will often increase toward the end of the project, when the bulk of the core functionality work has already been performed.

The strategy that is the opposite of accelerating, decelerating, is a strategy to be avoided. The motivation behind decelerating is often based on shifted priorities. In this case, pausing or canceling is usually the preferable option because better projects are most likely waiting in the funnel.

Summary

A project portfolio represents the vision of the organization. It is composed of active projects and a funnel of potential projects. These projects and programs need to be regularly assessed and evaluated to align the portfolio content with the corporate strategy. Because a portfolio needs to adapt iteratively to changes within the organization, we reviewed typical actions to influence the content of the agile portfolio. These were Go, No-Go, Pause, and Accelerate.

Before projects enter the portfolio, they are commonly sent through an approval process that comprises idea collection and business cases. We evaluated this process and introduced new ideas about how agile projects can support this initiation process.

In addition, we highlighted the four biggest challenges of project portfolio management and how agility addresses them. We also saw tips and tricks on how to overcome these challenges. In this context, we covered the risk-reward diagram, the penalties associated with project switching, and how we can combine smaller projects to create a project with sufficient critical mass to bring about substantial visionary changes in an organization.

Tip Here are a few suggestions for successful portfolio management:

- Always have the funnel of project proposals filled and prioritized.
- Avoid project switching.
- Constantly evaluate the effectiveness of your metrics.
- Remember that canceling a project is not negative.
- Don't mix agile and nonagile projects in one portfolio.

Chapter 8
Resource Portfolio Management

Our primary focus in the previous chapter was the project portfolio and project initiation and selection processes. Now we will turn our attention to another portfolio in the organization: the resource portfolio. The biggest component of a project's cost is most likely personnel, and it's an element that is dynamic, variable, and even volatile. This is especially true for the agile workforce. For that reason, in this chapter we'll discuss various practices for bringing agile talent into the organization and for sharing knowledge among experts of agile practices within the organization. And we'll see potential ways for matching resources to projects. We'll look at the entire agile team—employees, consultants, trainers, coaches, and mentors—and we'll investigate some of the opportunities resource portfolio management will bring to these roles and the organization itself.

Defining standards in knowledge and education is often related to certification, so we'll also take a closer look at the position of certification in the agile community. Because some agile teams work co-located, we will also look at the challenges of agile development in globally distributed development efforts.

Balancing the Resource Portfolio

A resource portfolio captures important information about the personnel of an organization. This portfolio contains information about all the employees, coaches, trainers, mentors, consultants, and so on who are potentially available for project work. This portfolio can also contain the individual's experience (quantitative or qualitative), background, and areas of professional interest. The project portfolio, as we saw in the previous chapter, plays a dominant role in the overall portfolio management strategy. Once the projects are prioritized and scheduled for execution, resources should be allocated. All we need to do is assign the best matching talent to the projects. Sounds simple, doesn't it? Unfortunately, this step often proves much more difficult than we might anticipate. In this section, we'll take a look at the following challenges and attributes that make resource portfolio management difficult:

- Lack of vision.
- Too many projects and not enough resources.
- Projects require different skills.
- Lack of feedback from resources.

Lack of Vision

I mentioned earlier that the resource portfolio is aligned with the project portfolio for staffing and allocation purposes. That is only partially correct. Ideally, the resource portfolio in an agile environment benefits from iterative cycles of training. But because of short project cycles and retrospectives in between iterations, the project selection process is much faster than the process of transforming and updating the skill set of internal employees. Therefore, the resource portfolio should be synchronized not only with the project portfolio but, more important, with the project funnel. In other words, the best time to allocate resources and get appropriate skills transferred is the period from when a proposal enters the funnel until the project is initiated. Employees and external resources waiting for the next assignment can use the time for training, self-study, and even certification.

The funnel is a great source for innovation; projects in the funnel are often connected to new gadgets and technologies (software or hardware). The required skills for such projects are not easy to find, but active resource portfolio management can monitor the changing priorities in the funnel (especially within the top-10 list) and react accordingly. Funnel management (also known as pipeline management) is not new to agile practices, and agile portfolio management embraces funnel management.

Truth be told, nothing is more frustrating to employees than when they are typecasted in their organization only because of a lack of resource management. The same is true, of course, for external vendors, with the exception that external resources are more likely to transition to another assignment faster. A successful human resources strategy includes a personal development plan for the individuals. Remember that "once a Java developer" does not mean "always a Java developer." If resources are demanded as early as the introduction of a project to the funnel, personal career paths are derived from it. Employees will feel fully integrated into the corporate strategy and its execution. For example, a team member will know that she will be staffed on a very promising project two months from now. Portfolio management requires looking out into the future; the resources are no exception.

The agile rhythm of the projects allows professionals to more easily take a break from an active project for one iteration and focus on skill development. It is also easier for professionals to jump back into another project, because iterations provide clear boundaries, similar to a mini-project. This technique prevents task switching, whose negative effects we discussed in earlier chapters, because the employee is fully committed to a professional education. Although there is a performance penalty for project switching—from a project to an educational break and back to the project—this penalty might be justified in certain situations. Examples include a major critical project in the pipeline for which the project personnel need to be prepared or updating the skill set of an employee for the current project. Some project team members might not be as productive as they could be because of some missing fundamental training. In this case, a short break for training and its associated switching penalty might be justified because of the long-term benefits to the project.

In the context of motivation, let me point out two areas that many professionals have differing views on: vacations and work breaks. You can compare agile projects with a commuter train ride that makes lot of local stops. The departure and arrival times are, as a result of routine and frequency, very predictable. The distances between stops are also often similar in length, just like iterations. Why not use these "stops" to jump off and on a train, especially because you can do so without interrupting the overall journey of the train?

Full-time employees in the U.S. usually have much less vacation time than the rest of the Western world. In addition, it is also common for Americans to schedule their fewer days off around public holidays (Thanksgiving, Labor Day, and so on) and create frequent long(er) weekends. The lack of overall vacation time and the inflexibility to schedule a longer vacation does not always work well with the personal needs and desires of employees. I've met many professionals in the U.S. who have changed jobs solely to procure a longer vacation by using the time in between jobs.

So why not offer your workers periodic time-outs that are the length of an iteration, maybe even more? You could even allow employees to use vacation time or take unpaid time off. Just to be clear, because of the concentration of vacation time around the public holidays, real progress in projects is much lower at those times anyway. The time between Thanksgiving and New Year's, for example, is very low in productivity because of resource constraints. And if you think you can easily eliminate the employees who would switch jobs for longer vacation breaks, think again! First, the employees with this vision typically know their market value and are confident that they will find (or have found already) another opportunity. Second, their personality is usually very dynamic and open to new opportunities and challenges, which is not a bad profile for agile developers. And last but not least, they might find an opportunity with your competitor. To make a long story short, the time box of the iterations can be used not only to measure the progress of the project but also to accommodate the team members' needs for extended breaks, vacations, and other time off. That flexibility opens new horizons for each team member in terms of relieving fatigue, enjoying vacations, and increasing job satisfaction. It also allows team members to take vacations at times other than during the holidays when resources are already strained. Delegating the team holiday schedule to the team is in line with self-managed teams. Having "vision" in terms of resource portfolio management means that you have vision with regard to the organization's needs and the individual's needs. And they are not always conflicting needs.

An unhappy workforce will sooner or later be marked by an increase in attrition. Attrition is expensive for an organization in many ways. For example, it brings with it the cost of hiring replacements, lower team productivity, and more important, the cost of benefits not being realized because of a paused project. Those factors can have a big impact on the bottom line of the project and the organization's portfolio management strategy.

By the way, many agile processes make a clear statement about overtime. Extreme programming was one of the first methods that condemned overtime that would last more than a week. In agile projects, reducing overtime is not seen as the organization doing a favor for the development team but as a means of keeping productivity high.

Too Many Projects and Not Enough Resources

Having too many projects is an issue I've already mentioned with regard to project portfolio management, but a lack of resources intensifies this issue even further. In addition to the administrative aspects of the project portfolio being affected, what will happen if too few available resources are too thinly spread? Generally, software engineers try to keep the wheels in motion, help wherever possible, and follow the assignments they are being asked to work on. But what if there are more assignments than anyone can handle? Eventually, the employees will reach their limits.

We know from an earlier discussion that switching personnel between projects or between tasks within a project always comes with a significant productivity penalty. Likewise, assigning resources to more than one project or having too few resources on a project will require frequent role changes and will also hurt productivity. Instead of engaging in a strategy of task switching, reprioritize and reduce the number of projects and then fit the amount of resources to the projects. This solution might also be suboptimal, however. Let's see why.

Imagine that executive management will actually need more projects delivered than resources available. That scenario is quite common. Management is aware of the resource constraints, but the fact that there are too few resources does not help them with their business decisions. Gaining business momentum while reducing the amount of projects does not go hand in hand.

Why not outsource additional work? This is an extremely powerful and quick way of increasing staffing resources that will get the job done, even when projects are performed off site in isolation. This solution is not unique to agile development, but outsourcing agile projects provides great opportunities. Review your project portfolio and identify important projects that could be executed by a contractor. Staff these projects with consultants, or subcontract the entire project to an external provider. Have the vendor follow your agile delivery model and communicate the necessary metrics required at the end of each iteration. Also let the vendor run the entire project, either on site or off site. If you are interested in more detailed information about the progress of the work, attend the daily stand-up meeting either by teleconference or in person. Attending the daily stand-up meeting will give you an accurate, firsthand impression of the progress of the project.

In a model like this, the hiring organization is still in the driver's seat and determines the length of the iteration, specifies the length of the contract (extended iteratively), and evaluates the progress. The metrics and the retrospectives the vendor compiles and conducts will help you stay involved with the external project without burning any internal resources, except a small amount of your own, of course. No agile vendor can hide behind a shield of months-long requirements work without delivering working software.

This outsourcing approach is especially powerful for a project requiring technologies that will be used for that project only, in which case a heavier internal investment in the relevant skills does not seem appropriate and effective. That is also true for more common (perhaps "hip") technologies, where external skills can be found easily. Even though the hiring organization might have the skill set to get the project staffed, using external resources might be more cost effective. The outsourcing model effectively ensures that the hiring organization has enough staff to complete the projects it needs, and it takes away the pressure on the organization of succeeding with only its own personnel.

When you staff your projects with external resources, agile development will expose the promised capabilities of vendors very quickly. Perhaps it will take more time for less experienced software development organizations to isolate these vendors. But at the latest it will take only a few iterations by an underperforming vendor for their cover to be blown.

Confident and capable agile vendors will sign an initial short-term contract for a few iterations with an option to extend on certain deliveries. The short delivery cycles are in sync with the iterative-incremental development process and will not create an additional burden, as illustrated in Figure 8-1.

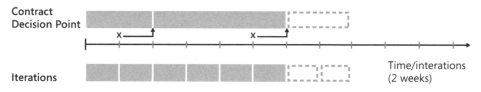

FIGURE 8-1 Agile contracts

Another solution is to recruit not only employees but also coaches, mentors, and instructors and thereby increase the staff for more upcoming projects with external help. A similar model is described in more depth in the following section.

Either way, reactively hiring employees or staffing projects with subcontractors is suboptimal in terms of resource portfolio management. These are only possible workarounds to increasing the available resources. Ramping up external teams through outsourcing can be very time consuming, sometimes taking as long as hiring employees. And who guarantees that the external vendor has free cycles and resources to take on additional projects? A more strategic view on resources will decrease the need for additional external resources—the internal resource pool must be prepared for projects ahead of time.

Projects Require Different Skills

As the saying goes, if all you have is a hammer, everything looks like a nail. If the entire IT team is expert in Java, your next project will most likely be another Java project. Even worse, if Java software engineers are on the bench, they are watching out for new Java opportunities. The same is also true for any other technology.

On the other hand, a diverse resource pool without duplicate skills among members might not be useful either, because larger projects will need a larger concentration of similar skills to get the major groundwork covered. One developer with Java skills on a multimillion dollar Java project is not sufficient.

The best possible mix will lie somewhere in between these two extremes.

Instead of selecting projects based on the available skills in the resource portfolio, projects should be selected according to their impact on the future of the organization. But transforming and educating internal employees to match the skills needed to meet the exact desired completion date for visionary projects is extremely challenging, if not impossible. To meet the completion date in a timely manner, organizations use a variety of educational techniques to fill the gap. The idea is to get the staff equipped with the right knowledge and jump-started via the application of the techniques in their project. Agile companies offering training and mentoring services usually fill the talent gap in this way. Achieving such flexibility and availability with personnel (internal or external) comes with a price tag, but keep in mind that the increased costs are often only a fraction of the financial potential of a project.

A combination of training, mentoring, and consulting with experienced subcontractors provides three benefits:

- Knowledge transfer through formal training
- On-the-job training and application
- Progress on the project itself

Organizations that are transitioning to agile development are often especially interested in coaches, who are people who provide educational and professional training. The advantage of using coaches is that they can provide hands-on instruction to a particular role in a project while bringing other team members up to speed on a certain topic. In rare situations when adequate resources for a project cannot be hired, coaches can also educate external resources on the project. That is beneficial, however, only for the individual project and not for the organization because external resources will likely leave the organization after the project is completed, taking their newly acquired skills with them.

In terms of educational services, coaches can provide formal classroom training, facilitate short but highly targeted workshops, or transfer knowledge in one-on-one sessions with individuals on the team. Their professional services are equivalent to other external consultants who are responsible for deliverables. Because their responsibilities are very challenging to juggle, coaches are usually more expensive to hire than other external consultants. For that reason, many organizations, to reduce the overall cost structure of the project, remove coaches from their projects as soon as the project team is fully equipped with knowledge and techniques needed.

Figure 8-2 demonstrates that the knowledge transfer and educational portion of a project's costs are reduced over the course of the iterations. The portion dedicated to project progress increases slightly, but most important, the overall participation of the coaches decreases. Who is picking up the steadily decreasing portion of the coach's work and delivers the rest of the work that keeps the project progressing? Your employees! Figure 8-2 shows how this results in a project whose costs significantly decrease over the iterations.

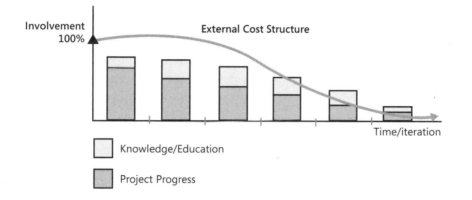

FIGURE 8-2 External coaches—education, progress, and costs

Coaching programs instituted for a particular project often start with formal training, which introduces the fundamentals and vocabulary of specific techniques to be used in the project. To increase the effectiveness of the coaching program, the classroom training can be provided by additional instructors other than the project coach. They work in parallel and complement each other. In a shared model like this, the coach will focus on the actual progress of the project and is responsible for the knowledge transfer to the project team, while the instructor or instructors deliver the formal education without a direct connection to the project context. Once the fundamental training is completed, the coach or instructors might not be needed anymore, which reduces the cost of the program even more. Larger projects that employed more than one coach can also reduce the number of project coaches over time until only one coach is left, and that coach has only sporadic involvement or works only part time. In this way, instead of using agile reporting purely for project progress, you can also use it to provide a system of incremental knowledge acquisition for team members. Make training and coaching models measurable, and you can evaluate even the completed educational programs.

I have also had good experiences on projects using a slight twist to the coaching model just described. Instead of using a coach (or multiple coaches) and multiple instructors, the projects I'm referring to used only one coach. A project was staffed primarily with external contractors who had expertise in the technology being developed. The project team also consisted of personnel from within the organization who didn't have this expertise. While the contractors were making progress on the project, the organization's employees assigned to the project were being brought up to speed by the coach, through breakout sessions and one-on-one meetings.

Using this approach, the team had only one go-to person for coaching and the external consultants could focus on project tasks without being distracted from making progress on the project. That turned out to be a very effective coaching model.

In general, coaching, mentoring, and consulting will get your project off the ground faster. They introduce new techniques and practices while actual progress is being made. This model works especially well with agile projects because tasks from all skill sets (for example, developing requirements, programming, testing) are executed in every iteration in parallel, and this process is reinforced with every iteration over and over again. An agile project also keeps all the different resources together as a unit and prevents the problem of dealing with replacing resources that have already departed to the next project. Therefore, a resource portfolio will make consultants with agile skills quickly available, allowing executive management to focus on pursuing a number of good projects at one time. The iterations will also make it easy to reduce external mentoring and decrease the project cost structure as appropriate.

Lack of Feedback from Resources

Take a poll of the portion of your workforce that is close to completion of a project and ask, "What is your next project?" and "When will you start?" Based on my experience, a new project starts when the old one is completed. But when is the old one really completed? Most of the time, a project very quickly reaches the 10 percent, 25 percent, 50 percent, and even 90 percent completion mark. At each of these points, the team dynamics are good and the vision for the project is clear. Then comes the last 10 percent, which would make the project complete.

During this time, team members usually start a self-advertisement campaign within the organization, hopeful of finding opportunities for a follow-up project. This happens even in a matrix or functionally organized reporting structure and is not unique to organizations in which employees are organized by project. It is quite understandable that nobody likes to take a seat on the bench while searching for new prospects after a successful project completion. This advertisement campaign takes energy out of the current project and reduces morale. The decrease in productivity can have an impact on the forecasted final delivery date. The reason why resources are watching out for new opportunities, however, is because of a lack of transparency in the resource portfolio. If the employees could see the strategy laid out, they could react to new prospects without stalling on the current project.

Without resource portfolio management, not only do the employees not know their next assignment, the organization does not know it either. One reason for this is that the organization is busy closing the previous project to release the resources. Once the resource becomes officially available, valuable time ticks off the clock until a new project is identified.

While measurements of the progress trend of agile projects are inaccurate in early iterations, the predictability increases steadily in later iterations of a project. Not only can the project manager start estimating a more accurate final completion date, the portfolio manager can identify new projects for the employee. Instead of using bench time after a project's completion to reorient the professional, the portfolio manager can ease the employee's transition by taking action while the current project is still in progress. (See Figure 8-3.) I have also seen organizations in which the organization keeps future projects a secret until the current project is closed out. The advantage of this approach is that the team stays focused as a unit and focused on the current project. This approach requires each team member to have a lot of confidence in the resource portfolio management process.

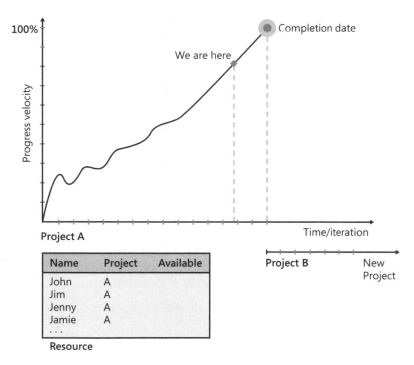

FIGURE 8-3 Resource transition between projects

The level of confidence in a successful resource portfolio management process expected from each employee is an important difference between management of traditional projects and portfolio management in agile projects. The progress of agile projects is evaluated after iterations. The new predicted final delivery date is derived from a series of completed iterations. The accuracy increases, and the end date is more reliable. The end date of a project is also the end of the last iteration. Therefore, the transition of resources from the closed project to a newly scheduled project is much more seamless.

The main problem in resource portfolio management, therefore, is not the lack of direction of executive management, but the lack of feedback from the project team about the status of their project. Agile metrics and project reporting (which we covered in Chapter 5, "Metrics") will set the stage for successful resource management and will provide important feedback to management. When the project team provides reliable metrics and feedback about the completion trends of its project, it effectively completes the communication loop with executives. This will allow executives to make sound decisions about follow-up projects and about assigning team members to upcoming projects.

Roles and Resource Pools

Traditional resource portfolio management often uses a "resource pool." Instead of containing information about actual individuals, the resource pool contains descriptions of roles—for example, project manager, business analyst, and so forth. To assign resources for new projects, the portfolio manager links the individuals to roles described in the resource pool. In Figure 8-4, John, a scrum master and business analyst in the organization, might be chosen for a project in either role.

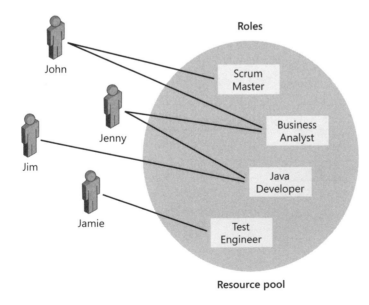

FIGURE 8-4 Roles and resource pools

The idea of resource pools is intriguing because project managers can staff their projects according to necessary roles within the organization. For example, suppose that for a particular project I need one scrum master, two business analysts, six developers, and two test engineers. After the roles are identified, matches are searched for and the project is staffed. Of course, the actual staffing of a project typically happens quite differently: word of mouth and individuals' reputations are more important for internal staffing than anonymous role descriptions. (See the "Corporate Networks" section later in this chapter for more information about searching for specific skills associated with individuals.)

Personally, I can see the value of resource pools and roles from a traditional human resources perspective—the required positions for each project simply must be filled—but agile projects are very situational and require the right person at the right time. That becomes obvious when you compare a traditional job description with the actual work an individual performs on an agile project.

Skills Transfer

When experimenting with agile projects for the first time, many organizations bring in external consultants to get the project done without initially looking at their own existing resources. That is quite understandable, considering that an organization would want to avoid obstructions related to missing skills when agile is first put into practice. The following sections introduce techniques related to the transfer of knowledge to and within your organization. That means that even after the services are delivered and the external provider walks away from you, your organization has acquired the knowledge. Transferring knowledge is always challenging, and agile projects add another twist to it. The agile manifesto insists on "people over processes and tools," which means that the employees' skills are more valued than written job procedures. You are investing in a person, not in a process. Although this is not necessarily an issue unique to agile development, it is especially true in agile projects because required skills are generally captured in a person's brain rather than in written manuals.

Agile Training

Agile training can be broken into on-the-job training and off-the-job training. Off-the-job training is foundational education, such as degree programs or continuous education programs in universities; on-the-job-training is related to skills acquired during company work hours, at the company's expense, and most likely directly linked to the task to be performed. A challenge with agile know-how is that the skills acquired through on-the-job-training typically challenge the foundational education of individuals that was acquired many years ago. The majority of project managers learned work-breakdown structures, Gantt-chart schedules, and critical path analysis, which are now being challenged by agile practices. A true transformation within an organization can occur only with individuals who have an open mind and are willing to expand on their educational foundation.

One pioneer in off-the-job agile training is the College of Santa Fe, which developed an MBA program with a focus on software design and management. The technical part of this program is covered using agile development techniques. I am very confident that other institutions will follow with similar programs and that more new agile professionals will enter the job market. For these professionals, it will feel unnatural not to perform projects the agile way. Until then, we need to stay focused on on-the-job training for agile practices.

The list of on-the-job training companies is extremely diverse. The companies usually focus on different agile practices, such as Extreme Programming, Scrum, Lean, Dynamic Systems Development Method (DSDM), or others. Additionally, the courses target different roles in the project—for example, project managers, developers, test engineers, and so forth. Because they are structured this way, the courses are relatively short and focused, and they provide a very effective platform for on-the-job training.

On-the-job training for agile development and project management is not as easy as it might appear. Agile practices are not acquired like the knowledge dispersed in a one-hour compliance training session. Unlike knowledge that can be transferred through traditional means such as lectures, knowledge of agile techniques needs to be acquired by practicing them. Learning by doing is the most effective method of learning for adults anyway. For example, the agile practice of pair programming is an extremely powerful tool for on-the-job training between two professionals

Let me give you an example. Showing a business analyst a template that is used to document a user story qualifies as a transfer of knowledge, but that knowledge is theoretical and lost within hours if not applied and practiced. In addition, knowing the template does not mean that the individual will write good user stories in the future. Practice is required to become a good author of stories, and much more practice is needed to become an expert. And the writing of the story is actually secondary anyway—the core competency is performing the business analysis to develop the user story. Developing business-analysis skills is much more time-consuming than learning how to capture the requirement. In this example, an expert is good not only at writing stories but also at challenging stories, the story template, and the application of the stories by a team. That level of knowledge is adaptive, powerful, and agile.

Based on my own experience, I doubt that pure online training courses are appropriate for the transfer of such detailed knowledge. Long-distance learning, however, with practice and review sessions might be quite appropriate. When the principles are taught in that way, the information has time to sink in and results in a deeper understanding through longer periods of reflection on the topic.

I also believe that a mix of different training methods is always a good idea. If you are looking to learn agile principles or trying to train someone in them, lay the foundation first.

Then focus on specific areas. And get into tool training last. Tools are simply a medium to get the job done faster and in a less tedious fashion. For example, a tool can capture estimation results, but it is not performing the actual estimation itself—that is still a responsibility of the agile team. That is why agile experts can very easily distinguish between useful and less useful tool features.

In summary, consider the following steps to successfully acquire agile skills or to assist others in acquiring them:

1. Build the foundation.
2. Apply to become a practitioner.
3. Specialize and become an expert.
4. Use and evaluate tooling.

Mentoring

Mentoring is the best way of providing on-the-job training when you consider the dedicated time spent between mentor and mentee. This method not only transfers knowledge and skills, it also enables the mentee to actually apply the practices within the project context. The mentee observes the skill first, applies it, and then receives feedback on it. Eventually, the mentee internalizes the best practice and repeats it when appropriate.

Mentoring has two components: it is educational, and it also keeps the project heading in the right direction. Although this method of skill transfer might be the most effective, it comes with a price tag because, unlike instructors or contractors who have one goal to pursue, the mentor has two. Organizations planning a large-scale agile adoption program might want to consider hiring an agile coach as part of its full-time staff or using *meta-mentoring*, in which a mentor teaches mentoring skills to the future internal agile coach and mentor. (Note, however, that meta-mentoring is similar to making a copy of a copy—fidelity decreases.)

Agile project activities are executed repetitively, iteration by iteration, and in parallel. This process creates an efficient review cycle for the mentoring program. After a few iterations, the mentor can step down from her role and move on to mentoring the next team. Retrospectives in projects with mentors include an educational assessment component that allows team members to reflect not only on project achievements but also on whether they have progressed on their personal (educational) goals.

Globally Distributed Development

For general resource portfolio management, success is not dependent on where resources are physically located. This is not true for agile development, so let's take a quick look at the impact of globally distributed development on the management of a resource portfolio.

A physical separation between individuals developing, implementing, and validating requirements creates challenges in agile projects, as shown in Figure 8-5.

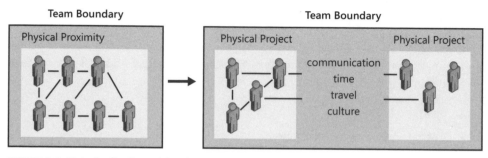

FIGURE 8-5 Globally distributed development

One of the strengths of agile development is the team's ability to cope with incomplete, ambiguous requirements. When requirements work is sent offshore, additional challenges arise due to geographical separation. Language barriers can make it difficult to communicate and clarify requirements. If the context of a requirement is not provided, the person who can provide the context might be thousands of miles and many time zones away rather than down the hall. (Incorrect assumptions might be made when answers are not readily available.) The same challenges arise for testing efforts in a globally distributed environment, where test objectives and test results might be ambiguous as well.

If the work is divided among a team that spans continents, verbal communication between team members in one team room is not possible. Modern communications media (instant messaging, e-mail, phone, and so forth) is used to fill the gap. The media itself introduces still more challenges, such as infrastructure needs and availability issues. Please do not underestimate the impact of this type of organization of team members. For example, some organizations (for security and other reasons) do not allow instant-messaging systems, access to certain servers, or e-mail attachments. Alternative communication methods that bypass these limitations are often suboptimal.

In addition to the physical separation of team members, personal separation occurs. Team members on the other side of the globe are productive in their own time zone and have their own holidays. Additionally, there are cultural differences in how people work together. In other words, it is much easier to talk to the person on the other side of the table than trying to reach a person by phone, but distributing a team globally might still make sense financially.

I have experienced the following simple challenge in several projects. It took almost 15 minutes to rally a virtual team for the 15-minute stand-up meeting. That much time passed before everyone had dialed in from various locations. Participants on cell phones lost connections, pass codes and dial-in numbers changed frequently and caused confusion, or the meeting time changed without everybody on the team being notified of the change. I'm aware that these are simple problems that can be fixed, but how can we efficiently negotiate requirements, remove ambiguity, and prioritize requirements if simple phone conversations turn into a challenge among distributed teams? The bigger question is whether agile development and globally distributed development are compatible.

The better the infrastructure, the higher the chances are that the two approaches will work together. A workable infrastructure consists of both teams having access to the same code base, instant messaging, speed-dial phones, international calling plans, access to networks (wiki, passwords, user rights), Web conferencing, reliable virtual private network (VPN) access, and also reliable people.

Having every team member globally separated does not seem to have a positive influence on morale and productivity. It seems that a separation of entire teams according to their project goals works best. Having one agile team working in one location while the other team works in a different location independently seems to justify a global separation. The project managers of both teams work to integrate the effort of the two teams on a periodic basis, with telephone calls daily or every other day.

I also believe that agile projects do best when all roles are represented at every site. Exchanging team members and having them travel across the geographical boundary is always a good idea to increase the width and depth of communication. For example, you could start rotating business analysts between the teams to increase work relationships through personal familiarity. The various relationships among team members are often the key for effective offshore communication. The same result could be achieved, of course, if the technical team members rotate with their business analysts in the opposite way. For cost reasons, however, the smaller offshore team usually travels and visits the larger teams. Short iterations are ideal for implementing these exchange programs. Daily stand-up meetings and even the retrospectives could be executed in an offshore setting with periodic exchange using electronic media.

Corporate Networks

Social networking sites have become very popular in recent years. Whereas some sites focus on the personal side of people's lives, other sites manage professional relationships. Many large organizations prevent employees from accessing social networking sites because they do not see the value, are concerned about potential productivity, and probably most important, see the sites as potential security threats. Professional networks, however, hold much more value for an organization.

At first glance, a professional network on the Internet seems very similar to an in-house corporate network, with one difference: the reach is limited to the boundaries of the organization. If you put yourself in the shoes of a corporate recruiter, you might see such sites as a great resource for finding talent for your resource pool. For example, suppose one of your employees is a brilliant business analyst. You found her name on a professional network site. She not only knows a lot of people, she also has recommendations from previous jobs and is part of a professional community (for example, Agile Alliance). You search for other candidates who are also part of this community and live in your area. You might find people your current employee recommended in the past. Isn't that an endorsement you would find valuable? You will be surprised how many people are already indirectly linked to you.

In the same way that recruiters are keen on getting the best talent for a position, professionals want to find the job opportunities best suited to their skills. The game of job hunting (by professionals) and skill seeking (by organizations) are two sides of the same coin. Online professional networks empower both sides. Professionals can find new opportunities through their own professional network. And organizations looking to hire new people can complete the first level of reference checking, as U.S. companies usually do, much earlier in the processes by using these same networks.

When corporate networks are expanded beyond the boundaries of the corporate intranet, a company can broadcast news, offer jobs, and connect people with similar interests. This network might even be composed of a workforce that other companies are jealous of. That scenario, in return, will result in more interest on the part of professionals who want to become part of the network.

Certification

As of 2008, the agile community has no standardized certification program like other communities have—for example, the Project Management Professional (PMP) certification of the Project Management Institute (PMI). It appears that some people like certification and others do not. Then there are people who like the benefits of certification in general but are divided about the way that professionals are actually tested.

Although for many professionals (such as electricians, lawyers, and accountants) a certification program is a common procedure and widely accepted, the agile community has not found an official and consistent voice yet. Therefore, individual agile methodologies have decided to implement their own certification programs—for example, Scrum, DSDM, and Rational Unified Process (RUP). Depending on the methodology, the certification is awarded for different levels of expertise (entry, intermediate, and expert), and some programs require professionals only to participate in a training session. Others have more elaborate certification systems, such as completing multiple-choice tests, demonstrating work experience, and assessing hypothetical situations. It is true that behind every certification program is a business model, but it is also true that certification creates a community and an identity for professionals within a certain field.

Especially for large organizations that are adopting agile resource portfolio management principles, certification offers a tremendous value. A resource pool, which captures the roles being played within the organization, can be associated with certificates available in the market. Just as an example, if you need a scrum master on your next project, you can require a Certified Scrum Master who has gone through the training class. In-depth descriptions of the candidate's work can be largely replaced by the course description and objectives.

Summary

This chapter introduced another important portfolio in your organization, the resource portfolio. We saw the challenges associated with resource management and how agile development projects tackle them. We saw the different internal and external roles needed to transform a project or organization into one that uses agile development principles. The chapter emphasized that agile projects are ideal for on-the-job-training—achieved through consulting, mentoring, and coaching—because the transfer of knowledge and the effective implementation of that knowledge can be assessed using the same iterative rhythm. At the end of the chapter, we touched on the topics of the challenges for resource portfolio management in a distributed environment and professional certification.

Chapter 9
Asset Portfolio Management

The asset portfolio is the last of the three portfolios we'll discuss that are important for a successful portfolio management strategy. This portfolio is also known as an *application portfolio*. Systems, applications, and related hardware investments are captured in this type of portfolio. Although assets are more static than projects, portfolio managers still need to monitor the operational aspects of an organization to harvest ideas for new projects and allocate potential resources. That process will, in turn, influence project and resource portfolio management and bring us full circle back to the previously introduced portfolios.

Balancing the Asset Portfolio

In contrast with the project portfolio, the asset portfolio contains materialized projects—for example, a system from a completed project that is in operation. An asset is an outcome after development projects have been completed—in our context, that is mostly likely an information system. But assets can also be systems that have been acquired commercially over the shelf (COTS). Both examples commonly consist of software and hardware, including their financial components (such as rental, service, and licensing costs).

Because the assets are often created by executing projects, the project portfolio is a major source of assets for asset portfolio management. The output of the project portfolio turns into an input for the asset portfolio. But because the assets require personnel for maintenance and operation, assets are also connected to the resource portfolio. Many organizations new to portfolio management focus first on project portfolios to gain insights into struggling projects and overcome the issues. I agree it is the portfolio of agile projects that can expose organizational impediments quickly. On the other hand, 70 percent of all costs are sunk into systems after the projects are completed. These are the systems that we capture in an asset portfolio. The cost aspect is reason enough to take a closer look at this portfolio and how agile development practices can be used for this type of portfolio.

In this chapter, I'll tackle three issues associated with maintaining, updating, and replacing legacy IT systems:

- First it's an asset, and then it's a roadblock.
- Is built to last a positive attribute?
- What's the total cost of ownership?

First It's an Asset, and Then It's a Roadblock

I think every company has at least one of these systems—a system (asset) that was a good idea many years ago but then turned into a roadblock. The asset ran and ran, like a Volkswagen bug. However, over the years, the technologies changed not only once, but perhaps twice or more. As a result, the technology of the system is outdated and the business logic most likely is too. That is a deadly combination for the organization. Why?

Finding talent to support these roadblock systems gets harder and harder. Imagine all the Assembler systems or COBOL systems that still serve essential business processes. Even today, when we are surrounded by superior technologies, the majority of crucial business applications are still associated with technologies from the 1970s, 1980s, and 1990s. Because there are fewer and fewer resources available in the marketplace that can modify these systems, continuing to use them eventually will drive us into an organizational dead end. That becomes obvious when we take a look at the course offerings of universities. The number of universities in the U.S. offering COBOL or mainframe courses to their students is getting lower and lower. I would not be surprised if these courses vanish soon or if they already have in most universities. That means even organizations that are willing to pay any price for modifications of these systems might at some point hit technical boundaries.

Of course, a system might continue providing benefits even though it has not been kept up to date. That is something we discussed earlier in this book in more detail. However, these benefits steadily decrease over time. Sooner or later, the benefits will reach zero and might even turn negative. (See Figure 9-1.)

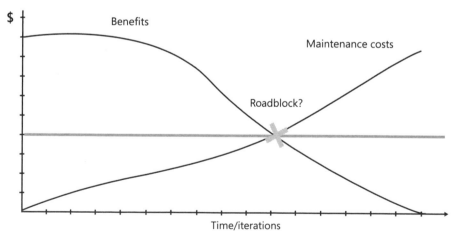

FIGURE 9-1 An asset turning into a roadblock

The critical point that defines when the system turns into a roadblock is the moment when the benefits are less than the costs to operate the asset. So what are these costs? They are very much related to the quality of the system. The quality, however, is a systemwide constraint that starts with iteration zero. The better the quality of a system is, the slower is the pace at which the system will turn into a roadblock.

Although the term *asset* has a positive connotation, it might not always be a positive thing. In the light of a financial analysis, an asset might be seen to be a break-even proposition or even a negative one.

Let's take the following typical scenario as an example. A mainframe system needs to be changed to accommodate a small enhancement request. As a result, the entire system must be retested. That is even true if only one line of code is added or modified. The reason is that the entire system must be recompiled and relinked. And in that case, who guarantees that the system will still operate correctly? Programmers often feel they have control of a system and a good understanding of it, especially when only minor changes are needed. But in reality, it is a risky business. The side effects of quick bug fixes and changes could be enormous. Every time I see monstrous old systems, I remember the saying, "Never change a winning team." That is, of course, true only if the asset is actually winning something for the organization.

Object-oriented technologies, on the other hand, require only a recompilation of the affected components. That isolates the testing efforts into small areas and reduces the time spent on testing the potential side effects of the changes. Assets built with object-oriented technology are easier to adapt to their environment and are much more cost-effective during maintenance.

Even after applications are recognized as roadblocks, organizational dynamics sometimes change and prevent a solution from being developed or implemented. For example, executives might decide to freeze the budget spent on these roadblocks to eliminate further costs. In this case, the system becomes further outdated over time and provides fewer benefits. That is problematic and not a good solution for the long run.

Alternatively, the system could be rewritten with more state-of-the-art technologies and architectures. The idea is to implement a technical replacement of the system. In reality, however, the supporters of rewriting systems often want to go through this exercise because the system is not capable of addressing new features. It is a dilemma—instead of rewriting the application, what they really want is new functionality. I've seen numerous projects kicked off as a simple rewrite effort, where everyone involved thought they had a good handle on the scope of the project. Days into the effort, the project scope increased dramatically, with team members deciding things like, "While we are rewriting the system, let's get rid of the following defects..." or "Let's use this opportunity to make the new system better than its predecessor." Keep in mind that from a business perspective, rewriting a system will lead to the same result. From a cost-benefit perspective, who inside the management team would endorse a project like this? Financially speaking, a 100 percent conversion project would not produce any additional return on investment (ROI). Only added or improved features can contribute to ROI.

I hope these examples illustrate that when assets turn into roadblocks, hardly any emergency rescue is available. The systems have run into in a dead end for a reason, and benefits will deteriorate over time. Either an old system is maintained at a high cost to the organization or a new system replaces the roadblock. Keep in mind, an "as-is" vs. a "to-be" analysis of the roadblock will often lead to different interpretations of the type of replacement needed. That analysis should include answers to questions such as the following:

- What defects are currently known?

- Which functionality is outdated?

- What functionality is missing?

- Which functionality should be removed?

Maintaining an expensive roadblock (asset) also creates additional disadvantages. Incorporating changes to old systems has an impact on the cost structure because minor updates turn out to have a big price tag. These high costs are directly linked to time spent working on the updates. Think about the personnel who are blocked from performing more productive work by having to work on maintenance. It is a simple resource constraint you need to be aware of before you allocate resources to a maintenance project.

A big challenge for organizations maintaining legacy systems is that the system is in operation and might manage live customers, accounts, or transactions. Replacing such a critical system requires the entire functionality to be converted before it can be exchanged with the new system. The longer the transition period is between the old and new systems, the more business interruption it can cause. When the new system is in operation and the first transactions are executed, there is hardly any way back in terms of data consistency. Many systems, including off-the-shelf applications, have an upgrade mechanism but don't provide a downgrade option to reverse the effects the new version has caused. The point of transition, therefore, has to be carefully selected.

In terms of replacement strategy for legacy systems, there is no clear answer. The better the pre-warning system of the asset portfolio, the earlier potential roadblocks can be determined. Let's take as an example the concept of technical debt. Technical debt is the unfinished work accumulated from the previous release. The higher the technical debt, the lower the chances are that the asset will contribute positively to the bottom line as initially planned. This debt could trigger a new project to renovate the system.

But let's focus on more positive news. When replacing a system, you can take advantage of the iterative-incremental development process again. Large systems can usually be grouped into certain categories of functionalities—for example, inventory management and sales transactions as elements in a system for a bookseller. When building these units of functionality, you can identify pockets with the biggest pain points of the asset. Let's assume that the sales transaction functionality is error prone and cumbersome for the sales personnel. That will cause unnecessary internal costs. In addition, the store would also like to make the sales transaction available through an online shopping cart. For that reason, you decide to expose the inventory to the front end, but you keep the actual inventory management functionality behind the scenes, untouched.

Grouping functionalities and prioritizing the to-do list can now help the store with a step-by-step transition from the old system to the new system. The asset will continue to stay in the asset portfolio, but an additional project proposal is added to the funnel. If the project is funded, the project is spun off as a typical agile project. Resources maintaining the asset can build, for example, wrappers and interfaces for interacting between future and existing components of the system. These wrappers allow easy access to the already existing functionality. XML and SOAP come to mind as newer trends in technology to accommodate these efforts. Even if all the details of the underlying roadblock cannot be understood, wrapping the functionalities and providing interfaces will help in using existing elements. One way to accomplish this is to use two teams working in parallel. The first team will be dedicated to the newly instantiated agile project, and the second team will work only on crucial defects and maintenance efforts for the legacy system. The team dedicated to the newly instantiated agile project will remove the bottleneck functionalities and develop the given interfaces for integration with the legacy system functionality. Both teams can synchronize the efforts through daily stand-up meetings and retrospectives.

Is *Built to Last* a Positive Attribute?

Remember what we said about the outdated technologies from the 1970s and 1980s earlier in this chapter? How do you think people in the 2040s will judge the technologies we use today? I believe it will all sound very similar.

I remember an e-mail I received in the mid-90s from a colleague who had a very green philosophy. His e-mail signature said something like, "The bytes of this e-mail were 100% recycled." Considering that any software system is a collection of bytes, we can relatively easily delete an e-mail, a component, or even an entire system and therefore recycle the bytes. This concept is extremely powerful compared with industries where projects are much more physically rooted. For example, consider the construction business. How much more difficult is it to demolish a building and remove the rubble? We already take advantage of software being so flexible whenever we download systems stored on servers on different continents. After completing a download, we can instantly use, evaluate, or just delete the systems or applications again.

Because of waterfall practices, however, systems in the past were planned entirely up front, in one large chunk. That required coming up with an estimate and scope definition before the project was kicked off. Executives often learned the hard way that what was not included in the initial scope was not delivered at the end. It is not surprising that executives are interested in harvesting the benefits of the 10 million projects developed over the years for as long as possible. Unfortunately, the technology chosen for a project might not have been the best choice at the time of release—and even if it was the best technology back then, it probably isn't the best technology available anymore.

Times change, and sometimes they change while the project is in flight. Especially for large projects, the need to build something to last seems to justify its cost. With the waterfall approach, we look for standards, develop costly frameworks, and observe industry trends to justify these technical decisions and their related costs. The IT industry is famous for trying to build something substantial and classy that has a long-term impact. None of those revolutionary new releases in the past (for example, Microsoft Windows 95) are still as cool or leading edge as when they were released. Other products have also been developed over a long period of time only to hit the market when the technology has already evolved again—for example, the release of OS/2 by IBM.

The problem with this approach is that you must make decisions about the architecture based on the overall requirements specification. That is a large collection of features, functional requirements, and nonfunctional requirements. It is common in waterfall projects for these specifications to reach hundreds of pages.

The Standish Group released statistics about features in existing systems that might help us see these features from a different angle. The Standish Group reported that on average 45 percent of the features and functions in systems are never used and 19 percent are rarely used. That means roughly 64 percent of all systems contain features that are never or rarely used but were paid for! In contrast, only 13 percent of the features and functions were often used, and 7 percent were always used.

These findings provide strong support for the use of agile development practices, where unnecessary features and functions are eliminated early in a project and are never added while the project is in progress. In terms of the asset portfolio, however, they mean that the implemented but never or rarely used features need to be maintained. Therefore, an organization is investing indirectly in the same unused features again! When you consider that the ratio of the costs of system development to the costs of system maintenance is 30/70, the costs of these features are even more staggering. That's why it is so important to look at the real requirements again, even if a system should only be replaced. You want to avoid building the same unwanted features all over again.

What we also learn from these statistics is that large projects might not be as large as they seem at first. If you eliminate all the unwanted requirements, the system can be delivered earlier than expected and realize benefits faster. Because the project was not as big of an investment as anticipated in the first place, the lifespan of the system in production could be much shorter and the system would still be very profitable. Even better, the smaller solution and quicker time-to-market delivery often generate even more requirements and feedback that can be used for the next project. The asset portfolio that contains systems that are originally developed with agile development practices can now be dynamic itself. Laying out the

IT strategy for decades is as difficult as planning a long-term waterfall project. Why not look at the assets from a shorter perspective and let the assets improve incrementally?

We do not want to create a throw-away attitude that changes the strategic system landscape with every iteration. The idea is to offer more than one fresh start to get to the right asset. In other situations, development cycles are shortened through agile development practices, but also the utilization rate is lower. As a result, executives are much more willing to invest again in similar but better projects earlier. That increases the rate of innovation of the business. It also reduces the chance of producing patchwork solutions, which are developed over years of added enhancement requests, and it also reduces the creation of roadblocks. Let's redefine *built to last* as *built to last as long as really needed*.

If your system has delivered most of the benefits it has to offer and is getting harder to change, think about recycling bytes and replacing the entire system, increment by increment. Most likely, technology has also changed since your system was built and there are better ways to provide the same functionality rather than starting all over again. That is good for business, good for innovation, and good for the bottom line.

Total Cost of Ownership

Let's take a look at total cost of ownership from a totally different perspective. Let's assume we are buying product in a store—for example, a cup of yogurt. This product usually comes in a plastic cup with an aluminum lid and is marked with a price—let's say, 89 cents. When we look at total cost of ownership, we need to look at all costs of owning this product. For example, producing the plastic container and the foil polluted our environment. The fumes and other waste products will have an impact on us and future generations. Delivery trucks moved the merchandise across the country to the store. The consumer also needs transportation to get to the store and back from the store, and most likely the product will end up in a plastic shopping bag, which will end up in a landfill that costs the taxpayer money to operate and maintain. After the consumer has the product, she might decide to store the product for a few days in the refrigerator, which requires electricity. The spoon to eat the yogurt will need to be washed (consuming soap and water), and the cup and lid will be disposed of as well. That will also generate waste-related costs.

The short story is that the product purchased for 89 cents might turn out to cost society hundreds of dollars. The price of the yogurt contained the cost to produce and distribute but not the costs to society. The latter are costs that are assumed by other sources, the society and the taxpayer. For IT systems in a business organization, the society is the organization and its stakeholders. All the costs have to be seen as *total* and cannot be deferred.

When we estimate IT projects, we also commonly estimate the production costs of the system (project) only. The consumer of the product, which is the organization installing the system, has many more costs to digest. There are also additional costs to other members of the society, which are the employees and potential users in the organization itself. These costs include the training of users, installation, hardware resources (either purchased or rented) to host the systems, networking and transportation of data, licenses, the salaries of troubleshooting personnel or staff monitoring daily events, manuals, and team administration, as well as the costs to deactivate a system after years of operation. Whenever you deploy or release systems, keep in mind that eventually, even though this might not affect you personally, somebody will need to collect the waste again and recycle the bytes.

Assessing asset portfolios in an iterative rhythm can expose some of these costs early and more clearly. If total ownership of some assets exceeds the benefits to the organization that will use the system, the purpose and value of the asset will need to be revisited.

Summary

The last of three common portfolios, the asset portfolio contains systems in operation. We revisited the cost structure of systems from a total cost perspective and learned that organizations often outlive their IT infrastructure. Technical progress and changed business strategies will cause these shifts. To show how to prevent these assets from turning into roadblocks to the organization, I covered how agile development practices can ease the transition when systems are replaced or retired after their benefits have expired (or nearly expired) or when assets turn out not to be profitable.

Chapter 10
Portfolios in Action

This chapter closes Part II, "Defining, Planning, and Measuring Portfolios." It will provide an overview of how the three portfolios we've been discussing interact and influence one another. We'll take a look at a sample portfolio dashboard, and we'll examine a fictional scenario in which we manage an agile portfolio. The scenario will demonstrate how the portfolios interconnect and evolve over time.

The Portfolio Dashboard

Executives steer and lead organizations toward a vision. This vision represents a mental model of where the organization will be at some defined point in the future. Therefore, where we are today is point A, and where we will travel to is point B. The executives who play a role similar to the one of pilots need a condensed but meaningful set of information to make sound decisions while the project is in flight. As in a real flight, we will experience minor bumps, adjust altitudes to clear airspace for others, pass through some unexpected bad weather patches, and maybe even make an emergency landing.

As agile portfolio managers and executives, we will look at dashboards of metrics to get a high-level overview of the overall situation, but we will also need to interact with the individual project teams in person to gain more knowledge about the projects if needed. The dashboard consists of the three portfolios we have covered in the previous three chapters.

Our dashboard will consist of three portfolios:

- Project portfolio
- Resource portfolio
- Asset portfolio

Each type of portfolio has its own focus and needs to be managed differently, because the project portfolio has the biggest impact on the organizational vision and the resource portfolio has short-term staffing but also a long-term career development component. For example, if the project portfolio contains a very visionary project, the personnel need to be prepared and the portfolios aligned. The asset portfolio consumes the biggest portion of financial resources because systems are usually much longer in operation than in development. The costs accumulate and can easily exceed the costs for developing the system. Assets represent, therefore, a materialized vision (projects finished in the past that are now exploited and harvested to gain the promised benefits). A dashboard view considers all three portfolios and assesses the situation as a whole.

Every iteration reveals bottlenecks and issues but also opportunities. The dashboard is a condensed view of the information about each item within the respective portfolio. The portfolio manager puts the metrics derived from each project on the dashboard for analysis. The type of information gathered includes the following:

- Average velocity (progress)
- Average sum of open defects (quality)
- Average team morale (team health)

A Sample Scenario

Let's follow a development organization through three iterations. We will assess the portfolios by using common agile metrics that use the iterative rhythm of agile projects. We do this to get a feeling about how the three portfolios harmonize. An agile organization interested in implementing an agile portfolio management process will need to adjust the type of metrics shown in this example to its own environment. That is an ongoing task for portfolio and executive managers, who evolve their dashboard over time. For example, you might want to work with different quality metrics or to measure team morale differently in your organization.

First and foremost, all three portfolios are managed in parallel, as illustrated in Figure 10-1, and they share the same checkpoints between iterations. These checkpoints translate directly into the iterative rhythm. In the upcoming example, the checkpoints for all three portfolios are synchronized. Alternatively, the more static asset portfolio can be assessed less frequently than the resource and project portfolios.

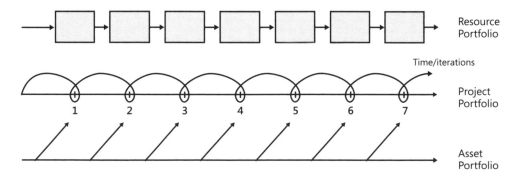

FIGURE 10-1 Evolution of the portfolios

The content of the project portfolio is very much influenced by the proposal funnel, the assets, and the capability of the organization to handle various projects, as represented by the resource portfolio. The portfolio manager monitors the project portfolio on an ongoing basis, but the asset and resource portfolios feed important decision-making information to the manager at the end of each iteration. Project personnel communicate their project's progress to the stakeholders during scheduled retrospectives. The resource portfolio can also be managed on an ongoing basis so that project resources can be adjusted between iterations. In addition, the asset portfolio can always initiate new projects, which will in turn draw more attention to the resource portfolio so that the talent can be allocated.

First Iteration

We will look at the first iteration of four projects: A, B, C, and D. The iterations for each project are two weeks long. (See Figure 10-2.) Our dashboard contains all three types of portfolio, and we also have a project funnel that is associated with the project and asset portfolios. The risk-reward diagram is shown in the upper-right corner of Figure 10-2. As you might recall from Chapter 7, "Project Portfolio Management," the risk-reward diagram is divided into quadrants that reflect the probability of success and the potential reward. Projects that have the highest potential return on investment are placed on the left side of the diagram; projects with the greatest chance of being completed successfully are placed in the upper half. So the potential "star" projects (those with a high probability of success and a high return on investment) end up in the upper-left corner. Conversely, projects with a low probability of success that offer only a small return on investment end up in the lower-right corner of the diagram.

Resources	
John	A
Paul	B
Mary	A
Pete	C
Frank	C
Sue	A
Nancy	C
Carol	C
Chris	A
Matt	A
Linda	B
Jimmy	D
Joe	D
Jill	D

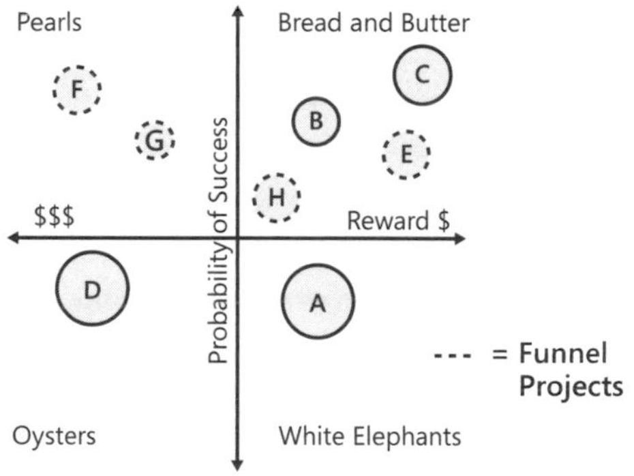

Project Funnel

	Cost	Benefit
Project E	200,000	300,000
Project F	1,200,000	4,000,000
Project G	350,000	1,300,000
Project H	90,000	120,000

Asset

Name	Cost/ Benefit
A1	94%
A2	20%
A3	180%
A4	250%
A5	25%

FIGURE 10-2 Dashboard after the first iteration

The risk-reward diagram in this case indicates that projects B and C offer mediocre returns and that project D is a speculative and risky project. Potentially high returns for project D have not been anticipated, and the project might be a prototype or proof of technology (POT) project.

Recall from Chapter 7 that project costs are indicated by the size of the circle. You can see that project A not only is categorized to be a killer project (high risk, low reward) but also is the largest circle and therefore consumes the most project resources. The quadrant for the potential stars (the upper-left quadrant, which is reserved for low-risk and high-reward projects) is, unfortunately, empty. Looking at the resource portfolio part of Figure 10-2, you can see another issue: we do not have any additional resources available to take on new projects, although good ideas are already waiting in the project funnel. The personnel dedicated to maintain and enhance the existing assets are not listed in the resource pool. Some assets, which are systems in operation or production, have higher total costs of ownership than benefits—for example, A3 and A4. Asset 1 is also close to turning into a roadblock.

To increase the pace of execution and the number of projects on the dashboard, the organization will start executing multiple processes in parallel. The length of the iteration will measure the beat. This approach requires the organization to use external agile consultants to execute additional projects quickly and to hire new employees for the longterm to carry out the organization's vision for the portfolio. Staffing through external consulting agencies allows for faster staffing because the project team, project managers, and executives do not need to go through a time-consuming hiring process. That way, a small but necessary bench of internal employees can be created. That creates flexibility.

In addition, assets A3 and A4 will be investigated to be replaced by submitting new project proposals to the project funnel. The proposals will not only replace the systems in operation but also significantly reduce the operational costs. For these projects to be approved, the proposals submitted must make a strong financial case to executives. In addition, project A will be canceled by executives at the end of an iteration, and the resources will be released so that they can be applied to a more important project proposal listed in the funnel.

Second Iteration

In the previous iteration, we decided to add more personnel and eliminate unpromising and unprofitable projects from our dashboard. The latter would free up even more resources, which we could then shift to other projects. Let's analyze Figure 10-3 to see how our decisions have affected the portfolios and how the situation has changed by the end of the second iteration (at the four-week mark, for example). First we notice that our resource portfolio increased because we added three external consultants.

Resources		
Name	Employee	Project
John	Y	F
Paul	Y	B
Mary	Y	F
Pete	Y	C
Frank	Y	C
Sue	Y	F
Nancy	Y	C
Carol	Y	C
Chris	Y	F
Matt	Y	F
Linda	Y	B
Jimmy	Y	B
Joe	Y	D
Jill	Y	D
Laura	N	G
Jenny	N	G
Stu	N	G

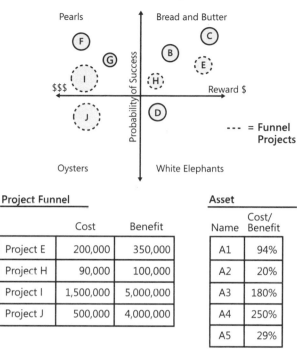

Project Funnel		
	Cost	Benefit
Project E	200,000	350,000
Project H	90,000	100,000
Project I	1,500,000	5,000,000
Project J	500,000	4,000,000

Asset	
Name	Cost/ Benefit
A1	94%
A2	20%
A3	180%
A4	250%
A5	29%

FIGURE 10-3 Dashboard after the second iteration

In the risk-reward diagram, notice that the portfolio managers or executives eliminated project A and that all project resources shifted to project F, which promises a high return. The newly acquired resources have been allocated to projects lined up in the funnel, and project G was initiated as a result by the executive team. Although the asset portfolio has not changed at all, fundamental changes were initiated by the executive team. Notice that new items (projects I and J) were added from the funnel. As a side effect of the new evaluation of the dashboard, project D was reassigned to the lower-right quadrant after we made a reassessment of it. Reasons we might have for doing this are that the POT might not have turned out as we expected or the benefits were less than we anticipated.

Third Iteration

After only three iterations, we can see how our portfolio has changed as a result of following a portfolio management strategy, as discussed throughout Chapter 7. Based on these common goals in portfolio management, we have

- Increased and diversified our portfolio without executing too many projects

- Shifted our focus toward visionary projects
- Emphasized the need for larger and substantial projects

Figure 10-4 reflects these changes after only three iterations.

Matt has been removed from project F and will now support project E, which was elevated from the funnel. That was also made possible because we hired two new employees and two more external consultants, all of whom were added to the resource portfolio. Project D was removed, and the resources from that project were reallocated (along with Matt from project F) to project E. In addition, the new hires and two new consultants are focusing on the very profitable project J. Project H has been downgraded into the killer section and will not be considered for an upcoming iteration.

Resources

Name	Employee	Project
John	Y	F
Paul	Y	B
Mary	Y	F
Pete	Y	C
Frank	Y	C
Sue	Y	F
Nancy	Y	C
Carol	Y	C
Chris	Y	F
Matt	Y	F
Linda	Y	B
Jimmy	Y	B
Joe	Y	D
Jill	Y	D
Laura	N	G
Jenny	N	G
Stu	N	G
Sam	Y	J
Alan	N	J
Ken	N	J

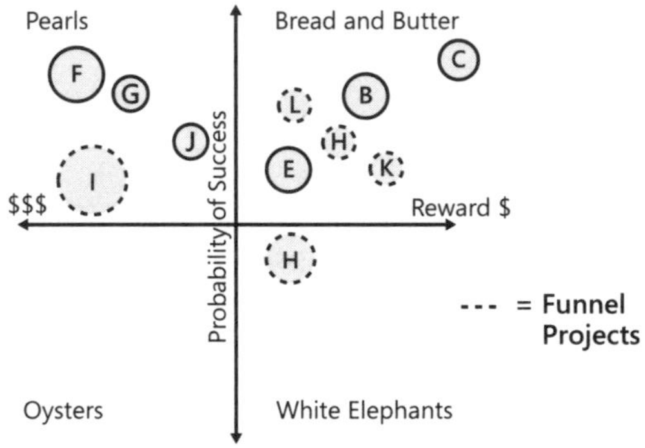

Project Funnel

	Cost	Benefit
Project H	90,000	100,000
Project I	1,500,000	5,000,000
Project K	700,000	1,500,000
Project G	150,000	500,000
Project M	200,000	300,000

Asset

Name	Cost/ Benefit
A1	104%
A2	22%
A3	205%
A4	300%
A5	15%

FIGURE 10-4 Dashboard after the third iteration

It is also interesting to see the development in our asset portfolio, where the costs related to our roadblock systems increased even further. That increase could have been caused by teams shifting their focus to resolving additional defects or debugging releases. A1 has also turned into more of a roadblock and now produces slightly more costs to the organization than benefits. In the upcoming iteration, we could submit an additional project proposal into the funnel to replace this asset as well.

The funnel has three other entries—projects K, L, and M—which might have come through project ideas suggested from within the organization. The assessed costs and benefits for these three proposals are very small, which makes them good candidates to be low-priority projects when the first completed projects roll out of the project portfolio. The completed projects will reduce the amount of resources currently tied to active projects.

Looking ahead, we can see that project I, which promises a high level of benefits, is still in the funnel. We should try to get this project out of the funnel and launched as quickly as possible. We should consider hiring new employees or external consultants so that we can tackle this project as soon as possible. Remember that this project has the potential to reduce the cost structure in our asset portfolio and promises to bring great returns to our organization.

Summary

This final chapter in Part II presented the fictional evolution of an agile portfolio. The intent of this chapter was to provide an example of how the three types of portfolios influence and benefit one another. For simplicity reasons, I ignored things such as the unique skill set of each employee, the technical dependencies that might exist between the projects, and on-demand access to external resources such as consultants. In reality, an organization might need many more iterations to get the same results.

This scenario showed how the asset portfolio is actively involved in overall agile portfolio management. We saw how roadblocks are converted into new project proposals in an iterative fashion. In addition, the resource portfolio was staffed according to the needs in the agile development projects.

Part III
Organization and Environment

During the previous part of this book, we implemented the most relevant three portfolios for a successful portfolio management strategy; project, resource and asset portfolio. By adopting these portfolios, we discussed the opportunities and potential for executives and project managers when agile development practices were combined. These opportunities included for example project metrics, return-on-investment, project selection process, human resources and operations. We concluded with a chapter which brought these isolated portfolios together to a combined agile executive dashboard.

This third and last part of the book will cover how agility will impact the traditional project management organization and its environment.

In Chapter 11, "Portfolio Management Using Scrum," we will illustrate how an existing agile process is elevated from a project to an enterprise-wide portfolio management strategy. Scrum, a very popular and successful agile framework, will be used to outline this proposal.

In Chapter 12, "Project Management Office," we will look at large organizations, which often establish a Project Management Office (PMO), responsible for the successful roll-out of processes throughout the entire enterprise. Because agility changes the project culture significantly, we will take a fresh new look at the role and responsibility of the PMO. Last but not least, we will be looking at common tools and techniques when applied in agile portfolio management.

Chapter 11
Portfolio Management Using Scrum

Developed in the mid 1990s, Scrum is now one of the most popular collections of agile project management practices in the agile industry. Influenced by lean thinking, which has its roots in the production process of Toyota, Scrum mapped these principles to software development. The result is a powerful framework for managing iterative-incremental projects. In this chapter, we'll investigate how Scrum practices can be extended and applied in the context of agile portfolio management. This chapter, therefore, is not intended to replace other introductory books about Scrum that provide much more in-depth information about this process framework. (The bibliography section at the end of this book provides additional references.) The scope of this chapter is limited to an example of how Scrum practices can be mapped to agile portfolio management.

Overview of Scrum

Scrum is not a process that is tailored to your organization but instead is a set of proven practices that are applied and executed as is. The Scrum rules, roles, work products, and vocabulary are therefore not changed to fit the organization, but the other way around. The rules of Scrum are strikingly simple, which we'll see in the subsequent sections of this chapter. But executing these rules is, in reality, extremely difficult to do. Because these challenges also exist with respect to agile portfolio management, I'll point them out as well.

But first, let's step back and see on a high level how the Scrum process is applied on an individual project. Take a look at Figure 11-1.

A *product owner* is responsible for the prioritization of the *product backlog*. The product backlog can be seen as a dynamic container of features, functionality, technical items, and issues that need to be implemented. Every team member can contribute to the product backlog, but the product owner prepares the backlog so that the important items are always estimated and prioritized. There is only one product backlog for each project. In terms of requirements, the product backlog contains, for example, the features of the user story or use case scenario.

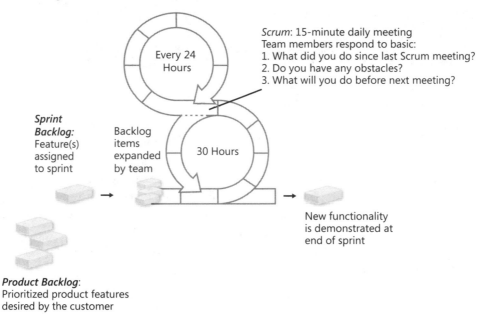

Every 24 Hours

Scrum: 15-minute daily meeting
Team members respond to basic:
1. What did you do since last Scrum meeting?
2. Do you have any obstacles?
3. What will you do before next meeting?

Sprint Backlog:
Feature(s) assigned to sprint

Backlog items expanded by team

30 Hours

New functionality is demonstrated at end of sprint

Product Backlog:
Prioritized product features desired by the customer

FIGURE 11-1 Time boxes, roles, and rules

The *sprint backlog* is a different type of backlog. It contains a subset of the features of the product backlog. Each sprint, which is a 30-day iteration, has one sprint backlog only. A sprint backlog contains the tasks that will turn the items from the product backlog into working software. These tasks are identified and estimated by the team, and each task should not amount to more than 16 hours of work. If the tasks are bigger than 16 hours of work, they are broken down into smaller tasks until they are 16 hours or less in length. The sprint backlog provides the direction of the sprint and provides a mechanism to prevent the team from overcommitment.

A user story, captured in the product backlog, will therefore break into smaller activities in the sprint backlog. The sprint backlog is owned by the team, and everyone can make changes to it. With the sprint backlog in place, team members can sign up for work listed in the sprint backlog during their sprint. Upon completion of the item, burn-down has been achieved and progress can be reported.

Every day, the project team meets for a daily Scrum meeting for 15 minutes. Each team member reports on progress, plans, and impediments to the rest of the team. The Scrum meeting provides a quick way of synchronizing daily team activities. It is the only standing meeting on the calendar of the team.

At the end of each sprint, the team demonstrates the progress to the customer and stakeholders using working software. In an ideal scenario, the stories of the sprint plan have been converted into working software. Once a sprint backlog has been defined and agreed upon, the sprint backlog is protected from changes. Over the course of the entire project, it is quite typical that the high-level goals from the original plan will be adjusted, but not for the current sprint. These adjustments represent the extremely important fine-tuning of features and requirements that is missing in traditional projects.

In Scrum, one person occupies a role that ensures that the project plays by the Scrum rules, and that person is the *scrum master*. Based on this short description of the Scrum process, you might have noticed that the scrum master role does not directly translate to the role of a project manager. Many of the traditional project management responsibilities have been delegated to other roles in Scrum; these responsibilities have been passed to the product owner and team members. For example, the team signs up for work, changes the Scrum backlog, and reports back to itself. That is quite different from having a project manager dole out work assignments, monitor team progress, and control reporting duties, which is the norm in traditional projects. In Scrum, the product owner is also continuously involved and shares important responsibilities related to determining the scope of the project.

Scrum Challenges

As simple as this model might seem, Scrum can be extremely challenging to do. The first challenging aspect is the mind shift required of all team members when they transition from traditional project management to Scrum. After many years of working in traditional project management environments, some workers won't easily adapt to a team-empowered environment. Signing up for work and reporting daily about accomplishments are tasks requiring a higher degree of self-motivation, which has not been fostered in a traditional project environment. It might take a while for every team member to feel empowered and take charge of his own work and schedules.

It is also not uncommon that the goals defined in the daily scrum meetings are too large, similar to weekly status reports in waterfall projects. The Scrum meeting that follows the meeting that set the oversized goal is when progress on the goal is reported back to the team. Often, this is when team members realize that the Scrum meetings are concerned with very small goals and accomplishments. Keep in mind that only eight work hours lie between the two meetings. How much work can possibly get done in this time frame?

Another different kind of challenge associated with the daily Scrum meeting is the reporting of impediments. The entire project team might face organizational obstacles that prevent them from getting their work done. By definition, the scrum master takes ownership of the impediments and tries to remove them as quickly as possible. In reality, these impediments expose fundamental weaknesses of an organization, especially if the organization is new to agile development. Based on existing hierarchies and politics, these impediments might have been disguised for a long time in traditional organizations. In Scrum projects, they become obvious right away.

The authority, strength, and willpower of the scrum master must be used to get them resolved as quickly as possible. A successful scrum master knows how to use the escalation mechanism within an organization to increase the priority of a particular issue, and he or she does not get tired of walking the hallways to talk with the people who can help get the impediment resolved. For example, waiting days for a user to gain access to a specific server might result in the entire project team being unproductive for that time period. Because of the short time frame of a sprint, time wasted in finger-pointing, or other such behaviors that delay the resolution of an issue, can cause the entire sprint to fail. A sprint that fails because of unresolved impediments reflects negatively not only on the project team but also on the entire organization, which should be creating and supporting a platform for productivity.

Another challenge typically arises in staffing the role of the product owner. In traditional development models, business analysts play a significant role during the requirements phase and hand over the specification to the design team. At this point, business analysts move on to their next assignment and define the scope for the next project. In addition, business analysts are not actually responsible for the outcome of the project; they simply prepare the requirements for the development team.

In Scrum projects, the situation is quite different. A business analyst participates in the project on an ongoing basis and is responsible for the correct interpretation and implementation of the requirements, which is the actual system rather than just the specification. Therefore, the role of a product owner in Scrum is better mapped to that of a project sponsor than to that of a business analyst. Characteristics of the product owner role are accountability, responsibility, and ownership. Many business analysts, because of hierarchical limitations in the organization, cannot fill the role of the product owner successfully.

Another important difference between Scrum and traditional descriptive processes is that Scrum is empirical, in the sense that the process can change based on practical experience. That means that not only does the team adapt the project scope to new situations throughout the execution of the project, but the team also adapts the process itself. For example, suppose that after a few iterations the project team agrees to move the daily stand-up meeting from 9 A.M. to 4 P.M. The self-organized team is empowered to do that. However, it is not empowered to skip the meeting altogether.

This section was not intended to provide a thorough introduction to Scrum. The goal was to set the stage for the following sections in this chapter. These sections present the Scrum process in the light of portfolio management and propose how Scrum principles can be elevated to the enterprise level.

Portfolio Backlogs

In Scrum, outstanding work is captured in backlogs. I do not like the term *backlog* because it gives the impression that the team is behind in its work or that the work is delayed, which is not necessarily the case. That is especially true in the context of portfolio management, in which the portfolio is a visionary and forward-thinking work product. However, to be consistent with the Scrum process and its vocabulary, I'll continue using the term *backlog*, even in the context of portfolio management. Ken Schwaber's two books, *Agile Project Management with Scrum* (Microsoft Press, 2004) and *The Enterprise and Scrum* (Microsoft Press, 2007), provide an in-depth introduction to agile project management with Scrum as well as practices for adopting Scrum across the entire enterprise. Within this chapter, we'll focus on how Scrum can be applied in the context of agile portfolio management.

As I've asserted many times already, the fundamental concept behind a successful portfolio management strategy is the concept of *portfolios*. These portfolios can be represented by and managed in a simple document or managed with a sophisticated portfolio management software product.

If we step back and look at the contents of a regular Scrum product backlog again, we notice that it describes features of a future system. The combined features will provide certain benefits to an organization. Now, if we elevate the idea of using a backlog for portfolio management to the next level, we can see a project as one big feature to be added to the organization that provides benefits to the organization. The combination of all projects is therefore a project portfolio. In other words, why not put the Scrum projects themselves into a backlog and call it a project portfolio backlog? The same is true for creating resource and asset management portfolios. We can include all three portfolio types in our definition of portfolio backlogs. The following sections provide a separate definition of each portfolio backlog.

Project Portfolio Backlog

The project portfolio backlog contains a list of active projects and a list of project proposals in the funnel. For each project, we can track attributes such as start date, forecasted end date, name, iteration length, benefits estimate, return on investment estimates, and a history of project metrics delivered by the project team iteratively.

In addition, the projects are iteratively assessed by executive management and allocated to a specific location in the risk-reward diagram. By categorizing projects according to the quadrants in the risk-reward diagram, executive management ensures that the project selection process is effective.

If a resource portfolio exists, team members can be listed in it. If not, the project costs must be captured at the project portfolio level. That value can be expressed as an average value for each iteration. The amount of resources allocated to a project is important to know to determine the size of the bubble in the risk-reward diagram.

With every project prioritized, the organization has a constant reminder about the most important projects in the organization and the ones that are challenged by the highest-priority proposals. This project portfolio backlog will then support the project selection process between iterations.

Resource Portfolio Backlog

The resource backlog includes internal resources such as employees and external contractors, including consultants, coaches, and instructors. In a more sophisticated resource backlog, job descriptions, titles, and internal compensation rates might be useful information to track.

Tracking the internal compensation rate is a common practice in large organizations. This is the average rate the organization pays its employees based on their position in the company. This rate can then be compared with the hourly or daily rate of external resources. It also includes retirement and medical benefits, as well as paid time off. These values are associated with rankings or job descriptions and might not reflect the actual compensation of a particular employee working on the project. Accumulating the resource rates enables an organization to put a price tag on a project. The price tag is used to guide executives in their project selection process.

It is a good idea to keep external resources in the resource backlog even if these candidates are not available. An unavailable resource could be brought back into the organization if needed at a later date or on a later project.

Even for organizations that distribute their projects globally, projects are still selected from a central location (for example, from the home office). For that reason, one resource portfolio backlog is sufficient. The resource portfolio should not be spread out or duplicated across geographical boundaries.

Asset Portfolio Backlog

The asset portfolio backlog is more static than the project and resource portfolio backlogs. It captures the systems currently in operation, including the teams needed to maintain and enhance them. That includes the personnel needed for hardware-related support such as service centers, help desks, and administrative offices. Similar to the projects in a project portfolio, the current assets are evaluated based on the benefits they are providing to the organization—only the evaluation is done less frequently. Therefore, beyond capturing administrative information about these assets, this backlog captures costs and the cost structure after the systems have been deployed. Dependencies on other assets in operations are also important. The dependencies between assets will affect the order in which systems are retired, replaced, or enhanced.

Roles

Portfolio management is not a one-person job. Portfolio managers require input from a variety of stakeholders—such as executive management, project management, the PMO, business sponsors, and potential stakeholders—to make the best decisions about ideas, proposals, projects, resources, and assets. The better the mix of stakeholders, the better the overall decision will be because the decision is based on a broader context. Keep in mind that the following roles are not Scrum roles; they are intended to complement Scrum.

Portfolio Owner

Similar to the role of product owner in Scrum, a portfolio owner owns one or more portfolios. The person in this role is responsible for the overall strategy and vision of the organization's development efforts, as well as for the execution of that strategy. This role could be filled by CTOs, CIOs, CEOs, or leaders of the PMO, depending on the structure and size of the organization. This role has to be assigned based on the organization's assessment of which person within the organization is the best candidate to perform the role of a portfolio owner.

This role is responsible for prioritizing portfolio backlogs. It has final decision-making authority on matters concerning the portfolio. The owner makes sure the vision and strategy of the organization mirror the portfolios. This is a much more detailed definition of the chief product owner described in the meta-scrum process, in which Scrum is elevated to address resource-staffing issues and cross-functional collaboration between Scrum teams and other organizational units within the organization. (For more information about meta-scrum, see the books by Ken Schwaber that were mentioned earlier.)

Portfolio Master

The portfolio master role is similar to the role of the scrum master. This role executes the Scrum rules, conducts the daily portfolio meeting, and removes impediments raised within the organization. A portfolio master performs a role similar to a high-level scrum master. Within the context of portfolio management, the portfolio master executes the Scrum process with the portfolio team. That is a different approach than the "meta-scrum" or "scrum of scrum" concept presented in Scrum literature.

Portfolio Manager

A portfolio manager is a Scrum team member. A portfolio manager prepares the portfolio dashboard for the portfolio owner. Just like the project manager at the project portfolio level of a Scrum project, the portfolio manager signs up for activities—for example, collecting metrics or working directly with a scrum master of a project to resolve impediments. This role can also feed the product owner role with additional objectives for the product backlog.

Organizations with a PMO might dedicate PMO members to the role of portfolio managers. The responsibilities include the preparation of new project proposals and keeping the backlogs up to date, which is necessary because of the iterative-incremental rhythm of agile projects. To provide the best possible information about the project, the portfolio manager might work closely with scrum masters inside the project. This close working relationship enables portfolio managers to generate the latest burn-down charts, metrics, and reports. Most important, the activities of the portfolio manager should not lead to creating more work for the project team. That restriction is in line with the agile value of "valuing working software over comprehensive documentation."

Just as the godfather of a child takes a deep interest in the child's activities, a portfolio manager might be dedicated to working with certain projects very closely. That could mean that the portfolio manager will participate regularly in daily scrum meetings and retrospectives. This approach will lead to a better assessment of the project without adding overhead to the project. This concept also supports the agile principle of "valuing individuals and interactions over processes and tools."

Portfolio managers also perform negotiations with external consultants and makes sure the best possible candidates are brought into the organization in a timely manner.

Activities

The following activities are performed when Scrum is applied in the context of portfolio management. These activities extend the vocabulary of Scrum and define what is unique when this agile process is applied to portfolio management.

Portfolio Sprint Planning Meeting

During the portfolio sprint planning meeting, the decisions about the upcoming sprint are made. For example, decisions are made about which projects will continue or be prepared for closeout, which resources will be hired, which assets are scheduled to be retired, and which proposals will be launched as new projects.

Portfolio Scrum Meeting

The portfolio master, whose role parallels that of the scrum master in a Scrum project, executes the daily portfolio Scrum meeting, which takes no longer than 15 minutes. Every portfolio manager reports on the progress of, the plans for, and the current impediments to daily portfolio management work. These impediments do not necessarily have to be organizational issues but can be issues raised by the individual teams. They can include cross-departmental collaboration and corporate policies. Through this mechanism, organizational issues are brought immediately to senior management's attention. The status each portfolio manager is reporting on can be related to the project, resource, or asset portfolio backlog.

Portfolio Sprint Review Meeting

The portfolio master facilitates the portfolio sprint review meeting. Similar to the a project team in the project retrospective, the portfolio team reflects on what went well with portfolio management during the past sprint and what areas need to be improved. This meeting is also used to improve the structure and content of the portfolio backlogs—for example, the refinement of the agile metrics.

Metrics

Just as project teams produce burn-down charts for individual projects, a portfolio team can produce an organization-wide burn-down chart, quality metrics, and team morale metrics. These values can be summarized by averaging or adding the available project metrics. However, this information has to be interpreted and used with great caution. Let's see why:

First, every project team will most likely have a slightly different perception of small, medium, and large when estimating story points. Therefore, the project reporting that takes place after a story point has been burned from one project can reflect something totally different from the reports in another project. That system of ranking work is fine within each project because the interpretation of a story point is very consistent in that context. Across a variety of projects, the consistency of the interpretation is not a given. The project forecasting, therefore, has to be based on each project's own historical data only. A comparison between projects is not useful—only a comparison of the iterations within a project is useful.

However, when this data is accumulated or averaged on an enterprise level and the data gets merged together, its usefulness becomes apparent. One story point in one project might translate to five story points in another project. If each team remains consistent with its story estimates, the average value of the sum of projects will also be consistent. In this case, executive management has an indicator whether, for example, January was a more productive month than February in terms of progress. These types of comparisons are valid for all the other project metrics as well. They become invalid only if a large number of projects are introduced that significantly influence the average values.

The second reason to exercise caution when using project metrics is that publishing the average values organization-wide can discourage teams whose metrics are below average. As discussed in earlier chapters, subpar metrics don't always indicate subpar performance. A team's focus in any given iteration can negatively affect the metrics of items outside that focus. Organization-wide metrics must be considered from various viewpoints. One might argue that they do not give an exact picture of the situation, so why bother? Others might say that these high-level metrics are not supposed to carry a detailed message.

Here is a positive example from a large retailer I worked with in the past. The most important metric was an in-stock quote. The in-stock quote represented how many products listed in the catalog were available in an actual store. The higher the quota (with the optimum quota being 100 percent), the higher the chances were that customers would find the merchandise they were looking for at the local stores. This metric was available in real time and visible in every building on every floor. No visitor or employee could escape from this information. Although the metrics were not very dynamic on a daily basis, they conveyed a strong message, especially during holiday seasons when stores had trouble filling their shelves fast enough. The strength of this metric was that the entire organization was constantly exposed to one overall high-level goal—in this case, maximizing the in-stock quote. From this example, you can see one way to take agile metrics compiled in the developmental part of an organization and share them throughout the organization.

In my opinion, when high-level metrics are understood and communicated effectively, they make strategic sense. An iterative-incrementally increasing organizational burn-down conveys that the organization digests more and more functionality. This information could turn into a productivity index and give the organization a relatively simple but effective overview of its productivity.

Scrum Certification

One big factor in the success of Scrum is the certification program, which is orchestrated by the Scrum Alliance. Since 2003, Certified Scrum Master (CSM) and Certified Scrum Product Owner (CSPO) certificates have been earned by participants in a two-day training course. More than 25,000 IT professionals have completed this course worldwide as of March 2008. It is, therefore, not very difficult to allocate trained personnel to all aspects of a Scrum-driven environment, including its portfolio management.

In addition, the Scrum Alliance recently started issuing additional certificates that target different roles within the organization. The dependencies, relationships, and certification paths are shown in Figure 11-2.

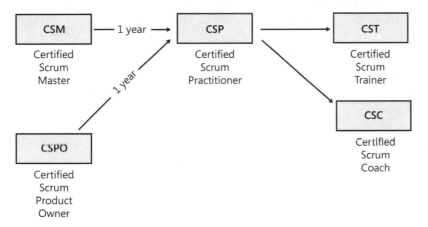

FIGURE 11-2 Scrum certification paths

After one year of practical experience as a scrum master, the CSM can apply to become a Certified Scrum Practitioner (CSP). The candidate will need to take an exam to demonstrate her acquired practical knowledge. Two more advanced certificates are the Certified Scrum Trainer (CST) and Certified Scrum Coach (CSC) certificates. After becoming certified, a scrum trainer can teach other professionals to become a CSM or CSPO. The Certified Scrum Coach is officially recognized as qualified to consult organizations using Scrum.

Although acquiring each certificate requires a significant financial commitment from the trainee, the certification process is well defined. First, the applicant receives formal training as a foundation of knowledge, that stage is followed by a by a period of real-world application of the principles, and finally applicants are allowed to teach and coach others. The process of certification follows a "learn, apply, and duplicate" paradigm.

Scrum certification offers great advantages for organizations—for example, it ensures that someone is on staff to clearly lay out the rules and responsibilities when projects are launched. During the hiring or contracting process, an organization can use the certification path laid out by the Scrum Alliance as a guideline for finding qualified individuals. Standardizing the certification program and the roles associated with each certificate makes it easy for interested organizations to map the certificates to the various resources in their resource portfolio backlog.

Summary

Scrum is ideal for agile project management. But can Scrum be used to manage a portfolio? This chapter provided a proposal on how the practices of Scrum can be elevated to and executed on an enterprise level. Based on the existing roles in Scrum, we applied the Scrum framework in the context of portfolio management. We added three backlogs: the project, resource, and asset portfolio backlogs. We extended the role of a product owner and scrum master to portfolio owner and portfolio scrum master. We also saw how a team of portfolio managers can work directly with individual Scrum project teams. Just like a project team in a Scrum project, the portfolio team plans sprints, reviews sprint activities, and conducts a daily Scrum meeting. We also looked at the latest Scrum certification program and how it could benefit the resource portfolio backlog.

Chapter 12
Project Management Office

A project management office (PMO) is traditionally a centralized organization that is commonly composed of a group of individuals who are experienced in project management, software development processes, or a combination of both. Especially in large hierarchical enterprises (for example, functional or matrix), the personnel of the PMO are expected to act as a communications bridge across various parts of the organization, harvest best practices across the enterprise, and leverage proven project management approaches. The PMO also prevents common project management pitfalls from occurring within the organization. Its other duties include standardization of processes and ensuring that the organization adheres to government regulatory requirements and certifications.

As we've learned, agile projects are managed and executed quite differently from traditional projects. This last chapter will focus on how agile project management and agile processes affect the PMO, and it will define the role and responsibility of the PMO in an agile enterprise.

The Challenges of Managing Agile Projects

Throughout this book, I have noted many differences between agile and traditional projects. Some of the changes required for agile projects—such as a short daily stand-up meeting—might seem minor compared with the implementation of iterative-incremental development. It is the entire collection of agile practices that fundamentally changes how projects get done in an agile organization. For example, if an iteration lasts only for two weeks, there is no room in the team's schedule for long meetings. The practices used for coordinating, estimating, planning, reporting, and of course developing have to fit the time frame of the iteration. In other words, agile practices work together as a unit, and eliminating one practice might compromise the project or even cause it to fail.

An organization can adopt agile project management incrementally. However, which agile practices are introduced and in which order must be carefully orchestrated. The PMO plays a prominent and vital role in the implementation of a successful agile project and portfolio management strategy. To understand the part played by the PMO, we need to define the role and responsibility of the PMO in the agile enterprise.

Let's discuss the major challenges when traditional PMOs face agile projects.

Agile Project Teams Are Empowered and Self-Organized

A traditional role of the PMO is to monitor the progress of the project team and make sure the project team works according to the established corporate policies and standards. This approach follows a traditional "command and control" paradigm. The foundation for team-work in an agile project, however, is built on trust and doesn't require an overseer. Instead, the agile project manager trusts that the team will try to deliver on its promises regarding the functionality to be delivered and the timeline for delivering it. In agile teams, the role of the project manager is inside the team's boundary, not outside. Trust between the project manager and the agile team is important not only for reporting but also for planning and estimating.

If agile projects are monitored from an external entity like the traditional PMO, the agile team will start reporting to entities outside the team's boundaries. That is basically the same situation that exists in a traditionally managed project, where teams report to a project man-ager who has more of an outside overseer role. A traditional PMO takes the leadership role in certain activities, such as compliance with regulatory requirements, and actively directs the agile team in a top-down management style. An empowered, self-organized team will, of course, not ignore corporate standards but build them into the team's work schedule according to its own chosen way to organize the project.

But there is another, more subtle, problem that appears if you add a reporting structure that has the agile team reporting to a traditional PMO. When traditional project teams report the project status to the PMO, they often do so through the project manager. This becomes a problem if the team is empowered and self-organized, as they are in agile projects, because the agile project manager is usually not familiar with all the details of the development work. The agile project manager's lack of familiarity with fine details is actually good because the project manager should focus on directing the project and should not get hung up on technicalities. If the agile project manager is expected to deliver project progress reports to the PMO in a traditional way, the project manager must drill down into the details and un-derstand them to successfully communicate the dependencies. How else could the desired level of status details be delivered? That brings us back to square one, where we had the "command and control" paradigm. By setting up a structure in which the project manager reports status to the PMO, we will reintroduce the complex communication hierarchy used before we introduced agile development practices.

If agile metrics are being used instead of traditional ones, the PMO can monitor agile projects closely. It is essential that the PMO know how to interpret these metrics. The PMO should also be invited to the retrospective meetings at the end of each iteration, where tan-gible progress is demonstrated to the stakeholders. If a PMO likes to be involved at points other than those in the iterative rhythm, members of the PMO can attend the daily stand-up meeting to get daily progress updates. If concerns (for example, compliance requirements, use of agile processes) from these in-person meetings arise, the PMO personnel can submit additional software or process requirements through the project sponsor or project manager directly to the team. Direct interference with the agile team, especially during the iteration, must be eliminated, even during the stand-up meeting, where non-team members are only observers. The relationship between the PMO and the agile projects must be based on trust and monitored solely through standard project metrics and personal interaction with the project manager only.

Agile Processes Are Empirical

When I say that agile processes are empirical, I mean that they evolve around a repertoire of practices. These agile practices have been proven to be effective many times in many real-world scenarios. When agile projects begin, the team uses either a collection of individual practices or an entire agile framework, such as Scrum, Lean, or XP (Extreme Programming), or a combination of them. The difference between traditional processes and agile processes is that the agile team adjusts to the processes while the project is going along, whereas a development team in a traditional process follows the same procedure from start to finish. I am aware that traditional projects plan for lessons-learned workshops after projects are completed and could potentially submit change requests to the PMO to adjust the existing process. Based on my experience, though, the existing processes are very static and hard to change. Lessons learned are often compromised because project team members have moved on to new assignments. Agile projects, on the other hand, adapt not only iteratively to new project requirements but actually adapt the process itself through retrospectives. These retrospectives are much more than the lessons-learned sessions of traditional projects because in addition to project experiences, process and personal experiences are also being shared among the team members. This iterative approach explores the project, process, and people from multiple angles.

In its traditional role, the PMO provides software development processes, commonly called a System Development Life Cycle (SDLC). One characteristic of the SDLC is that all projects in an organization follow a "one size fits all" process. As a result, each project steps through the same activities, produces the same documents, and reports on the same defined milestones. Standardizing an agile process to an SDLC on an enterprise level is impossible. What is possible, however, is to have the PMO actively participate in selecting which agile practices are used and in applying this collection of proven agile practices to other projects in the organization. Therefore, a PMO in an agile environment must work directly with individual projects instead of providing inflexible process frameworks.

Because a large process might not fit the needs of small projects, some organizations choose to offer a variety of development processes depending on the type of project. In this case, a small, medium, or large project would follow a variation on the process theme. The bottom line, however, is that the processes are still "one size fits all" solutions, but they're just provided on a different, more granular, level. These process frameworks are still static. That means these models still cannot serve the projects properly and cannot help them reach their full potential.

Another approach many organizations take to increase the application of the SDLC is to provide the process on a very high-level framework. Instead of a "one size fits all" process, the framework describes the general outline, similar to the cornerstone concepts of an agile process framework. Instead of defining all the details of a process, a high-level framework provides a general orientation for the user of the process. There is, however, a minor difference that causes many frameworks to fail to meet the needs of an organization. An enterprise-wide process framework is often not concrete enough, is often theoretical, and does not provide any applicable assistance to the project team. The framework is so elevated that it cannot guide the team members in their daily work. The result is that the teams will actually perform their own process and synchronize with the milestones outlined in the framework. These homegrown solutions, however, are not necessarily proven practices, and they might not work in conjunction with the framework.

Agile processes provide plenty of room for team interpretation and self-organization. In addition, agile processes are concrete, which means they will provide direct practical guidance for each individual on the team, including the project manager. These practical and essential cornerstones of the process translate directly into real actions for the entire agile team. The space between the cornerstones is unstructured and will be filled by the dynamics of the agile team.

During my career, I've seen plenty of traditionally managed organizations that had non-agile processes in place. Changing these processes was almost impossible due to bureaucratic procedures. Even making small changes such as replacing a template of a document was difficult. In cases like this, the organization had adapted to the process instead of the other way around. That led to a static process that did not match the dynamics of the organization. This situation became obvious when team members started a sentence with, "The process requires us to do X" instead of, "We do the following to achieve X." Agile processes, on the other hand, introduce a feedback loop to the PMO, which provides a mechanism to improve, evolve, and streamline the process to its full potential.

On one occasion, a PMO froze documents at certain milestones by converting the project documentation to PDF documents. By doing this, the PMO had a record of the project deliverables. We know by now what a negative effect this has on the requirement specification, for example. Although the members of that PMO knew and tolerated changes to the documents even beyond the milestones, the mechanism created an unhealthy work relationship between the PMO and its project teams. When I investigated the reasons for uploading PDF documents, I learned that the creators of the SDLC framework never thought of other document types or other milestones. After years in production, nobody challenged the framework, although almost everybody was convinced that there were better ways of executing projects.

Based on my experience, these SDLC processes have been adopted without giving them the time to prove themselves within their environment. Because the SDLC becomes part of a company's vocabulary—for example, "Did you freeze your requirements already?"—the company conveys the impression that this is the right way of doing things. This is one reason that so many projects fail and why 90 percent of projects fail to meet any of their time, cost, or quality targets. Many of these failed projects trace back to inflexible processes that create challenges, such as the ones discussed in depth in Chapter 2. As discussed, iterative, agile processes tackle exactly these issues.

Milestones Monitoring vs. Progress Reporting

Traditional processes divide a project into phases. These phases are separated by milestones. Prior to the start of a project, each project manager aligns the process with the master project plan and its milestones. A dilemma arises, however, when agile processes are introduced to an organization that is driven by such a phased model. This clash is quite understandable because agile processes simply do not line up with traditional processes in terms of timing and project deliverables.

A milestone in an SDLC, for example, occurs at the completion of an activity, such as at the "Requirements Completed" milestone. An agile project executes activities continuously, and a "Requirements Completed" milestone does not exist in agile projects. Agile project milestones are marked by the end of iterations, which are predictable and frequent. The difference is that the agile teams' report on and demonstrate tangible progress, which is measured in working software. In contrast, traditional milestones capture the completion of activities. For example, at the first milestone of a traditional project, the team reports solely on whether the requirements have been gathered. The agile team, however, reports on fewer requirements (because of the short iteration), which have been designed, programmed, tested, and integrated. Simply comparing the two teams on the accomplishments with regard to completed requirements instead of working software does not give the full picture of the current status.

With these two fundamentally different approaches, a PMO that embraces agility needs to provide an alternative way to measure progress for projects within the organization. The existing milestones used for traditional project management cannot be applied in the agile context; however, iterations are an ideal way of tracking the progress of the agile projects.

Best Practices for Project Management

A common role of traditional PMOs is to implement project management methodologies and make these available consistently within the enterprise. Project management frameworks like the Project Management Body of Knowledge (PMBOK) or Projects in Controlled Environments (Prince2) are very popular choices to reach that goal. In a survey of 252 organizations, the accounting and consulting firm KPMG determined that 69 percent of all project failures are related to lack of project management methodologies or improper implementation of them. The survey results show that even industry-wide project management frameworks are challenged when applied in practice. Spreading these practices blindly, therefore, could add unnecessary risk to an organization's development efforts. Filtering and promoting the best applicable practices is not only important on an organizational level but essential for each project.

Agile project management tackles many of the issues that resulted in the 69 percent failure rate of project management methodologies just mentioned. Agile principles focus on personal interaction and communication, even on a daily basis. The rules and vocabulary of agile processes are lightweight, which allows for a quick adoption of agile principles in the enterprise if more traditional methods are kept out of the way. Similar to the traditional project management frameworks, agile processes have solid cornerstones that give each project a clearly defined boundary. The gray area between these cornerstones will be specified and defined by each project team independently. Agile processes might at first seem like a loss of control for the PMO, but by the end of an iteration, which is only a few weeks away, the project metrics and working software that are delivered will demonstrate to the PMO that a new control mechanism is in place. The new control mechanism tracks progress according to project goals, not according to the project's movement in the overall process.

Traditional methodologies provide templates of work products, the exact sequence of activities is specified, and the roles are granularly defined. Therefore, the learning curve is steep and the application of the framework is often error prone. A PMO that promotes agile processes must be aware of the lightweight nature of these practices and handle them accordingly.

Defining the Roles and Responsibilities of an Agile PMO

Even though agile practices are lightweight and easy to implement, implementing them in a traditional management environment presents a challenge to a PMO. Although high-level process frameworks and the monitoring of project milestones require less involvement from a traditional PMO, agility demands the opposite. The personal involvement of PMO members, who will participate in agile projects by harvesting and sharing best practices, requires a new definition of the PMO.

The PMO must not only play a more active role, it needs to play a proactive role. The agile PMO is a servant leader for the project, which not only removes impediments for the projects on an organizational level but also tries to prevent the impediments from occurring in the first place. In addition, the members of an agile PMO can talk the agile lingo; evaluate practices, ideas, and concepts; and provide assistance in the adoption process. Because of the variety of these responsibilities, the role that every individual PMO member plays might vary.

For example, the most active role in an agile PMO could be a member who actually steps into the shoes of an agile project manager in a real project. Through retrospectives, the project manager not only optimizes the path for the particular project but can also feed the PMO with hands-on experiences. By being proactive, the PMO members ensure that agile practices are not only observed but actually applied. By having PMO personnel share both positive and negative experiences with certain agile practices or tools, the organization will eventually improve its processes.

A more distanced PMO role is the mentor, who works in collaboration with the agile project manager. Because a mentor has fewer commitments than a project manager, the PMO mentor can assist on multiple projects at the same time. The PMO mentor can also teach existing project managers about best practices in formal in-house training sessions.

You might notice that all these working models between the PMO and agile projects require a lot of dedication from the PMO to the project teams. This level of dedication consumes resources from the PMO. To perform successfully in an agile organization, the PMO most likely will need to be expanded from its traditional model.

A PMO can also be the center of excellence. It can include a pool of trainers, mentors, internal consultants, or even senior agile project managers who take on full responsibilities in certain key projects. Within a large organization, a PMO that consists of only one or two members will not be able to adequately fulfill these responsibilities. The PMO personnel will be distanced from the agile projects, with little insight into the actual agile practices being used and with even less room for duplicating those principles across the enterprise.

The PMO and Portfolio Management

The PMO is often wrongly mixed together with the activity of portfolio management. The PMO provides guidance regarding the initiation and execution of projects, and it seems natural to connect the PMO to the project portfolio. If you look a little bit closer, though, you'll notice a few differences that challenge this view of the relationship, especially in the context of agile portfolio management.

A PMO in an agile organization promotes agile practices and works very closely with the agile projects. As described in the preceding section, the members of the PMO might even be part of the agile project. The agile project portfolio, however, embodies the vision of the organization. This vision is based on the technical and financial feasibility of projects. In other words, the portfolio is forward thinking from a business perspective, whereas the PMO has a focus on project execution in the present. No doubt, there are synergies when it comes to project reporting through agile metrics, but the actual project portfolio should also be managed on an executive level outside the PMO or by someone in the PMO who can wear both hats.

Choosing the Right Tool for the Agile Job

In addition to establishing the SDLC, another typical role of the traditional PMO is to standardize the tools within the organization—for example, defining the use of Microsoft Office Project and providing the training to use it properly. The tools are often selected by the PMO, which evaluates the functionality of the commercially available applications. In addition, because these tools reach wide and deep within the organization, the PMO needs to acquire enterprise licenses from software vendors. The traditional PMO, then, has two important parameters to consider with regard to what tools to use: functionality and cost. Once the licenses are acquired, the tool becomes available to the organization and is pushed out to the projects.

Agile projects require a different process for the acquisition and use of tools. This process is summarized in the agile manifesto as, "Value individuals and interaction over processes and tools." A tool that might have worked for one project might not work for another project. Even worse, the tool might cause an additional bottleneck. The idea of providing a consistent and uniform way of project management through a tool rarely works. In my opinion, a tool decision distracts from the real need of the organization, finding its project management practices. For example, punching an estimate into an entry field of a software tool and pressing an OK button is much easier than applying the actual estimating technique and producing a number. The tools needed by an organization, therefore, might be as diverse as the various projects. Consistency and conformity might not always be an advantage; the opposite might actually be the case.

Agile projects are, in my opinion, better served if the PMO provides or collects reports of users' experiences with tools and makes those reports available across the enterprise. That way, team members can learn about the features of the tools based on the experiences others have had with the tool. The savings the organization might realize by purchasing enterprise-wide licenses are less significant if you consider the total costs of ownership of the tool. As a matter of fact, many of the tools used in the agile community are the result of open-source development and are available for no cost.

Overhead and Profits

From a cost perspective, the PMO often creates additional overhead in an organization. Even though the PMO provides services across the enterprise, the services are difficult to split across the cost centers, especially when the results affect the entire organization—for example, the choice of the SDLC. In addition, the services a traditional PMO offers are sometimes not desired. This is especially true of a PMO whose primary function is to monitor and control the projects. This responsibility might not be seen as a service to a project, but as an obstacle instead. I have witnessed project teams attempting to bypass the PMO to get their project done more effectively. When a relationship like this has gone bad, the responsibilities and services of a PMO need to be revisited. At the end of the day, the projects provide the benefits to the organization.

An important consideration is that a PMO serving agile projects might actually be profitable. With a pool of project managers assisting agile project teams directly, the services and costs can be linked to specific activities. The more involved the PMO is in the enterprise, the higher the chances are not only that the PMO is profitable but also that the profitability is measurable. The iterative rhythm of the projects not only is an ideal mechanism for evaluating the progress of the project and the chosen process, but it also can serve to evaluate the services provided to the project by the PMO and others. This model keeps everyone accountable and responsible for their deliverables.

Applying Models, Standards, and Regulations in an Agile Environment

Another service the PMO provides to the organization is keeping it in compliance with industry standards and models—for example, standards and regulations driven by the Capability Maturity Model Integration (CMMI) consortium, the Food and Drug Administration (FDA), or the International Organization for Standardization (ISO). Standards and regulations are often used to justify traditional processes in projects. That, however, is a myth.

Let's take the CMMI framework, for example. CMMI is a framework for process improvement and organizational maturity. The maturity is measured against specific criteria, which classify the exact level. The ability of an organization to reach a given maturity level, which ranges from 1 through 5, is also not related to implemented software tools or certain templates. Applying CMMI does not introduce an additional process that will compete with agile processes. The opposite is actually the case. CMMI focuses on improving the processes in place and, therefore, on improving the organization.

From the IT and PMO perspectives, software development and project management processes are in the spotlight. Earlier in this chapter, we discussed how agile processes are flexible and empirical. These attributes are the result of agile processes being revisited during every retrospective. Process improvement is therefore possible not only after projects are completed, but after each iteration. Reaching for a higher maturity level also does not mean that the project needs to produce more documentation. Progress in working software or results and conclusions drawn from the daily stand-up meeting are sufficient.

It is not the intent of this chapter to explore all possible standards and regulations in the industry. CMMI was simply taken as an example to illustrate that agile practices are not contrary to this mature model. If your organization or project has to comply with certain regulations, revisit the requirements of the standard carefully. Deliverables are not always documents, and an assessment of a project does not mean that documents will be inspected. If that is the case, agile projects might work just as well as traditional processes, perhaps even better.

Getting the Most from Your PMO

Based on the challenges described in the preceding section, let's wrap up this chapter by taking a fresh look at the PMO from the perspective of an agile enterprise. Here are some ideas about how the PMO might work more collaboratively within an organization than the traditional PMO.

Mentoring

When members of the PMO are assigned to become mentors to agile project managers, they can suggest and implement best practices in the project, which allows them to gain new insights into the day-to-day activities of the agile projects. Both parties keep their project knowledge up to date by exchanging information about latest trends and developments in the field of agile project management and about how these trends can be applied in the organization.

Staffing

An agile PMO can assist project teams by handling requests for direct or indirect staffing efforts. A "direct" request is one that asks the PMO member to jump into a project and provide hands-on services. An "indirect" request refers to a request for the PMO to work with the human resource department to recruit the best possible talent for the situation. From a portfolio management perspective, that is an active role for the PMO member in the management of the resource portfolio.

Training

In addition to actually delivering training courses and seminars within the organization, the agile PMO can leverage its communication channel with the training department. The PMO can support the training department in identifying valuable training vendors and courses for agile projects and preapprove services for quick training needs. In addition, members of the PMO can be dedicated to produce internal training courses executed as seminars, workshops, or "lunch and learns."

The PMO can group project team members for training courses, and it can coordinate the creation of training courses for the products the agile team has developed. These courses might be delivered to colleagues within the organization or to potential customers and end users outside the organization. While the agile development team focuses on the delivery of the actual software, the PMO can be the driving force within the organization to have the training material ready when the system is ready.

Manuals and Release Notes

Similar to its responsibilities regarding training courses, the PMO can facilitate the creation of product manuals and release notes. That role is especially crucial if the entire product documentation should have a consistent look and feel to the customer.

Release Teams

When large organizations decide to adopt agile practices, they commonly build releases increment by increment. These releases, however, are often internal, which means they are shown to stakeholders, end users, or focus groups. The goal is to get feedback and improve the system over time.

An extremely powerful option for agile projects is to release a partial system to production. That requires the use of a dedicated team of resources—let's call it a release project team. Organizing the release activities under the PMO has the advantage that not every individual project team needs to go through all the steps of releasing a system to production. A dedicated release team can handle this task, and the development team can concentrate on building the next increment.

Metrics

The agile PMO will help the active project teams produce the metrics needed. For example, new project teams might not know which metrics are required, which metrics are optional, and how to produce the metrics. The members of the PMO will provide the necessary guidance.

Status

The PMO personnel can attend daily stand-up meetings and retrospectives of the projects to gain additional insights into the projects not satisfied by the project metrics. Attending these meetings is optional, however, and the PMO member doesn't participate directly. These meetings should provide enough status information for stakeholders and eliminate the need for other formal status reports in the organization.

Portfolios

Last but not least, the portfolios need to be managed and information about them must be compiled so that executives can make decisions about the projects in the portfolio. This task will likely be a large chunk of the agile PMO's responsibilities. The PMO will help implement the strategy, facilitate the project selection process, calculate ROI, and perform the cost-benefit analysis as described throughout this book.

Summary

In this final chapter of the book, we saw the duties of the PMO in the light of agile projects. I described the roles and responsibilities of a traditional PMO and the impact agile projects will have on them. Here are some guidelines for an agile PMO:

- Create a partnership between the PMO and the project teams instead of a hierarchy.
- Value trust over control.
- Use retrospectives as the milestones.
- Remember that ownership and involvement bring out the best practices.
- Use tools to help with project tasks and accelerate the progress, not to do the work.
- Industry standards and models do not conflict with agile practices.
- Run the PMO like an agile project.
- Measure the services provided by the PMO.

Appendix
Additional Resources

Following is a list of other sources of information on topics discussed in this book. The list includes sources for quotes and statistics used in this book, as well as books, Web sites, and articles that cover certain agile topics in greater detail.

Books and Articles

Augustine, Sanjiv. 2005. *Managing Agile Projects*. Prentice Hall PTR.

Autry, James A. 2004. *The Servant Leader: How to Build a Creative Team, Develop Great Moral and Improve the Bottom-Line Performance*. Three Rivers Press.

Baker, Stephen. "Google and the Wisdom of Clouds." *Newsweek*, December 24, 2007 (available at *http://www.businessweek.com/magazine/content/07_52/b4064048925836.htm?chan=magazine+channel_top+stories*)

Boehm, Barry. 1981. *Software Engineering Economics*. Prentice Hall.

Brooks, Frederick P. 1995. *Mythical Man Month*. Addison-Wesley.

Christiansen, James A. 2000. *Building the Innovative Organization: Management Systems that Encourage Innovation*. Palgrave Macmillan.

Christiansen, James A. 2000. *Competitive Innovation Management: Techniques to Improve Innovation Performance*. Palgrave Macmillan.

Cockburn, Alistair. 2000. *Writing Effective Use Cases*. Addison-Wesley.

Cohn, Mike. 2005. *Agile Estimating and Planning*. Prentice Hall PTR.

Cohn, Mike. 2004. *User Stories Applied: For Agile Software Development*. Addison-Wesley.

Collins, James C. and Jerry I. Porras. 1994. *Built to Last*. Harper Collins.

DeCarlo, Doug. 2004. *eXtreme Project Management: Using Leadership, Principles, and Tools to Deliver Value in the Face of Volatility*. Jossey-Bass.

DeMarco, Tom. 2002. *Slack*. Broadway Books.

Derby, Esther, Diane Larsen, and Ken Schwaber. 2006. *Agile Retrospectives: Making Good Teams Great*. Pragmatic Bookshelf.

Finden, Adam. "Achieving Agility in Globally Distributed Software Development." Agile Journal, April 2006.

Gause, Donald and Gerald Weinberg. 1989. *Exploring Requirements*. Dorset.

Gause, Donald and Gerald Weinberg. 1990. *Are Your Lights On?*. Dorset.

Greenleaf, Robert and Larry C. Spears, Stephen R. Covey. 2002. *Servant Leadership*. Paulist Press.

Karner, Gustav. 1993. *Resource Estimation for Objectory Projects*. Objective Systems SF AB.

Klemmens, Roy K. "Project Estimation with Use Case Points." The Journal of Defense Software Engineering, February 2006.

Krebs, Jochen. "Managing an Agile Project Portfolio." Agile Development Magazine, April 2007.

Krebs, Jochen. "Taking Off to the Smart Shore" (3-part series). StickyMinds, October 2006 through January 2007.

Larman, Craig. 2004. *Agile & Iterative Development*. Addison-Wesley.

Lentz, Tiffany. 2007, "Agile Project and Management Metrics: Measuring Success Downward and Upward," Presentation at APLN-NYC.

Levi, Daniel. 2007. *Group Dynamics*. Sage Publications.

Pichler, Roman. 2007. *Scrum: Agiles Projekt Management erfolgreich einsetzen*. dpunkt Verlag (In German).

Project Management Institute. 2004. *A Guide to the Project Management Body of Knowledge, 3rd Edition*. Project Management Institute.

Rothman, Johanna. "An Incremental Technique to Pay Off Testing Technical Debt." Sticky Minds Weekly Column, July 17, 2006.

Rothman, Johanna, and Esther Derby. 2005. *Behind Closed Doors: Secrets of Great Management*. Pragmatic Bookshelf.

Rothman, Johanna. 2007. *Manage It!: Your Guide to Modern, Pragmatic Project Management*. Pragmatic Bookshelf.

Schwaber, Ken. 2004. *Agile Project Management with Scrum*. Microsoft Press.

Schwaber, Ken and Mike Beedle. 2001. *Agile Software Development with Scrum*. Prentice Hall.

Schwaber, Ken. 2007. *The Enterprise and Scrum*. Microsoft Press.

Shuja, Ahmad and Jochen Krebs. 2008. IBM Rational Unified Process Reference and Certification Guide: Solution Designer (RUP). *IBM Press*.

Smith, Preston. 2007. *Flexible Product Development*. Jossey-Bass.

Spector, Robert and Patrick McCarthy. 2005. *The Nordstrom Way*. Wiley.

Tabaka, Jean. 2006. *Collaboration Explained: Facilitation Skills for Software Project Leaders*. Addison-Wesley.

Thorp, John. 1999. *The Information Paradox: Realizing the Business Benefits of Information Technology*. McGraw-Hill.

Tockey, Steve. 2004. *Return on Software: Maximizing the Return of Your Software Investment*. Addison-Wesley.

Weick, Karl E. and Kathleen M. Sutcliffe. 2001. *Managing the Unexpected*. Jossey Bass.

Weinberg, Gerald. 1991. *Quality Software Management: System Thinking*. Dorset House Publishing.

Web Sites

http://en.wikipedia.org/wiki/Google

http://www.agilealliance.org

http://www.agilecmmi.com

http://www.agilejournal.com/articles/articles/better-guesstimating.html (Jochen Krebs)

http://www.agilemanifesto.org

http://www.allbusiness.com/management/1170568-1.html

http://www.apln.org

http://www.controlchaos.com

http://www.dsdm.org/certification/

http://www.eclipse.org/epf

http://www.ewave.co.il/www/articles/technical/PMO.html (KPMG Report)

http://www.gartner.com/it/page.jsp?id=506521

http://www.infoage.idg.com.au/index.php/id;707747065;fp;4;fpid;1197920176

http://www.informationweek.com/story/showArticle.jhtml?articleID=6501862

http://www.planningpoker.com

http://www.pmdoi.org

http://www.pmi.org

http://www.scrumalliance.org/

http://www.scrumalliance.org/training/

http://sporkforge.com/finance/cash_flow.php

http://www.standishgroup.com (Chaos Report, 1995)

http://www.umt.com/site/Why-Portfolio-Management_4.html

IT Project Management Research Findings at *http://www.dmreview.com/dmdirect/20040227/8165-1.html*

Netflix Story at *http://www.npr.org/templates/story/story.php?storyId=16411593*

Index

V

vacations, 141
value measurements. *See* metrics
value of individuals. *See* individuals, valuing
velocity (progress), 71. *See also* progress
virtual teams. *See* physical separation among team members
vision
    impeding, with small projects, 122
    lack of, 65, 140–142
    visionary features, 8
    visionary projects, 121
visual modeling, 76

W

waterfall-phased development, 17, 21, 22
    meeting goals, 95
WBS (work-breakdown structure), 32–33

weak matrix organizations, 57
Weinberg, Gerald, 113
Wide-Band Delphi method for estimating progress, 78
work breaks, 141
work package, 32
work-breakdown structures (WBS), 32–33
workforce. *See* people; resource portfolio management
writing manuals and release notes, 197

X

XP (Extreme Programming), 16

Y

"Yes, but..." syndrome, 23

Jochen Krebs

Jochen Krebs is an accomplished agile mentor and instructor. He is also the founder of Incrementor (*www.incrementor.com*), an agile coaching and training services company in New York. His focus is agile project management and requirements management, where he works directly with project management offices and their portfolios. During his 15+ year professional career, he has worked in various industries in several different roles—for example, as an object-oriented developer, project manager, instructor, consultant, and mentor. Jochen received his MSc from the Open University in Computing for Commerce and Industry.

Jochen is also the co-author of the RUP Reference and Certification Guide and has written numerous articles about agile practices in a variety of magazines. He frequently speaks at conferences and companies and spearheads the local chapter of the Agile Project Leadership Network (APLN) in New York. German-born, Jochen Krebs currently lives in Katonah, New York with his wife, Melanie.

What do you think of this book?

We want to hear from you!

Do you have a few minutes to participate in a brief online survey?

Microsoft is interested in hearing your feedback so we can continually improve our books and learning resources for you.

To participate in our survey, please visit:

www.microsoft.com/learning/booksurvey/

...and enter this book's ISBN-10 or ISBN-13 number (located above barcode on back cover*). As a thank-you to survey participants in the United States and Canada, each month we'll randomly select five respondents to win one of five $100 gift certificates from a leading online merchant. At the conclusion of the survey, you can enter the drawing by providing your e-mail address, which will be used for prize notification only.

Thanks in advance for your input. Your opinion counts!

* Where to find the ISBN on back cover

ISBN-13: 000-0-0000-0000-0
ISBN-10: 0-0000-0000-0

Example only. Each book has unique ISBN.

No purchase necessary. Void where prohibited. Open only to residents of the 50 United States (includes District of Columbia) and Canada (void in Quebec). For official rules and entry dates see:

www.microsoft.com/learning/booksurvey/